PRAISE FOR *PATIENTS IN PERIL*

"The relationship patients and their families develop with their primary physician has been identified as a key bedrock for the success of modern medicine. Dr. Coodley, in his book *Patients in Peril*, documents how that fundamental relationship is either crumbling or on the verge of crumbling...Dr. Coodley offers valuable diagnoses and solutions to the evolving crisis, solutions that should provide sustenance to interested citizens and political and educational policymakers alike."

> – Dr. David Rozansky, Professor of Pediatrics,
> Oregon Health Sciences University

"In *Patients in Peril* Dr. Gregg Coodley focuses on the demise of the traditional "family physician" or primary care physician (PCP) as a leading indicator of the disease affecting American medicine... The book is, in short, a thoroughly researched and experience-based diagnosis of what has become a growing endemic... The good news is that Coodley concludes his diagnosis with a treatment plan of desperately needed reforms. Let's hope the ailing medical system follows the doctor's orders."

> – Rick Seifert, Editor, *In My Time*

"Gregg Coodley's timely expose reveals an issue in primary care medicine that has unfortunately been lurking in the wings of clinical practice for decades, and will only get more complicated or worsen unless changes are made... Coodley outlines the issues, the history and problems and provides solid solution options... Gregg Coodley's most recent literary effort is a must read for everyone because someday, sooner or later, we'll all end up needing a primary care physician to care for us and that's when the hens will most certainly come home to roost."

- Dr. Barry Albertson

PATIENTS IN PERIL

The Demise of Primary Care in America

PATIENTS IN PERIL

The Demise of Primary Care in America

—— GREGG COODLEY ——

atmosphere press

Published by Atmosphere Press

ISBN 978-1-63988-626-5

Cover design by Ronaldo Alves

atmospherepress.com

Dedicated to the Doctors and Staff of the Fanno Creek Clinic

And to the Memory of Drs. Oscar and Eugene Coodley

ACKNOWLEDGEMENTS

I want to credit and thank a wonderful librarian, Sarah Vincuso, at the Providence Medical Library for her unstinting assistance in helping me obtain medical articles from the literature. I also once again want to credit the librarians at the Multnomah County Library for their help in allowing me to effectively use the research tools available to find material relevant to the book.

I want to thank the different primary care doctors, some of whom have chosen to remain anonymous, for their time and insights about their experiences. I need to thank Drs. Louise McHarris and Fred Barken for their thoughts and wisdom. I appreciated the useful insights of my colleagues at the Fanno Creek Clinic.

I want to thank my sisters, Lauren Coodley and Cheryl Coon, for their encouragement and very helpful feedback after reading the manuscript. They continued to make great suggestions throughout the process.

My agent, Susan Schulman, gave useful insight and advice throughout the process. I appreciate her hard work in helping to get the book published.

I want to thank the excellent staff at Atmosphere Press for all their hard work, suggestions and help during the publication process. In particular, I want to extend my thanks to Nick Courtright, Alex Kale, Albert Liau, Ronaldo Alves, Erin Larson and Cameron Finch.

Finally, I want to thank my wife, Karen, for her support, understanding and tolerance for all the time I spent working on the book.

Any errors in the book belong to me alone. I only hope there are not too many.

TABLE OF CONTENTS

The Village Doctor by Felix Schlesinger

(Courtesy, Wiki Commons)

INTRODUCTION

Once, Americans could count on having a personal, or primary care, physician. These doctors would see patients for new or chronic problems, recommend specialists and be there for patients both in the office and hospital. These days are ending, for primary care in the United States is rapidly disappearing. Where once 80% of American doctors were in primary care, now less than 20% of new graduates enter the field. Existing primary care doctors are retiring prematurely or changing fields to something easier or more rewarding. Many of the remaining primary care doctors feel demoralized, dispirited and defeated; rates of burnout and depression are at all-time highs. Experts predict increasing shortages of primary care physicians, a problem that already afflicts small towns and poorer sections of the cities.

It is patients who will lose most from the disappearance of primary care doctors. For primary care, and continuity of care with a physician over time, are both associated with improved patient care, greater patient satisfaction and lower overall costs. This book will endeavor to explain the roots of the problem, the travails of primary care in America, and how it affects patients. At its end, at what is the eleventh hour, it offers solutions to tame and reverse the crisis.

Primary care results in a long-term relationship between patient and doctor over time. In many cases this relationship expands to include the doctor caring for several family members of the first patient. This ongoing relationship is what most Americans want from their doctor. They want their primary care doctor to guide their care, suggesting referrals to specialists and tests based on the doctor's medical judgment.

This has been the pattern of most medical care in the United States over the last two hundred years. Primary care doctors remain the foot soldiers in the fight for health, delivering the basic and most personal part of each patient's care.

Primary care is distinct in another way, stressing the importance of the whole patient rather than a particular organ system or disease. More than any other aspect of medicine save psychiatry, it stresses the relationship between doctor and patient as the key to good health.

There is extensive evidence that access to primary care is associated with better outcomes, including more timely access to care, better preventive care, lower costs and mortality. The World Health Organization stated, "Evidence at the macro level is now overwhelming (that) countries with strong services for primary care have better outcomes at lower cost."[1] Increasing evidence demonstrates the value of primary care for patients. Having a primary care doctor means more preventive care, fewer emergency room visits and hospitalizations, and less costs for the health care system. It also leads to greater patient satisfaction and compliance with treatment. Studies among children, adolescents, adults and seniors all show these benefits.

Nowhere is primary care so threatened with extinction as in the United States. Almost all of the other developed nations spend far more on primary care than America. The amount of health care spending for primary care dropped even further in recent years, going from 6.5% of total US health care expenditures in 2002 to 5.4% in 2016.[2]

In 1940, 76% of doctors in the United States practiced primary care. Today it is less than a third of American doctors. Among new graduates, the number going into primary care is projected to drop below 20%.[3]

Meanwhile, the drop in the number of independent doctors in recent years is astonishing. In 2006 two thirds of primary doctors worked in independent practices. Today these are a rapidly declining minority of PCPs. From 2010 to 2018, unnoticed by the public, the number of PCPs employed by hospitals or other large corporations went from 28% to 50%, effectively doubling.[4]

The changes in the last twenty years have been rapid, overwhelming and yet little noticed by the public. In the olden days, say the year 2000, a patient would see her primary care doctor (PCP) for any new issue. Both PCP and patient would assume that their relationship would be long term. The primary care doctor would refer to specialists as needed. The emergency room doctor would call the PCP if their patient came there and discuss whether admission was needed. The PCP would also manage the patient if she was hospitalized. The PCP would see the patient for any acute illness as well as provide ongoing care for chronic illnesses. The primary care doctor would prescribe whatever medications the patient needed. The patient would get their vaccinations from the PCP. The PCP, circa 1980, would spend double the amount of time as they do today in a patient visit. They would draft a brief paper note that would take a fraction of the time they spent with the patient.

What of 2021? For a new problem, if they are lucky, a patient might see their PCP if they have one, or they might go to the quickie clinic in one of the pharmacy chains that have largely replaced local pharmacies, or to an emergency room. In the urgent care clinic, they could be confident of getting an antibiotic for their viral upper respiratory infection.

The bonds between patient and PCP have diminished. Patients who change to a different insurance often have to change PCPs. The insurer would insist that they see a physician in that insurance network. In addition, the decisions a PCP could make on behalf of his or her patients have greatly decreased. Referrals to specialists now take insurance company approval, as do many diagnostic tests. A rapidly growing number of prescription drugs now require insurance company approval as well.

If a patient is hospitalized these days, he would be managed in the hospital by a "hospitalist" or, more usually, a different hospitalist for each day he was in the hospital. Neither the emergency room physician nor the hospitalist would ever talk to the patient's regular doctor. Many times, the PCP wouldn't even get a timely report about the hospitalization afterward.

Vaccinations are different now. For some immunizations, Medicare will only pay for them in a pharmacy but not in the doctor's office. When the Covid pandemic struck, the powers that be relied on pharmacies as well as large municipal facilities as the site for a new vaccine, with PCPs being a poor later afterthought.

Primary care doctors' visits with patients often feel rushed for both parties. The PCP has to spend at least as much time completing the electronic health record as they actually spend with the patient. PCPs might want to call their patient about issues, but first they have to respond to a blizzard of questions, advice, admonishments and tasks from the insurance companies.

Chapter 1 lays out the history of primary care in the United States from colonial times up until the end of the twentieth century. For many of the changes we see today started then. As technology and financing increased, hospitals and the physicians who worked there rose in primacy. Since most specialists worked at hospitals, the increased money flowing to hospitals and for procedures benefited the specialist physicians most. American health care shifted from general practitioners delivering primary care to a system focused on the now more numerous and better paid specialists, helping to drive increased use of technology and generating higher health care costs. The personification of the best doctor shifted from Dr. Marcus Welby to Dr. House.

Chapter 2 goes into the evidence for the critical value and importance of primary care as well as the benefits of continuity of care for the patient with a single physician. The evidence is overwhelming and yet ignored.

The book then details in Chapter 3 the decline of primary care, showing both the decreasing numbers of primary care doctors and the unsuccessful efforts to reverse this. The academic bias against primary care, the massive debt load of new doctors and the huge disparity in income between specialists and primary care doctors all contribute to this worsening deficit in the number of new primary care doctors. In addition, existing primary care providers are increasingly dissatisfied, often quitting practice in their prime or retiring early. Causes of this unhappiness include loss of autonomy as independent physicians become employees of large corporations, the increasing insurance company interference in practice and the decreasing time, given the other demands, with patients. The rate of depression among these doctors is setting records.

Chapter 4 explores the increasing mismatch between medical training and what doctors do. In no area is this disconnect greater than in primary care. Primary care doctors principally were and are trained in inpatient medicine, even if it was always the lesser part of what they did. Now with the advent of hospitalists, primary care practitioners are effectively exiled from the hospital, leaving much of their training worthless, both a wasteful and unhappy state of affairs.

Chapter 5 explores the devaluing of continuity of care. When a patient's employer changes health insurance, the patient's long-time relationship with their doctor must yield to whoever is on the insurance company panel. It is clear which relationship is more important. While Americans accept this rationale for having to change doctors, it is not a feature of health care in any other major nation. Insurers often see both doctors and patients as interchangeable widgets. Yet this view does not lead to the best care or even the cheapest care. Dr.

Eric Cassell eloquently wrote, "The belief that medicine involves the application of impersonal facts to an objective problem that can be seen separately from the person who has it is the cardinal and emblematic error of twentieth-century medicine."[5]

Where once most patients who were hospitalized were cared for by their own doctors, they have now been replaced by "hospitalists," doctors employed solely for inpatient care by the hospitals. This change is the focus of chapter 6. Hospitals argued that "hospitalists" would be more efficient. The hospitals have indeed saved money by reducing the length of patient stays, resulting in increased hospital profitability. Subsequently, hospitals recruited hospitalists wholesale, creating a whole new specialty that diverted tens of thousands of physicians from going into primary care.

The consequence is that patients are no longer cared for by their own doctors when they are hospitalized. Hospitalists very rarely ask primary care doctors about their patients or communicate to them about the events in the hospital. The chain of continuity is broken. Yet evidence of better outcomes when patients are cared for by hospitalists is minimal. At least one large national study showed a markedly higher death rate for patients cared for by hospitalists compared to PCPS.

Is going to urgent care or to the hospital to be seen by someone the patient has never met really the best care? Evidence shows that it is not.

Perhaps the greatest source of unhappiness for primary care doctors is the increasing involvement of insurance companies in every aspect of medicine. The insurers claim that all of their interventions are designed to save money or improve care. Yet this claim is manifestly false. This is the subject of chapters 7-10.

Every physician had to be re-credentialed with each payor every year. Thus, the physician, already approved by their medical board and their local hospital, must repetitively fill out different forms for each insurer. There is a darker motive here too. By controlling who they credential, insurers can cut out troublesome doctors and force the others to be less troublesome.

Increasingly, for patients to get the medications their doctor prescribes, insurers require that the doctor's office fill out prior authorizations, special requests as to why they are needed. Doctors know that their opinion about what is best for the patient no longer matters. Nor is this micromanagement confined to the most expensive drugs where there is at least some excuse of cost saving. Doctors must do frequent prior authorizations for inexpensive generic drugs. This is so the insurer, who may have gotten a slightly better deal on a comparable drug, can make a few dollars more. No one discusses how it is legal for the insurance company drug purchasing agents to accept what is, in effect, 'kickbacks' from drug companies to put their medications on the preferred list. Estimates are that doing prior authorizations costs $60-70 billion dollars a year. The available data suggests that while prior authorization programs may reduce drug costs slightly, the overall health care cost often increases as patients have increased emergency room use and hospitalizations, not even including the cost above to the doctors to do these authorizations

Denials of patient medications creates excess paperwork for doctors, but those really at risk are patients. What happens when a patient develops a complication because the insurance refuses to pay for their regular medication because it is too expensive? For example, a patient with a well-controlled seizure disorder had her long-time medicine denied by her insurer as too expensive. She promptly had a seizure, fortunately not while she was driving.

Insurers increasingly determine which tests doctors can order for patients. What if the insurance refuses to authorize a CT scan, and the patient is later found to have a cancer that might have been detected earlier? Many times, the insurer makes the process of obtaining approval for tests so difficult and onerous that the doctor gives up. The loser from the ever more intrusive medical management by the insurance company is the patient.

Patients don't realize that the reason that their doctor cannot spend more time with them is the horrendous and increasing amount of time that must be spent providing information to insurance companies. The primary care doctor today sees fewer patients than twenty years ago, as the typical doctor now spends two hours on administrative work for every hour face to face with the patient. How much of that administrative work is beneficial to the patient? In truth, almost none benefits the patient, who suffers from their doctor being diverted from caring for them to caring for the demands of the insurer and the government. With each PCP seeing fewer patients, the shortage of doctors is exacerbated. Chapter 11 explores some of the ways primary care is drowning under trivia.

Chapter 12 explores how much insurance company involvement in patient care results in less time to care for patients. Increasingly, health care insurers, both public and private, are taking over medical decision-making under the banner of improving quality. The insurers assume that by guiding what the doctors do, they are raising the quality of care. Yet there is shockingly little evidence for the plethora of quality measures that doctors now must try to meet. Evidence suggests that primary care doctors would need more hours than in their whole work day just to meet these measures, with none left over for actual patient care.

The insurers, including Medicare and Medicaid, have piled on a rapidly growing list of quality measures, essentially "unfunded mandates," adding work to the doctor without adding income. Different insurers choose from over 2500 measures that they mandate primary care doctors must address. If only it all improved patient care. Doctors spend hours and hours trying to meet "quality measures." While some measures, such as mammograms or diabetic eye exams, do benefit patients, studies have shown many others are flawed and of dubious or marginal value to patients' health.

The electronic medical record was sold as a measure to improve efficiency and the sharing of information, yet the net effect has been to reduce patient care. The payors require so much data to be reported that almost all doctors see significantly fewer patients than in the days when they used written charts. The requirement that doctors use such systems or accept decreasing payments from Medicare forced many smaller practices to close and doctors to retire. Thus, the electronic record has contributed to the shrinking number of independent physicians. Evidence of improved outcomes or health care savings is almost non-existent.

Figuring out how best to pay physicians is the subject of chapter 14. Paying doctors for each service they deliver, called "fee-for-service," has been blamed for the rapid increase in health care costs over the last fifty years. Like democracy, fee-for-service is the worst system, except compared to everything else. The innovations in payment over the last twenty years have minimal evidence of improving quality, while always trending toward reduced physician autonomy, and massively increased administrative costs.

Under fee-for-service, the physicians are blamed for doing too much. Yet since the proportion of all health care costs due to primary care doctors is only 5%, it is ludicrous to assess excessive primary care visits as the cause of health care inflation. Twenty primary care visits cost less than a single day in the hospital. Thus, the basic premise, that fee-for-service payments to primary care doctors are a major cause of increased health care spending and must be changed, is flawed.

The alternatives of instead emphasizing value, quality and cost control sounds appealing on paper. In reality, the straightforward system of being paid for what one does has been replaced by increasingly byzantine, complicated formulas, requiring immense statistics and reporting to try to calculate quality, costs, use of technology and labor. The actual result of these complex machinations is a disproportionate benefit to the largest practices, such as doctors employed by large health care systems, at the expense of smaller, independent, rural and safety net physicians.

Patients don't realize how much of the current payments to primary care doctors comes from NOT PROVIDING care or services to patients. While the old system never paid doctors for more referrals or testing, the new arrangements pay them more if they refer less and test less.

Chapter 15 explores how the corruption of the new systems is invisible to the great and the good and the public. For example, private Medicare plans, known as Med Advantage, receive increased dollars the more complex conditions their patients have. Thus, these plans emphasize doctors finding and reporting such conditions so that the payors will get more money, with some trickling down to the doctors. Seniors think these plans want to improve their health care when they send nurse practitioners to their homes to do exams. Often insurers suggest these in lieu of annual exams by the patient's own doctor. There is no charity or kindness involved. The sole purpose of these visits is to game the system by recording more "high complexity conditions," raising the money companies receive from Medicare.

Even as the insurance companies act as doctors, sending more and more advice, suggestions and mandates to primary care doctors, the latest payment plans want primary care doctors to act as insurers. These contracts make PCPs responsible for "downside" risk. If a patient costs more than is budgeted, it is to be the PCP, not the insurer, who must pay money to cover this overage. All the incentive is to do less. Perhaps large health systems could tolerate such a risk, but the independent smaller practices don't have such deep pockets and will most likely be forced out of business.

Noting the increasing scarcity of primary care doctors, health care systems turned to physician substitutes, nurse practitioners and physician assistants. Many of these turn out to be wonderful, smart, compassionate health care providers. Many health maintenance organizations and public health clinics treat them as equivalent to doctors, often at a considerable cost saving. Yet their training is but a tiny fraction of the time required of physicians. Nurse practitioners receive 500 hours of clinical training compared to 20,000 hours for physicians. Treating them exactly equal to physicians with the idea that primary care is "simple care" devalues the training and work asked of physicians, leading to further demoralization and arguably worse care for the sickest patients.

Another innovation for patient convenience and profits is the twenty-first-century creation of urgent care and retail clinics, many run by huge corporations. They effectively skim off the healthier, more affluent patients who can meet their demand for cash on the spot while often refusing to see Medicare or Medicaid patients. Nor is this one-time visit always equivalent in quality to that provided by a patient's private physician who knows their history, their needs and wants and weaknesses. The very definition of primary care includes being the first contact for a patient with a new illness. The outside urgent cares interfere with continuity of care, frequently not even communicating about the visit to the PCP.

Primary care doctors traditionally took the lead in vaccinating their patients against different diseases. Yet the passage of the Medicare D program had the consequence that many patients could only get certain vaccines through their pharmacies. The change in policy has been so accepted that when the Covid vaccines became available, policymakers looked to the big pharmacy chains to expand vaccination efforts. In many states, primary care doctors had no role, despite their willingness, to give Covid vaccinations. Traditionally, doctors have had the greatest influence on their patients' willingness to accept vaccines. However, now only a few rare articles suggest that they could play a vital role in convincing hesitant patients to be vaccinated. Is it any wonder that primary care doctors feel forgotten and disrespected?

Thus, the death of primary care is a function of fewer and fewer and unhappier PCPs, each seeing fewer and fewer patients. Who wants to be a PCP given the loss of autonomy and increasing paperwork to increase insurance profits or meet mythical goals of "quality"? Nor do massive medical school debt and the reduced respect given to PCPs encourage new doctors to practice primary care. The result is patients who can't find a PCP.

This is not a theoretical future risk. Already there is a shortage of PCPs, particularly in small towns and poorer areas in the cities. This problem will worsen as the PCP shortage increases in the coming years.

Primary care doctors are less and less entrepreneurs or skilled artisans, instead becoming industrial workers, part of the proletariat, albeit a well-educated and well-paid variety. Chapter 19 explains how the majority now are employed by huge care systems, having opted for financial survival over independence. This rapid change has been driven by several well-meaning twenty-first-century government interventions in health care that end up rewarding the large and powerful at the expense of the small. Even as this change occurs, evidence suggests that bigger may not be better for patients, either in terms of care or cost.

The consolidation of medicine as smaller practices close leaves patients with fewer and poorer choices. Patients will confront the consequences when all health care in their town comes from a single hospital that employs all the doctors and is part of or allied with an insurance company. Monopoly or even oligopoly situations damages consumers, in this case, the patients, most of all.

The damage to primary care hurts patients the most. There is myriad evidence of poorer care when patients don't have a regular primary care doctor. Poor communication between hospitalists and primary care has been demonstrated to result in poorer outcomes and increased medical errors. When patients are hospitalized, without having their personal doctor there to act as the patient's advocate, the worth of patients who appear sick and diminished is often discounted.

Ironically, the decline in primary care is happening even as illness increasingly shifted from acute episodes to chronic diseases in the United States over the last one hundred years. Putting aside the Covid pandemic, the vast majority of Americans die from chronic diseases. Never would a regular doctor who knows the patient be more valuable than over this extended period of disease that most people encounter.

Some experts have long predicted that primary care will shift into a three-tiered model.[6] The very wealthy will still be able to see personal doctors under a concierge model, under which the patient pays a premium for extra attention from the doctor. On the bottom will be the poor, largely covered by Medicaid, with a large amount of care provided by community health centers. The rest of patients, if they can find a PCP, will have briefer visits with such doctors who are increasingly beleaguered by insurer and government demands for paperwork and demands to reduce costs and increase quality. I don't think this is a good outcome for patients.

In authoring the book, I have read the chronicles and arguments that others have written about primary care over the last thirty years. I have found much wisdom that I will try to share.

I have added to this background interviews with current primary care physicians from the three primary care specialties of general internal medicine, family medicine and pediatrics. This allowed me to understand better the experiences of other PCPs. In each chapter, I have reviewed and included recent writing and a huge gamut of the medical literature to see if it offers factual and statistical support to my arguments.

I come to this as the son and grandson of generalist physicians. My grandfather came to the United States as a teenager, taught himself English, somehow went to medical school, and practiced as a general practitioner in Los Angeles. My father graduated from medical school just in time to serve as a doctor in the Army in New Guinea and the Philippines during World War II. He took over his father's practice when his dad became ill, then later, as a general internist, added teaching to practice.

I went to the University of California for medical school at a time when it was almost free. I have been lucky enough to work in an HMO, practice and teach in an academic medical center and finally be the manager of and practice full time in a group of great independent primary care doctors for the last twenty-four years. I have enjoyed long relationships with many patients for decades. Even as I list the aggravations of practice in 2022, I still enjoy patient care.

There is an alternative future to the death of primary care in America. There are solutions to each of the problems discussed in the book. Many of these solutions would decrease the cost of health care for both the patient and the nation. Embracing simplicity can also allow existing PCPs to see more patients. Addressing the problems can also correct the imbalance between specialists and PCPs, encouraging more future doctors to become personal physicians for patients. The solutions would also create more satisfied PCPs, which is correlated with more satisfied patients.

Fixing this problem will help not just the doctors, but more importantly the patients, for health care is ultimately about them.

[1] John P. Geyman, "Beyond the Covid-19 Pandemic: The Urgent Need to Expand Primary Care, *"Fam Med,* January 2021; 53(1),50

[2] Sara Martin. Robert L. Phillips, Stephen Petterson, Zachary Levin, Andrew W. Bazemore, "Primary Care Spending in the United States 2002-2016," *JAMA Internal Medicine,* July 2020; 180(7): 1020

[3] Edward Salsberg, Paul H. Rockey, Kerri L. Rivers, Sarah E. Brotherton, Gregory R. Jackson, "US Residency Training before and after the 1997 Balanced Budget Act," *JAMA,* 2008; 300(10): 1174

[4] Carrie H. Colla, Toyin Ajayi, Asaf Bitton, "Potential Adverse Financial Implication of the Merit-based Incentive payment System for Independent and safety net Practices, *JAMA.* September 8, 2020; 324(10): 948

[5] Eric J. Cassell, *Doctoring: The Nature of Primary Care Medicine,* Oxford University Press, 1997, 46

[6] Lewis G. Sandy, Steven A. Schroder, "Primary Care in a New Era: Disillusion and Dissolution," *Ann Int Med,* 2003, 138: 265

Dr. Benjamin Rush
Stipple engraving by W.S. Leney, 1814

(Courtesy, Wiki Commons)

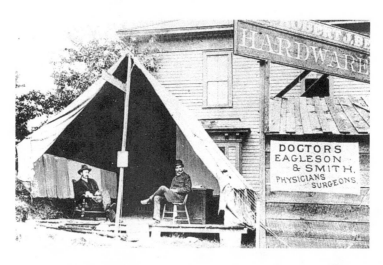

Doctors Providing Care in a Tent in Seattle after Fire of June 6, 1889

(Courtesy, Wiki Commons)

CHAPTER 1

Primary Care in America: A Background History

Doctors and medicine have been viewed very differently in other societies. The Romans considered doctors, who were mainly slaves and freedmen, an occupation of little esteem, while in the Soviet Union, doctors, who were mainly women, earned less than industrial workers. [1] Other societies esteemed physicians greatly.

When the American colonies gained independence, doctors stood somewhere between the two extremes. Originally, in Britain, there was a distinction between physicians who ranked above the lower level surgeons who did most of the hands-on work. This distinction did not last in America. Historian Paul Starr wrote, "All manner of people took up medicine in the colonies and appropriated the title of doctor." [2]

Medicine was a largely unpoliced profession. While some doctors received relatively good training while apprenticing to able practicing physicians, others simply declared themselves doctors and hung out a shingle. Since the number of effective treatments was so limited, this gave rise to lots of treatment with what was called "snake oil."

Medical treatment often was provided by the family who, given the state of medicine, may have been as least as effective as many of the doctors of the day. The rural character of the nation, along with the vast distances and poor transportation, made it imperative that patients have someone closer to take care of them than the chimera of a distant doctor in some far-off city. People used books such as William Buchan's *Domestic*

Medicine, which discussed how to deal with various disorders, to treat their kinfolk. Meanwhile, the limited economic resources of a relatively poor society made medicine a poor choice to make money.

Doctors were viewed with suspicion. The Jacksonian period in the 1830–1840s saw the elimination of even the weak licensure requirements in multiple states. Starr commented, "While some physicians were seeking to make themselves an elite profession with a monopoly of practice, much of the public refused to grant them any such privileges."[3] Even in states where licensure persisted, it did not usually require graduation from medical school.

Doctors in the 1800s were much less well paid and well regarded than in recent years. When Dr. J. Marion Sims returned home after deciding to become a doctor in 1832, his father exclaimed, "If I had known this, I certainly should not have sent you to college...it is a profession for which I have the utmost contempt. There is no science in it. There is no honor to be achieved in it; no reputation to be made."[4] An American medical journal declared in 1869, "In all of our American colleges, medicine has ever been and is now, the most despised of all the professions which liberally-educated men are expected to enter.[5] Doctors' income in 1860 was estimated to put them at the bottom of the middle class.[6] Medicine was further weakened by ongoing feuding between various kinds of practitioners.

Just as the rules for practicing medicine were weak, those for creating a medical school were almost nonexistent. The first medical school in the United States was opened in Philadelphia in 1765. The early 1800s saw a proliferation of new medical schools. By 1850 there were fifty in the United States compared to three in all of France.[7] New schools were opened by groups of doctors who were paid directly by students. After a prerequisite of only one course in natural and experimental philosophy, students were taught for three to four months for each of two years. Facilities were rudimentary, often with no lab or significant clinical practice. Since professors were paid by the students only if they passed the tests, exams were not difficult. Starr commented, "Any institution that raised its standards stood the risk of losing its students and its income."[8]

This was to change. Starr penned, "From a relatively weak, traditional profession of minor economic significance, medicine has become a sprawling system of hospitals, clinics, health plans, insurance companies and myriad other organizations employing a vast labor force."[9]

Several factors contributed to the rise of the medical profession. First, there were discoveries and new tools that medicine could use to prevent or treat illness, particularly occurring near the end of the nineteenth century. Doctors began to have more to offer.

Second was the growth of stronger licensing rules that gave patients more confidence that they would not be seeing a charlatan. The first strong licensure rule was enacted in 1877 when Illinois gave the state board of medical examiners the power to reject inadequately trained candidates, including those from disreputable schools.[10] Against the opposition of these schools, other states followed the path of Illinois.

Third, improved transportation with the advent of railroads and later automobiles meant that doctors could see patients with less time spent in travel. Doctors could see more patients, and since they didn't have to include as much travel time in their charges, their visits became less expensive. Doctors embraced cars early, with letters to *JAMA* in the first decade of the twentieth century noting that the time of a house call had been cut in half.

Physicians began being called general practitioners to emphasize that they offered medicine, surgery and often apothecary services.

Fourth, the last quarter of the nineteenth century saw

reforms in medical education starting at Harvard in 1871. Harvard put professors on salary, lengthened the school year to nine months in each of three years, added lab work and required students to pass all requirements to graduate.[11] Initially, the extra requirements caused a sharp drop in enrollment from 330 down to 170, but this number began to climb with more of the students having bachelor's degrees. Over the next twenty-plus years, most medical schools changed to a three-year program

The John Hopkins Medical School opened in 1893 and took things further. Hopkins required all entrants to have undergraduate degrees, offered a four-year training program and recruited distinguished practitioners from all over the country to teach. Hopkins created the modern model of two years of pre-clinical training followed by two years medical practice in the hospital under the supervision of the faculty.

While some schools began to follow the model of Hopkins, there were many that did not. The increased requirements increased the costs of medical training. Many students, particularly those from the lower classes, could not afford it. The result was the closure of many medical schools in the early 1900s, leading to shrinking numbers of doctors. From a high of 160 schools in 1906, the number had dropped to 131 four years later.[12]

In 1905 the Carnegie Foundation for the Advancement of Teaching selected Abraham Flexner, a well-respected educator, to visit and assess each of the medical schools in the United States. Flexner was to issue a report about his findings.

Flexner reported that many of the schools were substandard operations, sometimes operated on the side by doctors to boost their incomes. Most had no prerequisites for admission. Many required only a high school diploma. Graduation from some required only sufficient money to pay for a diploma. There was no system of testing to assess the medical knowledge or training of the graduates.

Flexner released his report in 1910. He called for schools to copy his alma mater at John Hopkins, probably the best American medical school of the day, with its high entrance requirements, excellent faculty, a rigorous four-year scientific curriculum and modern facilities and laboratories. Within a few years, most medical schools closed while only those with sources of wealthy support survived and copied the model of John Hopkins. The consequence was the development of a uniform system of medical education, with students at each school having to learn the same information. Students all had to pass standardized tests after graduation to assess their skills.

The Flexner report helped guide donations to medical schools from philanthropists, most prominently the Rockefellers, for several decades. Starr wrote that the staff of Rockefeller's General Education Board, "actively sought to impose a model of medical education more closely wedded to research than medical practice."[13] In addition, medical schools, tied to universities, embraced this model and the way it helped separate them from private physicians. In contrast, states wanted medical schools to supply physicians to meet local needs.

Starr wrote of the consequences of the uniform adoption of the Hopkins model, stating, "As American medical education became increasingly dominated by scientists and researchers, doctors came to be trained according to the values and standards of academic scientists. Many have argued that this was a mistake. They would have preferred to see only a few schools like John Hopkins training scientists and specialists, while the rest, with more modest programs, turn out general practitioners to take care of the everyday ills that make up the greater part of medical work. But this is not the course that American medical education followed."[14]

The decline in the number of doctors following the closure of so many medical schools worsened existing disparities in the number of available doctors, with shortages growing in poor and rural areas. The reduction also led to a decrease in doctors who were women, who were black, or who were working class, while deliberate discrimination against Jews, women and blacks added to this change.

A study by AMA President William Allen Pusey documented the effect, showing that more than a third of 910 small towns that had physicians in 1914 had been abandoned by doctors in 1925.[15] The ratio of doctors to the population dropped from 173 physicians/100,000 people in 1900 to 125 physicians/100,000 people in 1930.[16] Thus the shortage of primary care is not simply a new phenomenon. The difference was that almost all the doctors that existed before WWII were general practitioners rather than specialists.

This began to change starting in the 1930s. The proportion of doctors who were general practitioners began to drop. From over 76% in 1940, this dropped to 63% by 1949, to 45% by 1960 and then to 31% by 1966.[17]

There was also a large increase in doctors working in settings other than office practice from 1940 to 1957. Institutionally employed physicians increased from 12.8 to 26.5% of the profession in this time. Doctors in private practice declined not only as a proportion of physicians but relative to the American population. The 109/100,000 general practitioners in 1940 dropped to 91/100,000 by 1957.[18]

The post-war years also saw major growth in hospitals and increasing control by medical schools over them. Medicine became divided between faculty and trainees at the medical schools and hospitals, who had little long-term relationships with patients, and a declining cadre of general practitioners, particularly in the suburbs, rural areas and poorer communities, who maintained relationships with patients while increasingly being viewed as the poor cousins of the hospital-based specialists and academics.

Since there have been doctors, people have understood what it meant to have a regular physician. The term primary care itself is of recent vintage, at least in the United States. In 1966, two reports outlined the role of primary care. The American Medical Association Ad Hoc Committee on Education for Family Practice, chaired by John Millis, argued that each individual should have a primary physician.[19] The other report argued for a reform of general practice to add more training, "to balance the overemphasis on medical specialization."[20]

The 1960s–70s saw new residencies offering further training in primary care with the new specialty Family Medicine and in General Internal Medicine and Pediatrics. Primary care doctors would no longer simply be general practitioners whose one year of training post-medical school was much less than that of the specialists.

Primary care was noted to have some key features: 1) first contact access for each new medical need; 2) long -term care focused on the person rather than a specific disease entity; 3) comprehensive care; and 4) coordination of care when given elsewhere.[21]

Cassell explained, in his view, the three branches of primary care, saying, "Family physicians have a wider range of, if less clinical, skills and are more concerned with well persons. General internists are more concerned with sick persons, and their knowledge has greater depth but less breadth. General pediatricians are, by definition, interested in children and adolescents...Despite their differences, these disciplines share a fundamental concern with persons, sick or well.[22]

In the 1960s, the Johnson administration started two programs to increase care for the poor. One was Medicaid, insurance for the poor. The other was the opening of community health centers to deliver complete ambulatory care to underserved patients. Under the leadership of Dr. H. Jack Geiger, the first two community health centers were opened in Boston and Mississippi. The program aimed at bringing primary care to underserved communities.

Despite years of insufficient funding, the community

health center (CHC) project has now grown to 1400 community health centers serving thirty million people in impoverished urban and rural communities. The CHCs must serve everyone who wants care in their geographic area and provide primary care from infancy to end of life. They remain an important part of the provision of primary care, particularly to the poor.[23]

The sixties also saw the advent of Medicare, providing medical care to those over sixty-five. To win support for the program, Medicare followed the lead of Blue Cross in paying hospitals based on reported costs rather than negotiated rates while giving favorable rates for depreciation. As a result of this and other factors, the costs of Medicare would increase more than anyone anticipated. In addition, Starr commented, "Despite the widespread sense that federal policy ought to shift its emphasis to ambulatory care, the government was still putting big money behind hospital expansion."[24]

The next two decades were a time of increased income for many doctors. Many physicians benefited financially from the 1960s to the mid-1980s as Medicare paid doctors according to their "customary fees."

Yet the increased revenue for doctors and hospitals increasingly came from third parties rather than the patient directly. The percentage of bills paid by third-party payers, either the government or insurers, increased from 45% in 1965 to 67% in 1975. Health care spending rose at a rate far greater than other spending. Eventually, this would lead to a revolt by the payors to try to reduce such spending.

While the added revenues garnered by the health care system lifted all boats, it lifted some more than others. Starr observed, "Just as the financing system promoted overexpansion in some areas, it produced an undersupply of services in others. The incentives that favored hospital care promoted the neglect of ambulatory and preventive services; the incentives that favored specialization also caused primary care to be neglected."[25]

Yet, for most of this time, the generalist physician remained the hallmark of American medicine. Researcher Tim Hoff wrote, "The generalist physician of the past knew patients over long stretches of time, held their trust to make health care decisions for them and handled a large, diverse scope of work...a typical generalist practice in the 1960s or 1970s...(was) staffed with a physician or two, a supporting nurse, and perhaps one or two clerical staff. Records, notes and billing were all done by paper...there were only one or two insurance companies to deal with, and these companies rarely questioned physician decisions...Patients went to generalists for everything, were managed by generalists through their serious illnesses...Generalists were perceived as the appropriate caregivers for a wide range of clinical problems."[26] The television epitome of a doctor was Marcus Welby, "a veteran practitioner devoted less to magic bullets and more to exploring in-depth his patients' many problems from physical to psychological."[27]

Internist Fred Lafferty argued that a crucial change occurred in 1984 when the Center for Medicare and Medicaid Services (CMS) made significant changes. First, physicians could no longer bill patients beyond what Medicare paid. Second, CMS largely adopted the Blue Shield pay schedule, which heavily favored procedures and procedural specialties relative to primary care.[28]

Nevertheless, the percentage of Americans who reported having a regular or usual physician declined only slightly from 88% in 1975 to 80% in 1994.[29]

When I started my internal medicine residency in 1985, it was at the end of what, in hindsight, was a golden age for primary care, at least compared with what was to follow. Primary care doctors took care of their patients both in the outpatient setting and when they were admitted to the hospital. Medical training equipped doctors to do both. They did not receive frequent advice from health insurance companies on how to manage the patients. Almost any medication a doctor wrote a prescription for would be filled without question. Doctors in each of the primary care fields understood that there was important preventive care that they should recommend to their patients. The doctors' decisions to recommend tests or interventions were based on their own knowledge of disease rather than a cookbook list from an insurer.

Reimbursement for doctors was completely based on the services they provided, rather than being in large part dependent on meeting the goals defined by insurers. Medicare paid a set fee for each service. There was no financial incentive to deny services to patients. There was no incentive to list the most complicated diagnoses for patients since there were no private intermediary Medicare companies gaming the system to receive the maximum payment per patient.

There was no electronic medical record. At the cost of poor handwriting, doctor's medical visit notes took much less time to complete. Doctors didn't have to repeat a series of pre-scribed elements for each visit. Nor did they have to focus on sending lots of information every time to meet insurance company quality standards.

Doctors did not have to compete against multiple alternative non-physician substitutes. Private companies did not establish urgent care clinics to skim off the easy and most lucrative patient visits from primary care doctors. There were far more independent pharmacies instead of huge pharmacy chains establishing mini-clinics in their stores to make more money. Doctors could give any approved vaccines to their patients without restrictions.

Starr wrote in 1982 with amazement about how doctors seem to have kept their autonomy noting, "Modern medical practice requires access to hospitals and medical technology, and hence medicine, unlike many other professions, requires huge capital investments...Often the demands of technology are cited as the reason other self-employed artisans lost their independence. Medicine offers a case in point for those who wish to argue that technology is far from imperative in its demands for submission to organizational control."[30]

I suspect Starr would have come to a different conclusion now, almost forty years later. In the subsequent chapters we will explore primary care today and how it came to its current situation.

[1] Paul Starr, *The Social Transformation of American Medicine*, Basic Books, New York, 1982, 6

[2] Starr, 39

[3] Starr, 31

[4] Starr, 82

[5] "American versus European Medical Science," *Medical Record* 4, May 15, 1869, 133

[6] Starr, 84

[7] Starr, 42

[8] Starr, 43

[9] Starr, 4

[10] Starr, 102

[11] Starr, 114

[12] Starr, 118

[13] Starr, 121

[14] Starr, 123

[15] William Allen Pussey, "The Disappearance of Doctors from Small Towns," *JAMA*, February 12, 1927, 505

[16] Starr, 126

[17] Starr, 358-9

[18] Starr, 359

[19] JS Mills, "Citizens Commission on Graduate Medical Education," American Medical Association, Chicago, 1966

[20] Robert L. Phillips Jr., Andrew W. Bazemore, "Primary Care and why it matters for the US health system reform," *Health Affairs (Millwood)*, May, 2010; 29(5): 806

[21] Barbara Starfield, Leiyu Shi, James Macinko, "Contribution of Primary Care to Health Systems and Health," *The Millbank Quarterly, 2005:83(3): 457*

[22] Cassell, 12

[23] Sara Rosenbaum, Daniel R. Hawkins, "The Good Doctor – Jack Geiger, Social Justice and US Health Policy," *New England Journal of Medicine (NEJM)*, March 18, 2021; 384(11), 983

[24] Starr, 375

[25] Starr, 387

[26] Timothy Hoff, *Practice Under Pressure: Primary Care Physicians and Their Medicine in the Twenty First Century*, Rutgers University Press, New Brunswick, 2010, 7-9

[27] Hoff, 2

[28] Fred W. Lafferty, *The Major Cause of Rising Health care Cost with Decreasing Quality: A Scarcity of Primary Care Physicians*, Page Publishing, New York, 2015

[29] Dana Gelb Saran, "Defining the Future of Primary Care: What Can We Learn for Patients," *Ann Int Med*, 138: 248

[30] Starr, 16

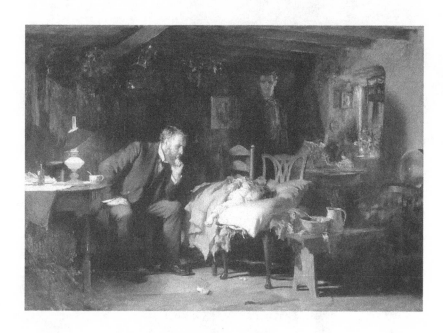

The Doctor's Visit – Luke Fildes

(Courtesy, Wiki Commons)

CHAPTER 2

The Benefits of Primary Care

As a primary care physician (PCP), I have always had a gestalt feeling that primary care improved the overall health of patients. Yet it wasn't until I started looking that I discovered the very large amount of research, both in the United States and in other nations, that showed that primary care doctors made a dramatic difference in health care outcomes.

First, evidence shows major benefits at the level of the overall population. Writing at John Hopkins, Barbara Starfield summarized this, noting, "Health is better in areas with more PCPs; second, people who receive care from PCPs are healthier; and third, that the characteristics of primary care are associated with better health."[1] Starfield and colleagues noted several studies showing that an increased number of PCPs was associated with lower mortality even after controlling for socioeconomic features, concluding, "The supply of PCPs was significantly associated with lower all-cause mortality."[2] The relationship between more primary care doctors and improved health has been documented in multiple other nations as well.[3]

Chang et al. compared outcomes in Medicare patients in a 2011 study. Patients in areas with the most primary care doctors had fewer hospitalizations for preventable conditions, lower mortality and no major difference in Medicare spending than those in areas with the fewest PCPs.[4] The strongest association was in areas with the most full-time equivalent primary care doctors delivering ambulatory care in an office or clinic rather than simply the number of internal medicine or family medicine doctors since these totals included doctors not delivering primary care.[5]

Macinko and colleagues reviewed all articles assessing the effects of primary care from 1985 to 2005. Macinko et al. concluded, "Primary care physician supply was associated with improved health care outcomes, including all-cause cancer, heart disease, stroke, and infant mortality; low birth weight, life expectancy, and self-rated health."[6] The review also showed a link to increased birth weight, life expectancy, and self-rated health.[7] The data suggested that an increase of one PCP per 10,000 population reduced average mortality by 5.3% each year.[8] In the year 2000, this would have translated into over 127,000 fewer deaths.[9]

Later studies confirmed the benefits of having more primary care doctors. In a study from 2005 to 2015, Basu et al. showed that adding one PCP per 10,000 people was associated with decreased mortality, equaling an increase in life expectancy of 51.5 days for a population of 100,000.[10] A 2021 analysis showed that patients living in counties with less than 1 PCP per 3500 people had a lifespan of 310 days less than those living in counties with a least one PCP per 3500 people. Again, adding PCPs to these areas would increase the average lifespan significantly.[11]

Another 2021 article confirmed these findings, noting that for each increase of one PCP in a county, around sixteen hospitalizations were prevented per 100,000 population each year. Additional PCPs also reduced premature deaths with a finding of fourteen years of life saved per 100,000 population for every additional PCP in a county in the United States.[12]

The benefits of primary care occurred at the individual level as well as in populations. Adults in the United States who had a PCP rather than a specialist as their regular source of care, "had lower subsequent five-year mortality rates after controlling for initial differences in health status, demographic characteristics, health insurance status, health perceptions, reported diagnoses and smoking status."[13] Starfield concluded, "People who identify a primary care physician as their usual source of care are healthier, regardless of their initial health.[14] Moreover, good primary care helped reduce the adverse effects of income inequality on health."[15]

It is not surprising that research also found that having a regular doctor resulted in better access to care, defined by a set of preventive and primary care utilization measurements, compared to those without a regular source of care.[16]

The benefits of primary care have been shown for adults, children and adolescents in both urban and rural environments. Having a primary care doctor reduced emergency room use among rural adolescents and among inner-city minority adults.[17] [18]

A study of children showed that, "expenditures for annual physician ambulatory services are higher for children whose usual source of care is a hospital outpatient department/ emergency room and who have no specific physician as a caregiver."[19] The author concluded, "Costs of care for children at these sites will be greater if, as is more often the case for poor children, no specific doctor provides care on a continuous basis."[20]

A study of children in three cities in New York State and New England led the authors to conclude, "For ambulatory care-sensitive conditions such as asthma, differential access to primary care could affect the likelihood of admission."[21] Importantly research found that it was not simply insurance that was necessary for improved care.[22]

Primary care was also shown to reduce overall health care costs. One study showed both better quality of care, and a linear decrease in Medicare spending as the supply of PCPs increased.[23] Several studies found that lower rates of hospitalization for, "ambulatory care-sensitive conditions," such as diabetes and pneumonia, were associated with receiving primary care.[24] [25]

Indeed, after thirty years in practice, I very rarely have to hospitalize patients with out of control diabetes or pneumonia. Those of my patients with those two conditions who get hospitalized for them almost always end up as inpatients as a result of a decision by an emergency room. When I can see them in the office and then see them again if needed in a few days, outpatient treatment can often be sufficient to address the malady.

First contact with a PCP for any new illness is important. Starfield noted the evidence, "that having a relationship with a primary care practitioner who can serve as an initial point of contact is strongly and statistically associated with less use of specialists and emergency rooms."[26] This point is worth considering later as we explore how the burgeoning number of acute/urgent care clinics has meant that, increasingly, the PCP is not the first contact for patients with new acute illnesses.

A recent review also gave evidence that the general checkup or physical performed by PCPs regularly for patients had important health benefits. Liss et al. evaluated nineteen randomized trials and thirteen observational studies with control groups. The authors concluded that checkups, "were associated with increased detection of chronic diseases, such as depression and hypertension; moderate improvements in controlling risk factors such as blood pressure and cholesterol; increased clinical preventive service uptake, such as colorectal and cervical cancer screening; and improvements in patient-reported outcomes, such as quality of life and self-rated health."[27]

Fryer studied Colorado Medicaid patients, some of whom were given a primary care doctor and others who were not. While physician charges were slightly higher for those with a PCP, the decrease in emergency room and inpatient charges translated to a 15% overall decrease in costs for those with a PCP compared to those without.[28]

While more primary care lowers costs, more specialists

may raise them. Baicker and Chandra reported in a national study of Medicare patients, "States with more general practitioners use more effective care and have lower spending, while those with more specialists have higher costs and lower quality."[29] Another trial found that family physicians and general internists, after adjusting for patient mix, had lower utilization of resources and hospitalizations than specialists.[30]

Zhou et al. studied a sample of 5% of Medicare patients in 2008. For every 1000 patients in an area, adding a PCP reduced annual health care spending by $634 and reduced thirty-day mortality by 2.14%. In contrast, each additional hospital bed per 1000 patients in an area raised annual spending by $52, while each additional specialist increased costs by $1000.[31]

Franks and colleagues argued that one of the benefits of primary care was reducing excessive testing and overtreatment, observing, "Ironically, those who are not poor have greater access to care, are more likely to receive the more intensive care offered by specialists and are more likely to undergo invasive procedures...higher income not only improves access to appropriate care but also increases the risk of excessive care."[32]

It makes sense intuitively that a doctor who knows a patient will have a better sense of when the patient needs further evaluation. For example, I have several patients who frequently come into clinic with a complaint of chest pain. For these patients, my awareness of their past presentations allows me to avoid sending them all to the emergency room for urgent evaluation each time. Knowing that Mr. S had his chest pain go away when he started an anti-depressant means that I have less worry that I am missing a life-threatening diagnosis. I also know that Mr. S has had multiple prior trips to the emergency room with extensive screening for heart, lung and gastrointestinal disease that all turned up negative.

The length of time a patient has been with a doctor impacts

the cost of their care. Weiss and Blustein noted that longer ties were associated with decreased hospitalizations, with patients with a relationship of over ten years having odds of hospitalization roughly thirty percent less than those who had only been with their doctor for less than a year.[33] In addition, those patients with the extended ties cost Medicare over $800 dollars less a year than those with a relationship of less than a year with their doctor.[34]

Again, this makes intuitive sense. I am likely to know far more about a patient who I have seen for a decade than someone who may have only seen me once or twice. I am far less likely to send them to the emergency room for their complaints of abdominal pain when I know that they have had unchanged chronic abdominal pain for a decade. In the case of Mrs. C, she has had severe incapacitating anxiety for years. Her symptoms included chronic abdominal pain at every visit, yet a complete workup was negative. I suspect that this may be irritable bowel syndrome, where patients suffer very real pain, diarrhea and constipation, but not from a concrete secondary cause like a tumor. My knowledge of this patient, learned after almost two decades of seeing her, allows her to avoid repetitive, intrusive and even painful testing or sending her for multiple emergency room evaluations or hospitalizations.

Research has examined primary care versus specialty care. Starfield summarized the findings, stating, "Primary care physicians do at least as well as specialists in caring for specific common diseases, and they do better overall when the measures of quality are generic,"[35] Generic measures were those not linked to a particular disease, such as not smoking and increased exercise. Rosenblatt and others noted that some patients see a specialist for their majority of outpatient care, noting that the rate of preventive care such as flu vaccine was higher for patients who saw primary care for most of their visits than those seeing specialists as their primary physician.

Rosenblatt et al. concluded, "Principal care means something quite different for most specialists than it does for most generalists. Specialists...rarely provide a substantial amount of care beyond the boundaries of their specialty."[36]

Franks and Fiscella studied over 13,000 respondents to a national survey, reporting, "After adjustment for demographics, health insurance status, reported diagnoses, health perceptions and smoking status, respondents using a primary care physician compared to those using a specialist had 33% lower annual adjusted health care expenditures and lower adjusted mortality."[37] Franks and colleagues noted that, "the quality of care provided by specialists outside their specialties declines."[38]

Data also suggest that the proportion of primary care visits provided by specialists has dropped in recent years, with the proportion dropping from 8% in 1997 to 4.8% in 2010.[39]

This should not be taken as implying that specialists are incapable of providing broader care. Some specialists, such as many general surgeons or rheumatologists, are quite good at broad-based patient management. Other specialties want nothing to do with it. Still, since broad-based care focused on the whole patient, rather than particular organ systems, is what primary care offers, it makes sense that primary care would do that better.

Primary care doctors offer better preventive care. States with more PCPs have lower rates of smoking and obesity.[40] Studies also showed that a greater supply of family physicians, "is associated with earlier detection of breast cancer, colon cancer, cervical cancer and melanoma."[41] Shea and colleagues found that the lack of a primary care provider was the strongest risk factor for severe, uncontrolled hypertension among patients seen in the emergency room.[42]

Ku and Druss showed how rates of Covid-19 infection and death were higher in primary health professional shortage areas, places where the number of primary care doctors was below what was needed for care.[43]

Goodson noted that patients with the three key diseases of hypertension, diabetes and hypercholesterolemia benefit from early treatment.[44] Initial and early diagnosis of these conditions is most likely to come from primary care doctors. Primary prevention is clearly superior to secondary treatment once complications from untreated disease develops.

The benefits of primary care persist even under new payment models. Accountable care organizations were a new Medicare innovation that was part of the Affordable Care Act. An analysis of Medicare spending concluded, "spending was lower and quality of care better for Medicare beneficiaries served by larger independent physician groups with strong primary care orientations."[45]

A study showed that having regular primary care was more important than having health insurance in getting preventive care. The authors concluded, "Expanding insurance coverage alone will not result in levels of health care utilization for the poor commensurate with their need. A more successful strategy....(is) to ensure that each individual, regardless of income, can call upon a usual source of care who will provide comprehensive treatment."[46]

Twenty years later, another evaluation yielded similar results. While preventive care was most for those with both health insurance and a usual source of care, typically a PCP, DeVoe et al. found, "When directly compared with health insurance status, usual source of care has been found to be a stronger predictor of access to care and have a stronger influence of the receipt of preventive services and the likelihood of timely visits to health care facilities."[47] The authors also wrote, "The development of a continuous relationship with a medical caregiver is especially important for people with chronic illnesses and mental health problems. When people lack a usual source of care, their access to necessary services is reduced, which may result in poorer health outcomes."[48]

Others estimated the effect if the United States had a physician workforce made up of 50% primary care doctors. They showed that it would improve patient access to basic care, cut costs in terms of reduced income by subspecialists and reduce the cost of marginal tests and procedures by billions of dollars.[49]

What does not having a primary care dominant health system mean for the nation? Starfield compared the United States with eleven European and North American countries whose health systems are more oriented to primary care. The other nations had better health status, life expectancy, satisfaction with their health system, lower medication use and lower health care costs than the United States.[50]

Thus, the intuitive sense that having a primary care doctor results in better health outcomes at lower overall costs is backed by convincing evidence. Patients' belief that having a regular personal doctor is better for their health is demonstratively true.

---

[1] Starfield, Contribution, 459

[2] Starfield, Contribution, 461

[3] Starfield, Contribution, 462

[4] Jeanne M. Lambrew, Gordon H. DeFriese, Timothy S. Carey, Thomas C. Ricketts, Andrea K. Biddle, "The Effects of having a Regular Doctor on Access to Primary Care," *Medical Care,* 1996. 34(2): 2096

[5] Lambrew, 2102

[6] James Macinko, Barbara Starfield, Leiyu, "Quantifying the Health Benefits of Primary Care Physician Supply in the United States," *International Journal of Health Services,* 2007; 37(1):111

[7] Macinko, 111

[8] Macinko,111

[9] Macinko, 111

[10] Sanjay Basu, Seth A. Berkowitz, Robert L. Phillips, Asaf Bitton, Bruce E. Landon, Russell S Phillips, "Association of Primary Care Supply with Popu-

lation Mortality in the United States, 2005-2015, *JAMA Internal Medicine,* 2019; 179(4): 506

[11] Sanjay Basu and others, "Estimated Effect on Life Expectancy of Alleviating Primary Care Shortages in the United States," *Ann Int Med,* July, 2021; 174(7): 920

[12] Satya Preetham Gunta and Others, "Association of number of primary care physicians with preventable hospitalizations and premature deaths," *Postgraduate Medicine,* 2021, https://doi.org/10.1080/00325481.2021.2021038

[13] Starfield, Contribution, 463

[14] Starfield, Contribution, 463-4

[15] Starfield, Contribution, 469

[16] Judith D. Kasper, "The Importance of the Usual State of Care for Children's Physician Access and Expenditures," *Medical Care,* May, 1987; 25(5): 398

[17] Steven Shea, Dawn Misra, Martin H. Ehrlich, Leslie Field, Charles K. Francis, "Predisposing Factors for severe, Uncontrolled Hypertension in an Inner-City Minority Population," *NEJM,* 1992, 327:776

[18] Sheryl Ryan, Anne Riley, Myungsa Kang, Barbara Starfield, "The Effects of Regular Source of Care and Health Need of Medical Care Use among Rural Adolescents," *Arch Pediatr Adolesc Med,* 2001:155: 184

[19] Kasper, 397

[20] Kasper, 397

[21] James M. Perrin and others, "Primary care Involvement Among Hospitalized Children," *Arch Pediatr Adolesc Med, May 1996; 150: 479*

[22] Thomas G. Rundall, John R.C. Wheeler, "The Effect of Income on Use of Preventive Care: An Evaluation of Alternative Explanations," *Journal of Health and Social Behavior,* December 1979; 20(4): 484

[23] Starfield, Contribution, 473

[24] Starfield, Contribution, 479

[25] Janet M. Bronstein and others, "Primary care visits and ambulatory care sensitive diabetes hospitalizations among adult Alabama Medicaid beneficiaries," *Primary Care Diabetes,* 2022; https://doi.org/10.1016/jpcd.2021.10.005

[26] Starfield, Contribution, 481

[27] David T. Liss, Toshiko Uchida, Cheryl L. Wilkes, Ankitha Radakrishnan, Jeffrey A. Linder, "General Health Checks in Adult Primary Care: A Review," *JAMA*, June 8, 2021; 325(22):2294

[28] Donaldson, 64

[29] Katherine Baicker, Amitabh Chandra, "Medicare Spending: The Physician Workforce and Beneficiaries' Quality of Care," *Health Affairs*, April 7, 2004;W184

[30] Sheldon Greenfield and others, "Variations in Resource Utilization Among Medical Specialties and Systems of Care: Results from the Medical Outcomes Study," *JAMA*, March 25, 1992; 267(12): 1628

[31] Mo Zhou, Allison H. Oakes, John FP Bridges, William V. Padula, Jodi B. Segal, "Regional Supply of Medical Resources and Systemic Use of Health Care Among Medicare Beneficiaries," *JGIM*, 2018; 33(12)2127

[32] Peter Franks, Carolyn M. Clancy, Paul A. Nuttig, "Gatekeeping Revisited – Protecting Patients from Overtreatment," *NEJM*, August 6, 1992;327(6): 425

[33] Linda J. Weiss, Jan Blustein, "Faithful Patients: The Effect of Long-Term Physician-Patient Relationships on the Costs and Use of Health Care by Older Americans," *American Journal of Public Health (AJPH)*, December 1996; 86(12): 1745

[34] Weiss, 1745

[35] Starfield, Contribution, 477

[36] Roger Rosenblatt, L. Gary Har, Laura-Mae Balwin, Leighton Chen, Ronald Schneeweiss, "The Generalist Role of Specialty Physicians: Is there a Hidden System of Primary Care," *JAMA*, May 6, 1998; 279(17): 1369

[37] Peter Franks, Kevin Fiscella, "Primary Care Physicians and specialists as personal physicians: health care expenditures and mortality experience," *Journal of Family Practice*, August, 1998; 47(2): 105

[38] Franks, Gatekeeping, 426

[39] Samuel T. Edwards, John N. Mafi, Bruce E. Landon, "Trends and Quality of Care in Outpatient Visits to Generalist and Specialist Physicians Delivering Primary in the United States, 1997-2010," *Journal of General Internal Medicine(JGIM)*, February 25, 2014; 29(6): 947

[40] Starfield, Contribution, 477

[41] Starfield, Contribution, 477

[42] Shea, 776

[43] Benson S. Ku, Benjamin G. Druss, "Associations Between Primary Care Provider Shortage Areas and County-Level Covid-19 Infection and Mortality Rates in the United States," *JGIM*, 2020; 35(11): 3404

[44] John D. Goodson, "Unintended Consequences of Resource-Based Relative Value scale Reimbursement," *JAMA*, November 21, 2007; 298(19): 2308

[45] J. Michael McWilliams, ME Chernew, AM Zaslavsky, P Hamed, BE Landon, "Delivery System Integration and health care spending and quality for Medicare beneficiaries," *JAMA Internal Medicine*, 2013; 173(15): 1447

[46] Rundall, 405

[47] Jennifer DeVoe, George E. Fryer, Robert Phillips, Larry Green, "Receipt of Preventive Care Among Adults: Insurance Status and Usual Source of Care," *AJPH*, 2003;93:786

[48] DeVoe, Receipt, 786

[49] Marc L. Rivo, "Internal Medicine and the Journey to Medical Generalism," *Ann Int Med*, 1993; 119:147

[50] Barbara Starfield, "Is Primary Care Essential?" *Lancet*, 1994;344:

Waiting for the Doctor – Robert Lee MacCameron.

(Courtesy, Wiki Commons)

Approximate Percentage of American Physicians in General
Practice/Primary Care:

Early 1930s	87%
1940	76%
1949	63%
1960	45%
1970	37.3%
1994	32.3%
2010	percentage of new graduates going into primary care 25%

CHAPTER 3

The Decline of Primary Care

Despite the clear benefits of primary care, multiple factors have resulted in the decline of primary care in the United States.

First, the push for increased convenience has led to increasing numbers of patients going to alternatives for acute care, from emergency rooms to acute care clinics.

Second, insurance plans have increased patient deductibles and co-pays in an effort to reduce costs. This acts as a strong financial disincentive for patients to see their primary care doctor. Having a single preventive visit covered annually is often not enough for patients either with chronic illness or recurring acute issues.

These increased financial costs of seeing primary care doctors due to these insurance company policies are but one of several factors that may contribute to patients having a less positive view of their primary care doctor.[1]

Finally, beyond a general shortage of primary care, there is the problem of maldistribution. There are clearly areas with existing shortages of primary care doctors, particularly in underserved communities. Even as community health centers see expanded numbers of patients, there are increased difficulties recruiting primary care doctors.[2]

The number of primary care physicians varies greatly between states. A 2019 study showed Mississippi with the lowest primary care physician (PCP) to population ratio at 49.1 PCPs/100,000 people compared to 130.7 PCPs/100,000 in the District of Columbia.[3] Another analysis suggested that the more rural an area, the less number of primary care physicians.[4]

A particular area where there is a shortage of PCPs is counties with a large number of "dual eligible beneficiaries," patients who qualify for both Medicare and Medicaid on the basis of age or disability and low income. One-third of the counties with the higher number of these patients also were areas short of primary care physicians. This tended to occur most often in Southeastern states.[5]

Ironically, the United States needs primary care more than ever, given the rise of chronic conditions estimated to affect 50% of the population.[6] Problems such as obesity and diabetes are rampant, while millions are seen annually with cardiovascular diseases such as high blood pressure. As much as a quarter of Americans suffer from a mental disorder.[7] Primary care is the first point of contact and the manager of many of these problems.

The role of primary care in providing mental health care is crucial. Studies have shown that about half of patients with depression or generalized anxiety were first diagnosed by their PCP.[8] Given the shortage of psychiatrists, PCPs manage a high proportion of mental health issues for patients.

The last 100 years have seen an astonishing drop in the percentage of American physicians who practiced primary care. In the early 1930s, 87% of private practice physicians were in general care; by the early 1960s, this percentage had dropped to 50%.[9] Starting in 1960, increases in specialists began to outpace increases in primary care.[10] The number of primary care doctors as a proportion of the whole dropped further in subsequent years.

Unlike in many other countries, patients wanting to see specialists did not, at least until the last few decades, have to be referred by their primary care doctor. Specialists might have cared more about the absence of primary care if that meant the patient could not see them.

Starr explained how during and after World War II, "Students in medical school, like young doctors in the army, could see how general practitioners were treated. The universities generally did not want GPs to admit patients to affiliated hospitals. As the medical schools replaced part-time instructors with full-time professors from research backgrounds, they were also substituting new models of professional competence."[11]

Specialists were also noted to have a higher income than general practitioners, despite working fewer hours. Insurers paid more for physician visits in hospitals than in the office. Since the specialists were often hospital-based, this added to their income advantage over the GPs. At the same time, the hospitals were adding more residents in training, due to payments from the government that covered their cost and their role as cheap professional labor. Thus, the hospital-based specialists could be more productive as a result of the assistance from the residents, further adding to their higher income.

Studies showed that many students intending to become general practitioners switched to becoming a specialist during medical school. A study at Cornell in the 1950s reported that the proportion planning to become general practitioners dropped from 60% to 16% between the first and fourth years.[12] The study's authors attributed the change to the growing body of medical knowledge, quoting a student as writing, "I can see why specialization is the rage today. Medicine is so large now that a doctor doesn't feel confident unless he knows at least one field extremely well, rather than a little about all subjects."[13] The decline continued. From 50% in the early 1960s the percentage of doctors doing primary care plummeted further to around 35% in 1975.

The 1960s saw an attempt to stem this decline with the development and strengthening of residency programs in primary care. The specialty of Family Medicine was started while General Pediatrics and General Internal Medicine were advertised as alternatives for those wanting more training but still wanting to be a patient's personal physician.

In 1970 Congress mandated that graduate medical programs produce a majority of generalists. However, the legislation defined it as including all internists, family medicine and pediatricians in the first year of residency training ignoring the reality that many residents went into specialties later in training. As a result, while the legislative target was met, the actual result was the continued production of more specialists than PCPs.[14]

Nor did these efforts reverse the income differential between specialists and primary care. The percentage of doctors opting for primary care stabilized but did not go up.

This percentage of American doctors doing primary care stayed around 35% from 1975 to 2007.[15] More specific data from the American Medical Association showed slow further erosion as the percentage of primary care doctors dropped from 37.3% of doctors in 1970 to 32.3% in 1994.[16]

The problem of decreased primary care has been noticed for decades. Almost thirty years ago, in a 1993 editorial, Dr. Jerome Kassirer, then editor-in-chief of the prestigious *New England Journal of Medicine* , commented, "In internal medicine, in particular, the generalist is becoming an endangered species. For nearly two decades, training programs in internal medicine have been producing more subspecialists than generalists."[17] Kassirer pointed out that in contrast to Canada, "In the United States, policies on education and training are the domain of a decentralized, loosely associated collection of organizations."[18] Kassirer noted that the goal was that at least 50% of those training in internal medicine should become primary care doctors but that this objective didn't explain how that was to be achieved. Kassirer concluded, "If I were a program director...I would have no idea how to convince – or coerce – half of the graduating residents to pursue careers as generalists."[19]

The reduced number of primary care doctors didn't improve in the next decade. In a 2004 *NEJM* article, Dr. Ruth-Maire Fincher wrote, "Several factors have contributed to the decreased interest in primary care: renumeration is lower than that for subspecialties...educational debt has increased, the demands of practice are often incompatible with the lifestyles that students desire, and physicians are frustrated by the hassles of medical practice."[20]

The increase in the debts owed by medical students was striking. From an average of $27,000 for graduates of private medical schools in 1984, it increased to $135,000 in 2003. For graduates of public medical schools, the median debt went from $22,000 in 1984 to $100,000 in 2003.[21] By 2017 the median debt had increased to $192,000.[22]

A 2016 article found that 58% of graduating family medicine residents had over $150,000 in educational debt, with 26% owing more than $250,000.[23] This reflects the high cost of medical school. In 2018 the median cost of medical school was $243,902 for public schools and $322,767 for private schools.[24]

A 2005 report noted that the problem had worsened. In the prior five years, the number of US medical graduates matching in family medicine dropped 35%, while primary care internal medicine programs saw 33% fewer graduates entering the field.[25] Another analysis surveying graduating residents in internal medicine in 2003 showed that only 27% planned to become generalists, compared to 57% choosing to become specialists.[26]

Further studies showed the situation worsening. Hauer et al. reported in 2008 that while internal medicine was still a top choice for students, with 23.2% choosing it, less than a tenth of these or only 2% of students planned to go into general internal medicine.[27] In this survey, 4.9% of students planned to go into family medicine and 11.7% into pediatrics, while 2.3% were doing combined programs such as internal medicine/pediatrics.[28] Thus, less than 20% of students planned to go into primary care.

While most other nations have more primary care doctors than specialists, the situation is reversed in the United States. Statistics from 2010 showed that fewer than 25% of new medical school graduates were going into primary care, with changes over time suggesting that this percentage could fall below 20%.[29] A 2010 article stated, "These trends have now become so pronounced that it is likely that the primary care physician workforce will not replace itself over the next twenty years."[30]

Others pointed out the declining percentage of primary care doctors who were graduates of US medical schools and the increase in foreign medical graduates.

Concurrently primary care showed increased attrition, adding to the decrease in the number of primary care physicians.[31]

Primary care doctors saw a higher percentage of outpatient visits than their proportion of doctors. Of the 956 million visits Americans made to office-based physicians in 2008, 51.3% went to PCPs at a time when PCPs made up about one-third of physicians involved in direct patient care.[32] The primary care doctors in 2010 included 79,831 in Family Medicine, 71,487 in Internal Medicine, 44,933 in Pediatrics, 2999 in Geriatrics and a mere 9557 remaining General Practitioners.[33]

While primary care makes up over half of all patient visits in the United States, it makes up a much lower proportion of the costs of health care. Primary care accounted for only 5.4% of all health care spending in the United States.[34] In comparison, most developed countries spend 12–17% of their health care expenditures on primary care.[35]

The number of PCPs per capita in the population declined from 2005 to 2015, from 46.6/100,000 people to 41.4/100,000.[36] The greatest decrease was in rural areas as retiring doctors were not always replaced. In contrast, as I noted earlier, in 1900 there were 173 physicians, almost all general practitioners i.e. primary care, per 100,000 people in the United States.[37]

At least four different studies have projected huge shortages of primary care doctors within the next 5–15 years.[38] [39] [40] [41] Studies predict shortages of PCPs from 44,000 up to 52,000, or about a quarter of the total current number, by 2025.[42] A 2019 analysis put the shortfall at 49,300 by 2030.[43]

The increased need and hence potential shortage are not merely a function of decreased PCPs. It is further driven first by population growth. Second, the aging of the population requires an increased need for medical care, on average, for the population. Finally, the expansion of insurance to cover more people, while a worthwhile development, means more people looking to find a primary care doctor.

Michael Dill and Edward Salsberg, summarizing a workforce projection by the Association of American Medical Colleges (AAMC), wrote, "Shortages are likely to be manifested in a number of ways, some subtle and some not. This includes longer waiting times for appointments, increased travel distances to get care, shorter visit times with physicians, expanded use of non-physicians for care and higher prices...Any future shortages are likely to have an uneven effect...resulting in hardships for both poor urban and rural communities."[44] The AAMC analysis also concluded, "Our baseline projections predict a greater shortage in primary care than in any other specialty area."[45]

Worsening the shortage is the reality that the amount of time the average primary care doctor wants to work has decreased. Many doctors are aging and hence may not be able or desire to see the same volume of patients they once did. Issues of lifestyle have become more important. The increasing number of women PCPs has increased the desire to better balance the work/non-work division, resulting in fewer weekly work hours. Finally, employed physicians who have accepted a fixed salary in exchange for a fixed number of hours have, in many cases, accepted lower pay as the cost of more life flexibility. The entrepreneurial ethic of the independent physician led him to accept overwork as the cost of success; those working in corporate medicine may be less willing to accept it simply so their employer can be more financially successful.

Moreover, with the advent of electronic medical records, existing PCPs are seeing fewer patients each day, which further decreases the availability of PCPs for patients.

The number of foreign medical graduates setting up shop in the United States has helped but not solved the problem. International medical graduates are more likely to practice in rural and underserved areas. They are a sizable fraction of current generalist physicians in the nation. International medical graduates have helped fill the gap in the supply of PCPs in recent years; if their numbers decrease, whether by limits on immigration or for other reasons, this could worsen the shortage of primary care physicians. The AAMC report noted, "If US MDs continue to select other specialties, the future of primary care practice is likely to rely increasingly on foreign medical graduates, osteopaths and non-physician clinicians."[46]

Understanding the decline in the number of PCPs, we must turn to the issues affecting the supply of potential new PCPs.

One factor in the decision whether to become a specialist or primary care physician is financial. A large study looked at the financial return on educational investment for a variety of professions in the United States. The highest return was for specialist physicians and attorneys, intermediate for dentists and business people and lowest for primary care doctors. The researchers concluded that, "students can expect a poorer financial return on their educational investment when they choose a career in primary care medicine than when they choose a procedure-based medical or surgical specialty."[47] The authors admitted that nonfinancial factors play a role in the choice but argued, "Policy makers would be remiss, however, if they ignored the powerful influence of up-front costs of professional training and students' concerns about their ability to repay their debts."[48]

Compensation for primary care doctors is roughly half or less than that of almost all specialists.[49] This calculation is affected by some non-procedure specialties, such as rheumatology or endocrinology, where the discrepancy is not so large. Some procedure-based specialists make far more. Internist Louise McHarris commented, "There needs to be better parity between primary care and specialists...specialists getting 50% more rather than five times more would be fairer."[50]

Another study looked at factors influencing specialty choice among osteopathic physicians. For the two-thirds who chose non-primary care specialties, key factors included student debt and the income and prestige of these specialties.[51]

Students with more debt were found, not surprisingly, to be more likely to choose a high-paying specialty career than primary care.[52]

It is clear that income plays a key role in medical students' choice of specialty. Dr. Norman Levinsky noted, "The anticipated income and number of hours worked, especially in comparison with the medical profession as a whole, influence residents' choice of specialties. There is a striking linear correlation between the average income of physicians in each specialty and the success of residency programs in that field in attracting applicants."[53]

For many years, the existing gap in income between primary care and specialists has continued to widen.[54] Bodenheimer et al. identified four factors behind the widening gap. First, the volume of procedures has increased faster than the volume of office visits, benefiting the specialists performing the procedures. Second, the updating of fee schedules has historically been made by a specialist-dominated panel. Third, private insurers have more commonly paid more than Medicare for procedures to a greater extent than for office visits.[55] For example, a 2001 study showed that private insurers paid an average of 104% of Medicare fees for office visits and 133% for procedures and imaging studies.[56] Finally, Medicare, for many years, tried to limit overall costs. When costs exceeded these limits, Medicare reduced the conversion factor governing the payments per service. Thus, increased procedures helped drive reduced payments for service for the primary care doctors.[57]

The amount of money involved is huge. One analysis in 2009 suggested that students who choose a high-income specialty over primary care could expect an additional $3.5 million dollars in income over a lifetime.[58]

Medicare pays most of the cost of graduate medical education, the training of residents in various specialties. However, attempts to use this funding to increase the supply of primary care doctors has had mixed success. The Medicare Prescription Drug, Improvement and Modernization Act of 2003 redistributed 3000 residency positions in hopes of spurring more residents to choose primary care. While there was an increase in primary care training after this redistribution, the growth of non-primary care specialty training was twice as large.[59]

The Affordable Care Act also tried to redistribute residency positions to create more primary care positions, with a focus on those in underserved areas. However, there is skepticism about whether this will prove any more effective given the declining numbers of physicians choosing primary care. Chen and colleagues wrote, "The relatively small primary care gains seen after redistribution overestimate real workforce gains, given the loss of internal medicine physicians to further specialty training or to hospital-based careers."[60]

There is evidence that financial changes might impact the numbers choosing primary care. Rosenthal and colleagues surveyed graduates of six American medical schools. While only 27% were choosing careers in primary care, another 25% said that they would change to primary care if there were adjustments in income, hours worked or loan repayment.[61] In this 25%, most identified a narrowing of the income gap between specialists and primary care as the crucial factor that would make them change to primary care. Students with the most debt in this cohort were also the most likely to change to primary care if their debt could be eliminated.[62] If the results applied to the larger current student population, it suggests that financial changes could double the number of medical students going into primary care.

Among the non-financial factors influencing career choice in medicine is the students' estimation of the effect of that choice on lifestyle. A lifestyle of limited hours is likely an important factor in getting students to choose specialties where hours are fixed, such as being a hospitalist or emergency room physician. Medical students generally believe, "anesthesiologists, dermatologists, emergency physicians and radiologists, have more, 'personal time free of practice requirements for leisure, family and avocational pursuits and control of total weekly hours spent on professional responsibilities.'"[63]

If the students were to talk to primary care doctors, they would hear the downsides of a career that cannot be neatly shut off at closing time. Even for those PCPs employed by large systems, the work does not stop with the last patient appointment. The burdens of charting and catching up on paperwork mean that days frequently extend into the evening and weekend. When a primary care physician is taking care of a sick patient, he cannot simply stop because the clock hits five p.m. This is different from shift-based specialties such as emergency medicine or hospitalists.

A survey of graduating internal medicine residents noted the negative factors making primary care less appealing. These included, "trainees' perceptions of job dissatisfaction among primary care providers, lack of prestige, indebtedness, lower income potential, greater stress, bureaucracy changing consumer preferences away from primary care, and a lack of clarity about the future of primary care practice as other types of providers enter the field."[64]

In the last two decades, many of the physicians who train as generalists chose to become hospitalists rather than choosing primary care. The vast majority of the medical residency experience is in the hospital. Choosing to become a hospitalist is choosing the familiar, the thing for which one is best trained, rather than the unknown life of the primary care doctor.

We had our own experience with how jarring that could be when we recruited an excellent physician just out of residency. She was unprepared for the PCP life and, within six months, abandoned it to become a hospitalist. Subsequently, at our practice we usually try to recruit doctors who have been doing primary care already, for they have a much better idea of what they are getting themselves into. In general, our experience has been that residency does not really prepare you for what it will be like to practice exclusively as a primary care doctor. It is not simply understanding the medical problems as much as the mountain of demands placed on the primary care provider by insurers, as well as the expectations of the patients.

Training itself tends to bias medical students against primary care.[65] As Dr. Jack Colwill aptly summarized in the *New England Journal*, "The academic medical center itself is a major obstacle...Academic medical centers emphasize the application of science and technology to the treatment of disease in individual patients...in this environment, generalism tends to be defined in terms of the absence of specialization rather than in terms of its positive features of breadth, comprehensiveness and integration. Most medical education occurs in this tertiary care milieu, producing a major socializing force toward specialization."[66] One medical student stated, "I feel like medical school is always talking about 'the rare case this' or the 'rare case that' and it's always 'the primary care physician screwed up and couldn't find it for ten years, and then the specialist found it after all this time.'"[67]

Another negative factor is that the traditional outpatient rotations occur in hospital-affiliated outpatient clinics with disproportionate numbers of uninsured, non-compliant patients with mental health issues and substance abuse, with little continuity, thus giving a negative portrayal of life as a primary care doctor.

The evidence suggests that many students who enter residency with a plan to become primary care physicians change their minds during residency. Colwill commented, "The heavy orientation towards inpatients, organization of inpatient wards according to subspecialty, encouragement by faculty members to take up subspecialty fellowships, limited experience in primary care, and the limited number of generalists to serve as role models all contribute to this shift towards specialization."[68] A survey of forty-eight residents in family medicine found that half changed to another specialty before completing training. Those who stayed in family medicine were more likely to be from a rural area, be married, have a strong motivation for patient contact and expressed more humanistic than scientific interests.[69]

Another study looked at residents in internal medicine. Sixty-two percent changed career plans during residency. By the end, only 25% planned to go into general internal medicine.[70]

There is another new factor that may further contribute to the decline in the number of primary care doctors. Previously students and residents on inpatient rotations would encounter primary care doctors who would care for their patients. Since PCPs have been replaced by hospitalists in this role, students and residents have even less contact with primary care doctors. Instead, the new role model with whom they will spend much time is the hospitalist. A 2022 article reported that in 2018 71% of newly certified general internists chose to become hospitalists while only 8% chose to practice outpatient care as PCPs.[71]

Among graduating medical students, another factor cited in choosing to become a specialist is that of prestige. Every time someone talks about how the role of primary care providers can be filled as easily by a nurse practitioner or physician assistant, it is another devaluing of the field. Nor does filling out endless forms seem glamorous compared to battling cancer as an oncologist or heart disease as a cardiologist. The fact that the PCP must know how to treat all of these diseases seems buried under the appalling burden of paperwork the insurers and patients routinely assume that the PCPs will do. Somehow being a specialist became "special," while generalists were ordinary. Levinsky wrote, "There is a widely shared perception that the best and brightest students do not enter the field."[72] Levinsky gave the example of the Boston University School of Medicine, noting that over a fifteen-year period, "the percentage of honors students choosing primary care residencies decreased disproportionately."[73]

Writing in the *New England Journal*, Dr. Robert Petersdorf commented, "One must wonder why being a generalist is the norm for 50% of the physicians in Canada and 70% of those in the United Kingdom. My conclusion is that in our country, the generalist specialties suffer from the Rodney Dangerfield syndrome – they get no respect. The lack of respect not only is economic and academic, but also pervades all of graduate medical education and, ultimately, medical practice."[74]

Hoff quoted one medical student as saying, "You definitely get a sense in med school that the smart kids, the ones doing the best, are not going into primary care, and shouldn't, and the kids in the middle or lower end of the pack are the future primary care doctors."[75] Another said, "I think a lot of us view primary care as something beneath us, not as exciting as specialty care."[76]

Block et al. interviewed medical students, residents and faculty about their perceptions of primary care versus specialty careers. The authors wrote, "Respondents generally perceive primary care as not requiring high levels of expertise; nearly half believe generalists are not the best physicians to manage patients with serious illness."[77] Trainees reported little encouragement toward generalist careers and negative attitudes toward generalists among the faculty. The study reported, "Only 0.3% of students and residents perceive that faculty encourage academically capable learners to enter primary care. Only 15.8% of respondents report being encouraged to enter primary care by both faculty and peers."[78]

The disparagement of primary care as simple and not appropriate for managing serious illness in academia certainly doesn't help produce more primary care doctors. Block concluded, "The presence of a chilly climate for primary care in AHCs (academic health centers) represents a barrier to primary care career choice and education."[79]

Agreeing with this analysis, Wayne Guglielmo wrote in *Medical Economics*, "Compounding the problem (of income differentials) is graduates' perception that as PCPs, they'll occupy a lower rank in the medical pecking order."[80] Cassell noted, "A common error in thinking about primary care is to see it as entry-level medicine."[81]

Hoff noted how this perception is reflected in the changing role of doctors on television. In place of a PCP like Marcus Welby, "Contemporary television shows such as *ER, House,* and *Grey's Anatomy* shape our perception of the 'best' and 'coolest' doctors as superspecialists interacting with one another with hospital settings that are fast-paced, exciting, and attractively quirky, and where many diagnoses are made magically through the sheer brilliance and eccentricities of the physicians involved."[82]

As important as the inadequate replacement of new PCPs

is the unhappiness of current practitioners. Dr. Frederick Barken, in his combined memoir and analysis of primary care, *Out of Practice,* wrote in 2011, "I chose to resign from the practice of internal medicine ten to fifteen years earlier than is usual, but still with dignity, as I saw the quality and personal satisfaction of primary care medicine eroding."[83]

The 1990s saw a near doubling of the number of patients covered by HMOs, with a huge increase in the number of PCPs employed by them, not always happily. As early as 1992, a survey of HMOs reported that they were experiencing a shortage of PCPs and that PCP turnover was important. The tighter rules and decreased autonomy of PCPs with the HMOs may have contributed to increased unhappiness among PCPs. Grumbach et al. found that many HMOs gave financial incentives to limit referrals or to increase productivity that many PCPs felt compromised patient care.[84] Since evidence has shown that overall PCP job satisfaction was the most powerful predictor of PCP turnover, the increased job turnover of PCPs in the 1990s is a clue that all was not well in the field.[85]

A 2002 physician survey revealed that general internists had lower job satisfaction than either specialists or family physicians. Factors that correlated with more dissatisfaction included younger age, longer work hours, increased time pressure during office visits and more patients with complex psychosocial problems.[86] Conversely, satisfaction was higher when physicians had more control over their practice and perceived that their work demands were reasonable, two components that may decrease as independent practices are replaced by employee physicians.[87] Another survey showed dissatisfaction among PCPs greatest in Internal Medicine, followed by Family Medicine and least in Pediatrics.[88] I could speculate that this correlated with the amount of exposure dealing with Medicare and the Med Advantage plans.

Even Pediatrics is challenged. Pediatrician Stephen Berman commented, "Pediatricians currently have a more limited amount of time to spend with families during their visits. These shorter, less comprehensive visits are less satisfying to the families and pediatricians and undermine the value of continuity. Health plans attempt to purchase services at the lowest price possible...to remain financially solvent despite these low payments, pediatricians see increasing numbers of children for shorter visit times."[89] A retired Kaiser pediatrician commented on the changes in her workplace over time, saying, "The tradeoff is that you give up control...I always felt like I was hurrying through."[90] She noted that the job had become harder, stating, "Mental health was a huge change from when I started...It felt like we were on our own trying to figure it out."[91] She added, "Society has changed...parents are less present. Over the years, I saw so much mental health stuff that I wasn't equipped to take care of."[92] She concluded about her HMO experience, "People with mental health issues, you get the same amount of time as an ear infection."[93] Still, she felt that her job had not been as hard as the PCPs for adults, stating, "The Internal Medicine people, as a rule, they were just swamped."[94]

Abigail Zuger reported that physician satisfaction with the job dropped significantly from the 1970s to 1990s. While in 1973, less than 15% of physicians reported any doubts about choosing a career in medicine, the number had climbed to 30–40% in the 1990s.[95] Zuger found that dissatisfaction increased with the expansion of managed care and was also driven by fear of malpractice, lack of time and role as "double agents" trying to save money for the insurance companies.[96]

In a different analysis of primary care doctors, satisfaction among PCPs dropped dramatically from 1986 to 1997, with the majority of PCPs unhappy with the amount of time they had with individual patients, their autonomy and leisure time.[97]

A 2007 survey of primary care physicians reported that two-thirds would not choose primary care again if given the choice.[98] Another survey of PCPs in 2012 showed that they did not recommend primary care as a field. Instead, when asked to choose, they were more likely to recommend that those interested in primary care become a nurse practitioner.[99] This was true among both PCPs reporting satisfaction with practice and those dissatisfied with their practice.[100]

The decreased time PCPs have with patients is married to increasing patient assertiveness. One PCP observed, "People think they know everything from Dr. Google...They would find the wrong information and wouldn't let go."[101]

The negative effect of time pressure on PCPs' job satisfaction is worth more comment. A study showed that specialists had an average of fifty-one minutes for new patients, in which they focused on one organ system. General internists (39 minutes) and family physicians (34 minutes) had less time for new visits, during which they had to manage all of the patients' myriad issues, provide preventive care, meet quality markers as well as deal with psychosocial issues.[102]

Moreover, the time PCPs had with patients greatly decreased compared to the past as the advent of managed care, increased administrative work, and financial pressures caused PCPs to see more patients in a shorter amount of time. Studies have shown that patient satisfaction is related to the time they spend with their physician, so shorter visits that are perceived as more rushed lead patients to more negative views of their doctor while decreasing doctor satisfaction with the process.[103] [104]

The Kaiser pediatrician explained , "Twenty minutes was the usual visit. We were only allowed extra time for the first visit for depression and the first visit for attention deficit disorder...we couldn't say no if patients walked in late."[105]

Luft et al. looked at the differences between PCPs who cover other issues during an acute care visit, which has been called "max-packing," versus those who focus only on the acute issue. Those PCPs who covered multiple issues lowered overall health care costs, with better clinical quality metrics, fewer specialty referrals and greater patient satisfaction. However, the cost was another forty minutes, on average, on the electronic health record, compared to those PCPs who just focused on the acute issue.[106] This is another case where what is better for the system is worse for PCPs, for this extra time on the computer is uncompensated.

A 2014 survey of American physicians showed that 20% planned to reduce clinical work hours within the next year. A quarter of those responding reported that they would leave their current practice within two years, with 37% of these retiring and another 10% moving to an administrative position where they would no longer practice medicine. The major factors listed were burnout, unhappiness with electronic medical records and work-life balance.[107]

Burnout is defined as work-related emotional exhaustion, fatigue, and depression, occurs among people without prior psychopathology and can manifest as decreased work performance and effectiveness.[108] Thus physician burnout can hurt both the doctor and potentially their patient.

Burnout in primary care starts as early as residency, with published burnout rates among primary care residents varying from 40 to 78%.[109] Another study showed that, "perceived (lack of) control over the practice environment was also the single most important predictor of physician burnout."[110] As the book will show, physician control over their work has diminished dramatically in the last two to three decades.

Burnout in primary care has two negative consequences. First, burned-out physicians are unlikely to motivate new graduates to follow in their footsteps. Second, increasing burnout is associated with decreasing work hours.[111] Thus the shortage of new docs becoming primary care doctors is aggravated by existing PCPs cutting their hours. This reality leads to the conclusion that the number of primary care physicians is probably declining faster than is known.[112]

Those outside medicine often underestimate the non-financial factors affecting physicians. A 2019 study showed elevated levels of burnout (44%), sadness (11%) and clinical depression (4%) among American physicians.[113] Family Medicine and Internal Medicine were among the specialties with the highest level of burnout at 48% and 49% of physicians, respectively. When doctors in a field have negative feelings about their work life, it becomes increasingly difficult to recruit new graduates to work in that area. For physicians, the biggest sources of unhappiness were, "too many bureaucratic tasks (59%), too many hours at work (34%), the increasing computerization of practices (32%) and lack of respect from administrators, employers, colleagues and staff (30%).[114] Income was only the fifth most important issue.

A repeat survey in 2021 showed similar findings, with 21% of physicians reporting being depressed. Again the biggest source of burnout was too many bureaucratic tasks. One physician was reported to comment, "I barely spend enough time with most patients, just running from one to the next, and then after work, I spend hours documenting, charting, dealing with reports. I feel like an overpaid clerk."[115]

High debts also correlate with increased stress, cynicism and suicidal thoughts.[116] This suggests that the greatly increased debt of more recent medical graduates has contributed to burnout in primary care.

Decreasing physician autonomy has been shown to be a huge factor in burnout among primary care doctors. In a study of family physicians, the authors reported, "Dissatisfaction was much more likely when the family physicians felt they did not have: (1) the freedom to make clinical decisions that met their patients' needs; (2) a sufficient level of communication with specialists; (3) enough time with their patients; (4) the ability to provide high-quality patient care; (5) the freedom to make clinical decisions without financial conflicts of interest; or (6) the ability to maintain continuing relationships with their patients."[117]

A family physician with a large hospital-owned medical group told me, "The treadmill that you feel you are on...We need to push volume and see more patients to make a living... A lot of docs feel like they don't have control of their schedule."[118] He added, "A lot of my friends working for Kaiser are still feeling the treadmill...they feel like they are being pressured to see more patients."[119]

Another study by Grembowski et al. looked at causes of dissatisfaction in primary care doctors. They concluded, "We found that primary physicians are more dissatisfied in offices with a greater number of physicians, in a group rather than solo offices, and when they do not own the practice...salaried employment in large medical groups may be a risk factor for physician dissatisfaction."[120]

A survey compared PCPs and specialists in terms of factors limiting optimum patient care. PCPs noted significantly more problems, including inadequate time for patient visits, the patients' inability to pay for needed care, reduced availability of specialists for their patients, lack of communication from other doctors, and patient non-compliance with treatment compared to specialists. Both PCPs and specialists reported that care decisions rejected by insurance was the biggest barrier to best patient care.[121]

The collapse of independent practice and the consolidation of PCPs into large hospital or investor-owned practices in the last two decades seems likely to worsen PCP loss of autonomy and unhappiness with the job.

To address burnout, numerous intervention programs have been proposed. Most showed small benefits.[122] Interventions directed at individual doctors, such as mindfulness or cognitive behavioral strategies, were particularly ineffective, while those directed at organizational issues, such as schedule changes or reduced workload intensity, seemed to be more useful.[123]

In a June 2020 *New England Journal* commentary, Hartzband and Groopman noted that the pillars supporting intrinsic motivation and a sense of well-being for doctors are autonomy, competence and relatedness, or sense of belonging. They wrote, "Physicians now endure a profound lack of control over their time...Competence was once viewed as having a deep fund of medical knowledge and exercising judgment appropriately with each patient. Under recent health care reforms, it has been redefined as compliance of various metrics...competence has also become a matter of checking off boxes in the EHR...many doctors feel that the system is increasingly driven by money and metrics."[124]

Lifestyle issues have increased in importance for medical students over recent decades. Studies have shown preferences for a shorter, more controllable lifestyle as a key determinant of choice of careers within medicine.[125] The draw of careers with fixed hours, from radiology to dermatology to emergency care to hospitalists, compared to the extended hours involved in primary care should not be underestimated. Such an appeal increases if you can get paid more while working fewer hours compared to primary care. Or if you can work fewer hours, get paid more, not have to deal with much paperwork or psychosocial issues and have what is regarded as a more prestigious specialty.

Importantly, studies of practicing physicians also showed that increased work hours were strongly associated with increased physician dissatisfaction.[126]

Strikingly, the electronic health record (EHR) is a major cause of burnout in primary care doctors. A study of faculty and residents in nineteen primary care programs revealed that over a third had symptoms of burnout. Seventy-five percent of those reporting burnout attributed it at least partially to their electronic health record.[127] Eighty-five percent of doctors surveyed reported that the use of the EHR negatively affected their work-life balance, with burnout increasing the more time they had to spend on the EHR.[128]

Another negative factor for PCPs is the increasing fragmentation of care. One of the biggest factors cited as to why medical students chose to become PCPs was the appeal of providing continuity of care.[129] Fincher noted that PCPs, "used to provide long term, continuous care. Now hospitalists provide inpatient care, and patients in a managed-care system may see a different physician each time they seek outpatient care. These forces have eroded the traditional bond between physician and patient, which was what attracted many doctors to primary care in the first place."[130]

Another issue that gets little attention is the issue of acute versus chronic care. Chronic diseases, "are the major cause of medical care utilization, disability and death in the United States."[131] Yet studies have suggested that American medicine, "casts chronic diseases in a negative light," making primary care, "seen as the field of chronic disease," less attractive as a career.[132]

While malpractice claims are not the main factor affecting primary care doctors' happiness on a day-to-day basis, they can prove a very negative impact when it does happen. Zuger noted the emotional cost of even unsuccessful malpractice suits, stating, "No matter what the background or outcome of a suit, physician-defendants routinely describe feelings of shame, self-doubt and disillusion with medical practice that may persist for years."[133]

Since the primary care doctors' sense of self-worth is often strongly linked to their relationships with their patients, it can prove very disillusioning when a patient instead attacks the doctor. I have seen primary care physicians who have decided to get out of the field after having to endure even an unsuccessful malpractice claim.

As an aside, it is amazing how attorneys handling these claims do not have any sense that the doctor should take it personally. I had to give a deposition for an attorney who was suing the emergency room but reserved the right to sue my partner and our practice, whose patient she represented. When I ran into her later at a social event, she had no memory that anything unpleasant had happened. I will say that doctors take it very personally.

Barken echoed this when he wrote, "A local attorney once told me: 'Relax. Most suits are frivolous. They are just a cost of doing business.' I contend that no suit is frivolous if you are the defendant."[134]

Negative feelings among primary care doctors may further hasten the decline in numbers of PCPs. Writing in *JAMA*, Shanafelt et al. commented, "given the particularly high rates of burnout in some primary care disciplines (e.g., family medicine and general internal medicine), burnout could amplify workplace shortages and affect access to care."[135]

Sinsky and colleagues also documented the excess health care expenditure due to PCP turnover, noting evidence that when PCPs leave their practice, the costs for their patients increase. Sinsky et al. found an average of increased excess costs of over $86,000 per PCP who left their practice, totaling over $979 million in excess costs annually.[136] Sinsky et al. noted of the 316,471 total PCPs, 152,205 are expected to experience burnout, and 11,339 leave their current practice each year based on prior national studies.[137]

The problems resulting from reduced numbers of primary care doctors are clear to some. Goodson wrote in a *JAMA* commentary, "Without a robust, well supported, appropriately compensated and self-sustaining generalist workforce, the majority of the US population will not be able to benefit from the powerfully effective interventions for the asymptomatic patients whose only contact with the health care systems is through generalists. Furthermore, broad and affordable universal access to health care will not be possible without a solid base of generalists who can deliver care and organize appropriate referrals."[138]

There is certainly an ongoing call to expand the number of doctors graduating in primary care. One approach is to expand the number of residency positions in primary care. Petterson and colleagues estimated that there would be a need for an additional 44,000 primary care doctors by 2035 but that the current production rate would fall short by 75% (33,000) of this total. They argued that there needed to be an increase of 21% in the number of primary care residency positions to meet the shortfall.[139]

Other experts have argued that simply creating new residency positions will be ineffective without other reforms, noting that, "programs are struggling to fill these seats with qualified candidates."[140]

Physician recruitment agencies have confirmed the increasing shortages of primary care physicians, noting that they lead the list of physician recruitment searches. One recruiter commented, "Increasingly, primary care is one of those things Americans don't want to do."[141]

Our practice's experience over the last twenty-four years gives anecdotal confirmation of the declining numbers of those choosing to go into primary care. Twenty years ago, we recruited excellent physicians by running ads in one of the national journals. This changed over time. First, our ads only drew queries from foreign medical graduates (FMGs) seeking positions in order to maintain their visa status. After a while, even FMGs were no longer responding. We were forced to go to medical recruitment firms. Yet most of the time, they offered only candidates with marginal interest in primary care, such as someone laid off from a research position. Most of our recent new doctors come from other places in Portland, particularly among those wanting to leave large systems for more autonomy.

In the last year, we have recruited two doctors who decided to close their solo practices after over twenty years. However, while good for our clinic, it more reflects how hard it is for primary care doctors to continue in solo practice. From a state or national capacity standpoint, it doesn't grow the pool of primary care doctors.

Unfortunately, it is clear that there just aren't that many new primary care docs in the pipeline.

In the following chapters, we will explore some of the challenges confronting existing primary care doctors.

---

[1] Gordon Moore, Jonathan Showstack, "Primary Care Medicine in Crisis: Toward Reconstruction and Renewal," *Ann Int Med,* 2003;138:245

[2] Christopher B. Forest, "Strengthening Primary Care to Bolster the Health Care Safety Net," *JAMA,* March 1, 2006; 295(9): 1063

[3] Karissa Merritt, Yalda Jabbarpour, Stephen Peterson, John M. Westfall, "State Level Variation on Primary Care Physician Density," *American Family Physician,* August, 2021; 104(2): 133

[4] Jordan C. Gemelas, "Post ACA Trends in the US Primary Care Physician Shortage with Index of Relative Rurality," *Journal of Rural Health,* 2021; 37: 700

[5] Wendy Y. Yu, Sheldon M. Retchin, Peter Buerhaus, "Dual-Eligible Beneficiaries and Inadequate Access to Primary Care Providers," *Am J Manag Care,* 2021; 27(5): 212

[6] Hoff, 4

[7] Hoff, 4

[8] Hoff, 93

[9] Institute of Medicine, *Primary Care: America's Health in a New Era,* National Academy Press, Washington DC 1996, 155

[10] Macinko, 112

[11] Starr, 358

[12] Patricia L. Kendall, Hanan C. Selvin, "Tendencies Towards Specialization in Medical Training," quoted in *The Student Physician,* ed. Robert K. Merton, George G. Reader, Patricia L. Kendall, Harvard University Press; 157: 153

[13] Kendall, 163

[14] Rivo, 147

[15] Macinko, 112

[16] American Medical Association, "Physician Characteristics and Distribution in the United States," 1995/1996 Edition, Chicago, 1996

[17] Jerome P. Kassirer, "Primary Care and the Affliction of Internal Medicine," *NEJM*, 328(9):648

[18] Kassirer, 148

[19] Kassirer, 149

[20] Ruth-Marie E. Fincher, "The Road Less Travelled – Attracting Students to Primary Care," *NEJM*, August 12, 2004; 351(7):631

[21] Tod Ibrahim, "The Case for Invigorating Internal Medicine," *American Journal of Medicine (AJM)*, September 1, 2004; 117: 365

[22] Mantosh J. Dewan, John J. Norcini, "We Must Graduate Physicians, Not Doctors," *Academic Medicine*, March 2020; 95(3):337

[23] Julie Phillips, "The Impact of Debt on Young Family Physicians: Unanswered Questions with Critical Implications," *J Am Board Fam Med*, March 8, 2016: 177

[24] Dewan, 337

[25] Robert A. Garibaldi, Carol Popkave, Wayne Bylsma, "Career Plans for Trainees in Internal Medicine Residency Programs," *Academic Medicine*, May, 2005; 80(5): 507

[26] Garibaldi, 507

[27] Karen E. Hauer and others, "Factors Associated with Medical Students' Career Choices Regarding Internal Medicine," *JAMA*, September 10, 2008; 300(10): 1154

[28] Hauer, 1154-55

[29] Edward Salsberg, Paul H. Rockey, Kerri L. Rivers, Sarah E. Brotherton, Gregory R. Jackson, "US Residency Training before and after the 1997 Balanced Budget Act," *JAMA*, 2008; 300(10): 1174

[30] Robert L. Philips, Primary Care, 808

[31] David S. Meyers, Carolyn M. Clancy, "Primary Care: Too Important to Fail," *AJM* 2009; 150(4): 272

58

[32] National Center for Health Statistics, "Health, United States, 2010 with Special Feature on Death and Dying," Hyattsville, Md, 2010

[33] Agency for Healthcare Research and Quality, "The Number of Practicing Primary Care Physicians in the United States," last revised July 2018, Rockville, Md https://www.ahrg.gov/research/findings/factsheets/primary/pcwork1/index.html

[34] Kevin Grumbach, Thomas Bodenheimer, Deborah Cohen, Robert L. Phillips Jr, Kurt C. Strange, John M. Westfall, "Revitalizing the U.S. Primary Care infrastructure," *NEJM*, September 25, 2021; 385(13): 1156

[35] Robert L. Phillips Jr., Linda A. McCauley, Christopher F. Koller, "Implementing High-Quality Primary Care: A Report from the National Academies of Science, Engineering and Medicine," *JAMA*, June 22/29, 2021; 325(24): 2437

[36] Basu, Association, 506

[37] Starr, 126

[38] Stephen M. Petterson, Winston R. Liaw, Carol Tran, Andrew W. Bazemore, "Estimating the Residency Expansion Required to avoid projected Primary Care Physician Shortages by 2035," *Ann Fam Medicine*, March/April 2015; 13(2): 107

[39] Stephen M. Petterson, Winston R. Liaw, Robert L. Phillips, David L. Rabin, David S. Meyers, Andrew W. Bazemore, "Projecting US Primary Care Physician Workplace Needs: 2010-2025," *Ann Fam Med*, 2012; 10:503

[40] Jack M. Colwill, Janice M. Cultice, Robin L. Kruse, "Will generalist physician supply demands of an increasing and aging population," *Health Affairs (Millwood), 2008; 27(3): w232*

[41] Michael J. Dill, Edward S. Salsberg, "The Complexities of Physician Supply and demand Projections Through 2025," Association of American Medical Colleges, November 2008, http://www.aamc.org/workforceposition.pdf

[42] Petterson, Estimating, 107

[43] Dewan, 337

[44] Salsberg, 7

[45] Salsberg, 26

[46] Salsberg, 8

[47] William B. Weeks, Amy E. Wallace, Myron W. Wallace, H. Gilbert Welch, "A Comparison of the Educational Costs and Incomes of Physicians and Other Professionals," *NEJM,* May 5, 1994; 330(18): 1280

[48] Weeks, 1280

[49] Goodson, 2309

[50] Louise McHarris, Interview with Gregg Coodley, July 22, 2021

[51] KM Stefani, JR Richards, J Newman, KG Poole, SC Scott, CJ Scheckel, "Choosing Primary Care: Factors Influencing Graduating Osteopathic Medical Students," *J Am Osteopath,* June 1, 2020; 120(6): 380

[52] Julie Phillips, 177

[53] Norman Levinsky, "Recruiting for Primary Care," *NEJM,* March 4, 1993; 328(9):658

[54] Thomas Bodenheimer, Robert A. Berenson, Paul Rudolf, "The Primary Care-Specialty Income Gap: Why It Matters," *Ann Int Med, 2007;* 146: 301

[55] Bodenheimer, Primary Care-Specialty, 302-4

[56] Bodenheimer, Primary Care-Specialty, 304

[57] Bodenheimer, Primary Care-Specialty, 304

[58] Julie Phillips, 178

[59] Candice Chen, Iman Xierali, Katie Piwnica-Worms, Robert Phillips, "The redistribution of graduate medical education positions in 2005 failed to boost primary care or rural training," *Health Affairs (Millwood), January 2013; 32(1): 102*

[60] Chen, 107

[61] Michael P. Rosenthal and others, "Influence of Income, Hours Worked, and Loan Repayment on Medical Students' Decisions to Pursue a Primary Care career," *JAMA,* March23/30, 1994; 271(12): 914

[62] Rosenthal, 916

[63] Ibrahim, 365

[64] Garibaldi, 510-511

[65] Michael E. Whitcomb, Joshua J. Cohen, "The Future of Primary Care Medicine," *NEJM,* August 12, 2004; 351(7): 711

[66] Jack M. Colwill, "Where Have all the Primary Care Applicants Gone?" *NEJM*, 326(6):391

[67] Hoff, 116

[68] Colwill, 391

[69] Agnes G. Rezler, Summers G. Kalishman, "Who Goes into Family Medicine?" *Journal of Family Practice*, December, 1989; 29(6):652

[70] Colin P. West, Carol Popkave, Henry J. Schultz, Steven E. Weinberger, Joseph C. Kolars, "Changes in Career Decisions of Internal Medicine Residents During Training," *Ann Int Med 2006;* 145:774

[71] Bradley M. Gray, Jonathan L. Vandergrift, Jennifer P. Stevens, Bruce F. Landon, "Evolving Practice Choices by Newly Certified and More Senior General Internists," *Ann Int Med*, July, 2022; 175(5): 1022

[72] Levinsky, 656

[73] Levinsky, 656-7

[74] Robert G. Petersdorf, "Primary Care Applicants – They Get No Respect," *NEJM*, February 6, 1992; 326(6): 409

[75] Hoff, 114

[76] Hoff, 115

[77] Susan D. Block, Nancy Clark-Chiarelli, Antoinette S. Peters, Judith D. Singer, "Academia's Chilly climate for Primary Care," *JAMA*, September 4, 1996; 276(9):677

[78] Block, 679

[79] Block, 682

[80] Wayne G. Gugielmo, "A Mixed Job report for Primary Care," *Medical Economics*, May 16, 2008, 28

[81] Cassell, 27

[82] Hoff, 2

[83] Frederick M. Barken, *Out of Practice: Fighting for Primary Care Medicine in America*, ILR/Cornell University Press, Ithaca, 2011, 1

[84] Kevin Grumbach, Dennis Osmond, Karen Vranizan, Deborah Jaffe, Andrew B. Bindman, "Primary Care Physicians' Experience of Financial

Incentives in Managed care Systems," *NEJM*, November 19, 1998; 339(21): 1516

[85] Sharon Bell Buchbinder, Modena Wilson, Clifford G. Mellick, Neil R. Powe, "Primary Care Physician Job Satisfaction and Turnover," *Am Journal of Managed Care 2001: 7:702*

[86] Tosha B. Wetterneck and others, "Work life and Satisfaction of General Internists," *Archive Internal Medicine*, March 25, 2002: 162:651

[87] Donald K. Freeborn, "Satisfaction, commitment and psychological well-being among HMO Physicians," *Western Journal Of Medicine*, January 2001; 174: 13

[88] J. Paul Leigh, Richard L. Kravitz, Mike Schembri, Steven J. Samuels, Shanaz Mobley, "Physician Career Satisfaction Across Specialties," *Arch Int Med, July 22, 2002; 162:* 1577

[89] Stephen Berman, "Continuity, the Medical Home and Retail-Based Clinics," *Pediatrics,* November 2007; 120(5):1123

[90] Anonymous, to Gregg Coodley, June 21, 2021

[91] Anonymous, June 21, 2021

[92] Anonymous, June 21, 2021

[93] Anonymous, June 21, 2021

[94] Anonymous, June 21, 2021

[95] Abigail, Zuger, "Dissatisfaction with Medical Practice," *NEJM*, January 1, 2004; 350(1):69

[96] Zuger, 71-73

[97] Alison Murray, Jana E. Montgomery, Hong Chang, William H. Rogers, Thomas Inui, Dana Gelb Safran, "Doctor Discontent: A comparison of Physician Satisfaction in Different Delivery System Settings, 1986 and 1997," *JGIM,* 2001; 16: 451

[98] Hoff, 104

[99] Catherine M. DesRoches, Peter Buerhaus, Robert S. Dittus, Karen Donelan, "Primary Care Workforce Shortages and Career Recommendations from Practicing Clinicians," *Academic Medicine,* May 2015; 90(5): 671

[100] DesRoches, 674

[101] Anonymous, June 21, 2021

[102] Wetterneck, 654

[103] Chen-Tan Lin and others, "Is patients' perception of time spent with the physician a determinant of ambulatory patient satisfaction?" *Arch Int Med,* June 11, 2001; 161:1437

[104] David A. Gross, Stephen J. Zyzanski, Elaine A. Borawski, Randall D. Cebul, Kurt C. Strange, "Patient satisfaction with Time spent with their physician," *Journal of Family Practice,* August 1998; 47: 3

[105] Anonymous, June 21, 2021

[106] Harold S. Luft, Su-Ying Liang, Laura J. Eaton, Sukyung Chung, "Primary Care Physician Practice styles and quality, cost, Productivity," *Am Journal of Managed Care,* April 2020; 26(4): e127

[107] Christine A. Sinsky, Lotte N. Dyrbye, Colin P. West, Daniel Satele, Michael Tutty, Tait D. Shanfelt, "Professional Satisfaction and Career Plans of US Physicians," *Mayo Clinic Proc,* November 2017; 92(11): 1625

[108] Christina Maslach, Wilmar B. Schaudel, Michael P. Leiter, "Job Burnout," *Ann Review Psychol,* 2001; 52:422

[109] Sandy L. Robinson, Mark D. Robinson, Alfred Reid, "Electronic Health Record effects on Work-Life Balance and Burnout within the 13 Population Collaborative," *Journal of Graduate Medical Education,* August 2017, 479

[110] Freeborn, 16

[111] Tait Shanafelt and others, "Longitudinal Study Evaluating the Association Between Physician Burnout and Changes in Professional Work Effort," *Mayo Clin Proc,* April 2016; 91(4): 422

[112] Harold Sax, "Leaving (Internal) Medicine," *Ann Int Med,* January 3, 2006; 144(1): 58

[113] Leslie Kane, "Medscape National Physician Burnout, depression and Suicide Report 2019," *Medscape,* January 16, 2019; https://www.medscape.com/slideshow/2019-lifestyle-burnout-depression-6011056

[114] Kane, 2019

[115] Leslie Kane, "Physician Burnout and Depression Report 2022: Stress, Anxiety and Anger," *Medscape Internal Medicine,* January 21, 2022

[116] Julie Phillips, 177

[117] Jennifer DeVoe, George E. Fryer, J. Lee Hargraves, Robert L. Phillips, Larry A. Green, "Does Career Dissatisfaction affect the Ability of Family Physicians to Deliver High-Quality Patient Care," *Journal Family Practice,* March, 2002; 51(3): 227

[118] Anonymous, to Gregg Coodley, June 24, 2021

[119] Anonymous, to Gregg Coodley, June 24, 2021

[120] David Grembowski and others, "Managed Care and Primary Physician Satisfaction," *J Am Board Fam Pract,* 2003; 16: 391

[121] Satish P. Deshpande, Jim DeMello, "A Comparative Analysis of Factors that Hinder Primary Care Physicians and Specialist Physicians' Ability to Provide High Quality Care," *Health Care Manager,* 2011; 30(2): 172

[122] Maria Panagioti and others, "Controlled Interventions to Reduce Burnout in Physicians: A Systemic Review and Meta-Analysis," *JAMA Internal Medicine,* 2017; 177(2): 195

[123] Panagioti, 201

[124] Pamela Hartzband, Jerome Groopman, "Physician Burnout, Interrupted," *NEJM,* June 25, 2020; 382(26): 2486

[125] E. Ray Dorsey, David Jarjoura, Gregory W. Rutecki, "Influence of Controllable Lifestyle on Recent Trends in Specialty Choice by US Medical Students," *JAMA,* September 3, 2003; 290(9): 1173

[126] Dorsey, 1177

[127] Robinson, 481

[128] Robinson, 479

[129] William J. Kassler, Steven A. Wartman, Rebecca A. Silliman, "Why Medical students Choose Primary Care Careers," *Academic Medicine,* January 1991; 66(1): 41

[130] Fincher, 631

[131] Ibrahim, 368

[132] Ibrahim, 368

[133] Zuger, 72

[134] Barken, 184

[135] Tait D. Shanafelt, Lotte N. Dyrbye, Colin P. West, "Addressing Physician Burnout: The Way Forward," *JAMA,* March 7, 2017: 317(9): 901

[136] Christine A. Sinsky, Tait D. Shanafelt, Liselotte N. Dyrbye, Adrienne H. Sabety, Lindsey E. Carlasare, Colin P. West, "Health Care Expenditures Attributable to Primary Care Physician Overall and Burnout-Related Turnover: A Cross Sectional Analysis," *Mayo Clin Proc*, February 25, 2022; https://doi.org/10.1016/jmayocp.2021.09.013

[137] Sinsky, Health Care Expenditures

[138] Goodson, 2310

[139] Petterson, 107

[140] Hanyuan Shi, Kevin c. Lee, "Bolstering the Pipeline for Primary Care: a proposal from stakeholders in medical education," *Medical Education Online*, July 5, 2016; 21:32146, http://dx.dai.org/10.3402/meo.v21.32146

[141] Gugielmo, 8

1889 Graduates of Leonard Medical School

(Courtesy, Wiki Commons)

CHAPTER 4

Medical Training: The Job and Education Mismatch

Medical training has evolved over time in America. However, the rapid changes of the last thirty-five years have meant that the training and the actual job have increasingly diverged, particularly for primary care. Medical education has three components: undergraduate education, medical school and residency. Undergraduate "pre-med" education consists of a core of science and math classes in college required by medical schools in order to consider applicants. This includes biology, chemistry, physics, organic chemistry, and calculus. Most are also required in high school. The ostensible rationale for requiring this training is that it is a necessary basis for being a good physician.

Let us look at how true this turns out to be in practice. The greatest utility belongs to biology. From understanding cells to the role of genetics and DNA to the basic tasks of respiration and digestion, it is very difficult to make a case that college biology should not continue to be a required foundation for all physicians.

However, the case for the others is harder to sustain. In making this assessment, we need to acknowledge that high school students get basic exposure and understanding of chemistry, physics and calculus, and often organic chemistry. In addition, there are medical specialties that depend more on understanding the components of these disciplines. For example, understanding light is crucial to an ophthalmologist. Anesthesiologists and lung specialists need to understand laws of gases and liquids, pressure and volume, subjects that all fall under the rubric of physics.

Yet I cannot recall a case where calculus is used by a practicing physician. Organic chemistry involves the memorization of large numbers of compounds and how they interact. Again, I cannot remember an instance when I utilized it since I studied it. Physics is of interest in my life outside of medicine, but has not been important within the profession.

It is not that these disciplines are without merit. They may be particularly important for scientists doing "bench" or laboratory research. However, requiring at least a year each of physics, organic chemistry and calculus in college, after these have also been required in high school, carries a significant "opportunity cost." By that, I mean that students cannot study other things that may be of more utility or interest.

In addition, removing the requirements for this repetition of basic science courses could allow the shortening of medical education, which currently encompasses a minimum of eleven years from college through residency training. Nor is this length of training a universal standard. In Britain, medical education, including undergraduate and medical school, is combined into a five to six year program rather than the eight in America, yet British physicians are considered among the best in the world.

Perhaps the real unspoken reason for these undergraduate requirements is an attempt to weed out potential applicants to medical school. We then just need to ask whether these criteria, when irrelevant to actual practice, are the best way to pick the best future doctors.

Colwill argued that the types of students selected are less those likely to go into primary care, writing, "The selection of medical students emphasizes academic achievements – especially in science – and places relatively less emphasis on students commitment to service,"[1]

Medical school traditionally involves two more years of

classroom work, followed by a third year where students spend a period of time doing each of the basic clinical disciplines, such as two months of surgery, two of obstetrics/gynecology, two in pediatrics, two in internal medicine and so on. Finally, the final year usually gives the student more ability to choose additional time in these and other specialized disciplines in order to help decide what field they wish to pursue.

The bias against primary care in medical training is astonishing. A survey of 2000 academic faculty, residents and medical students revealed that they saw primary care as requiring less expertise and being less difficult than specialty work and saw PCPs as inferior in the management of even common problems such as asthma and back pain.[2] Less than half of 1% of students and residents felt that academic faculty encouraged capable students to go into primary care.[3]

The first two years of classroom work in medical school need to be reexamined. No one would question the utility of studying anatomy or pharmacology for future physicians. However, there are subjects that are more questionable, at least in the way they are taught.

In medical school, we also memorized each of the components of the Krebs cycle. The Krebs Cycle is the process by which cells use oxygen to create energy. I had memorized it previously in high school and again in college. I regret to say that I forgot the steps involved shortly after each time, and it has never come up again since that first year in medical school.

My medical school was different from most in delaying anatomy until the second year. Our first year was dominated by biochemistry, divided into six to seven different segments, if memory serves. The faculty were concerned that the school not be seen as "soft" due to its location in San Diego. Thus, shortly after the first year began, we were told that if we failed any one of the segments, we would have to repeat the entire year. Moreover, 10% of the class would fail each segment to avoid grade inflation or for more obscure reasons. A fellow student described it as taking a nice stroll through the woods only to discover that the last 10% to finish would be shot. As a result, the nice walk turned into a crazed run to avoid being in the last 10%.

I was fortunate enough to not fall into the 10% failing for any segment. Yet by the time the year was over, my medical school class had lost a large percentage of its black and Hispanic members. I would like to think this was not the intention.

At the time and in hindsight, this was a terrible educational strategy if the goal was teaching knowledge to help doctors practice good medicine. For very little I learned that year, save pharmacology, was of use in my career as a physician. We had to memorize the structure of each of the amino acids, a useful adjunct for an organic chemist, but a crazy waste of time for a PCP. I have never had a single patient consult me for my knowledge of the structure of an amino acid, which is fortunate since I can't remember a thing about it.

The end of medical school is followed by one of the most ludicrous events in American medical education. Annually over 4000 Americans graduate from allopathic, osteopathic and international medical schools but are unable to obtain a residency position. Without at least one year of residency, these doctors are unable to practice in any state in the country.[4] While a quarter of these will get a residency position later, the other 3000 have basically trained for no purpose. The waste and cost of their medical education is a loss not simply for the individuals, but for the health care system. Such waste has been calculated to equal 12,000 years spent in medical schools and $750 million in costs each year.[5] As we contemplate the increasing shortage of primary care doctors, not training these 3000 plus medical school graduates each year so they can practice medicine is a lost opportunity.

Almost all graduates of American medical school now go

into residency, a minimum of three to seven more years (or more with the option of subspecialty fellowships). The bulk of the training is in the inpatient setting. In part, this is because residencies are hospital-based. Residents are a crucial source of cheap labor for hospitals. The pay of residents has increased from thirty-five years ago when we calculated that we earned less than the minimum wage for shifts lasting up to forty hours at a time. There are now more restrictions on the maximum hours residents can work. Still, residents cost hospitals a fraction of the cost of regular physicians. Hence there is a premium to use them to do hospital work as much as possible.

While in the past most medical school graduates went into practice as general practitioners after a single year of postgraduate training, this choice now is as rare as hen's teeth. Dewan and Norcini noted, "The purpose of medical training has moved from readiness for independent medical practice... to readiness for postgraduate training."[6] They noted that many residency program directors were opposed to the idea of general practitioners, stating that more years of training are needed to achieve competence. Dewan and Norcini argued that the training in primary care, even with a single year of residency as a GP (eight years of education, 110 weeks of supervised clinical training), still would far exceed that of physician assistants (six years, 45 weeks) and nurse practitioners (six years, 27.5 weeks) respectively.[7]

The residency years are challenging, to say the least. Doctors, like everyone else, talk about how in their day they walked ten miles barefoot in the snow to go to school. The first year of residency, called the internship, was the worst.

My internship routinely was filled with days that could last, when we would be "on call," thirty-four hours in a row, from seven a.m. to five p.m. the next day, overnight in the hospital.

This type of workload, with accompanying sleep deprivation and fatigue, along with the crucial need to quickly become competent so as to not cause harm to patients, doesn't make for perfect happiness. I remember being resentful, irritable and depressed at times, particularly during internship.

When I had to draw blood on a patient at three a.m., I resented them. I resented not being able to sleep. I can't remember the details, but I am sure I didn't take well to criticism from faculty about how I should have done things better. I acquired a reputation, at least among some of them, of being unhappy and difficult. With the benefit of hindsight, I can admit that there was some truth in this.

The second and third years of residency were better. At our city hospital, the third-year medical resident on call ran the wards and intensive care unit after hours, assisted by the second-year resident who was on call. Increasingly feeling competent to manage anything that came along was a wonderful tonic, although exhaustion did not vanish. The intern, angry at the patient whose veins made blood drawing hard in the middle of the night, transformed into a resident who felt calm and in control running "codes," when patients suffered a respiratory or cardiac arrest.

Thus, my residency training saw me running the intensive care unit after five p.m. and putting in catheters into the right side of the heart. We put tubes into the chest and extracted fluid from the spinal canal. We did the painful procedure of determining patients' oxygenation by a puncture of their radial arteries.

These procedures gave me increased self-confidence in my skills. Yet, I have done none of them since finishing residency in 1988.

One was young and at times felt invincible. I did a month of alternating twenty-four-hour shifts running the intensive care unit at the public hospital where I trained with one of the other residents, which I vaguely recall us thinking of like an ironman triathlon. These extra shifts allowed me to spend two months working in a clinic in a tiny village in Chiapas, Mexico, encountering malaria, typhoid, and tuberculosis, while translating the patients' histories, already translated into Spanish by an interpreter from their native dialect, in my mind from Spanish to English and then back again.

Reforms in residency training followed the death of Libby Zion, the daughter of a prominent reporter, which was attributed to overworked exhausted residents. Limits were placed on the hours residents had to work.

Yet more recent studies suggest that medical school and residency are still very difficult emotionally. Liselotte Dyrbye, writing about a national survey of trainees in 2011-12 noted, "Numerous studies have found that many medical trainees experience burnout...resulting from work-related stress characterized by emotional exhaustion, feelings of cynicism and detachment from patients (depersonalization) and a low sense of personal accomplishment."[8]

Dyrbye noted that her survey revealed, "Symptoms of depression, suicidal ideation, and a low sense of personal accomplishment were most prevalent during medical school... overall burnout, high depersonalization and high fatigue were most prevalent during residency/fellowship."[9] Dyrbye added, "Fatigue among medical students and residents/fellows was common, despite current hours restrictions intended to ensure that residents are adequately rested to deliver high-quality patient care."[10]

The residency years are indeed crucial. Yet even in the primary care disciplines the bulk of the training occurs in the hospital setting. The lesser time given to outpatient medicine is one reason many graduates, at least in internal medicine, opted to go for specialty training which revolved much more around the hospital than primary care. Colwill commented, "The curriculum focuses on the biologic sciences and hospital based specialty and subspecialty rotations rather than on epidemiology, behavioral sciences and primary care rotations... Subspecialty faculty members have the most contact with students and transmit their enthusiasm for their specialties to them. The selection process, curriculum and educational setting are all admirably designed to prepare subspecialists."[11]

The biggest source of funding for residencies is from Medicare, with another large fraction coming from the Department of Defense and the Veterans Administration. In 1994 Medicare payments for graduate medical education totaled $5.8 billion, averaging $70,000 per resident.[12] A small fraction of that was paid out as salaries for residents while the rest was income for hospitals, theoretically for the extra costs of teaching. Of course, the residents also served as cheap physician labor for the hospitals, which then benefited both from extra income and physician labor that was free to them.

The bias toward inpatient training was reenforced by the way Medicare financed graduate medical education. First, Medicare allowed payment only for teachers who were hospital employees. Outside primary care doctors who were recruited to serve as teachers were usually unpaid. This limited the number of primary care doctors who could afford to take the time out to teach. Second, resident time spent in an outpatient setting other than hospital clinics was excluded in the calculation of the amount of indirect payments hospitals would receive from Medicare; thus, it was in the hospital's financial interest to have trainees spend the maximum, if not all of their time in the hospital or hospital clinics.[13]

Compared to the money going into residency training, that specifically set aside for primary care was but a pittance. While in 1994, there was $5.8 billion overall for residency training, another federal program, Title VII of the Public Health Services Act, spent a total of $59.8 million dollars to support primary care.[14]

In the past, leaving aside the economic benefits for the hospitals, residency programs in the primary care specialties of internal medicine, pediatrics and family medicine legitimately could argue that doctors needed training in hospital work for their future practice.

Up to the last decade, primary care doctors took care of their patients both in the clinic and the hospital, so an emphasis on learning how to take care of severely ill patients in the hospital made sense. This may still be true in certain rural areas where doctor shortages are such that primary care doctors can still do everything, from outpatient clinics to hospital procedures. However, for the bulk of primary care doctors, inpatient work is no longer possible, having been assumed by "hospitalists." Procedures are the purview of specialists.

Thus, much of this clinical training is of less relevance to primary care doctors.

Even back in 2010, Hoff observed, "Almost no PCPs do hospital work anymore, yet all primary care specialties train their members almost exclusively in the hospital setting."[15]

The ability to care for sick patients in the hospital was invaluable for all the years that I could take care of my patients in the hospital. Yet as a primary care doctor in an urban setting, I am no longer able to care for my patients when hospitalized.

Even as so much of the PCP training became irrelevant, there were voices arguing that the solution was increased training. In 1994, UCLA School of Medicine decided to try to push further in the direction of giving general internists additional skills in hopes of attracting more graduates to general medicine instead of specialties. They offered an internal residency that was expanded from three to four years with the intention of letting general internists learn more subspecialty skills and the ability to do procedures. Dr. Dan Fogelman, who developed the program, explained that the goal was, "to create a cadre of comprehensive internists that could entice students into choosing general internal medicine."[16]

It is unclear to me what happened to this approach. Having general internists learn more procedure skills while there were already too many specialists doing these procedures may not have been productive. Nor would expanding primary care training by another year be attractive to most medical students.

Nevertheless, others also have argued that the solution for general internal medicine, at least, would be to increase the length of training beyond three years. A task force of the Society of General Internal Medicine that was dominated by academic physicians suggested increasing the length of training in a 2004 report.[17] They wrote, "The current training system is inadequate for the needs of the present and future general internist...we are skeptical that so much can be taught in our current three-year programs."[18]

Yet when the cost of loans and the lesser income to repay them is a major reason students don't go into primary care, it is crazy to think the solution is to add another year of reduced income for trainees.

Nor is the biggest problem today that internists don't learn enough skills. It is that they learn many skills that atrophy because they don't get to use them. Training primary care doctors so much in hospital medicine when inpatient work is increasingly the domain of hospitalists doesn't make sense. Nor does teaching internists how to do more hospital-based procedures when there is a surplus of specialists.

I can mention a specific example. A few years back, we had a primary care doctor talk about joining us. He had learned how to do colonoscopies while in the Navy and had been able to continue it at the Veterans Hospital. In order for a doctor to get hospital privileges to do a procedure, no matter how skilled they are, he must find others with similar skills who are willing to share call coverage with him. For this doctor, none of the gastroenterology groups that dominated at each hospital had any interest in covering for what would be a competitor. Here was an instance of primary care doctors being unable to use previously learned skills in doing procedures.

No matter how skilled I once was at putting in Swan-Ganz right heart catheters, no urban hospital would let anyone other than a cardiologist or similar specialist do this procedure. It may have been different in a small town hospital, but since I was a city rat, it was a skill that would never be used again after residency.

For most primary care doctors, the reality is that much, if not the majority, of the eleven years spent in medical education is now irrelevant. This experience is common to many, many primary care doctors.

The "wasted time" carries a large opportunity cost in terms of time forever lost. It also carries a real financial significance for this training is not cheap. Many primary care doctors finish with large debts from taking out loans to pay for it all. When they think about how much of their training was not useful, it can be demoralizing. Shortening and reducing the cost of training for primary care by eliminating irrelevant items would be a better strategy.

---

[1] Colwill, 391

[2] Block, 679

[3] Block, 679

[4] Harris Ahmed, J. Bryan Carmody, "On the Looming Physician Shortage and Strategic Expansion of Graduate Medical Education," *Cureus,* July 15, 2020; 12(7): 2

[5] Dewan, 337

[6] Dewan, 338

[7] Dewan, 338

[8] Liselotte N. Dyrbye, "Burnout Among US Medical Students, Residents and early Career Physicians Relative to the General US Population," *Academic Medicine,* March, 2014; 89(3):443

[9] Dyrbye, 446

[10] Dyrbye, 446-7

[11] Kasper, 391

[12] Molla S. Donaldson, Karl E. Yordy, Kathleen N. Lohr, Neal A. Vanselow, Editors, *Primary Care: America's Health in a New Era,* committee on the Future of Primary Care, Division of Healthcare services, Institute of Medicine, National Academy Press, Washington DC,1996, 196

[13] Donaldson, 197-8

[14] Donaldson, 198

[15] Hoff, 202

[16] Alan M. Fogelman, "Strategies for Training Generalists and Subspecialists," *Ann Int Med,* 1994, 120: 580

[17] Eric B. Larson and others, "The Future of General Internal Medicine: Report and Recommendations from the Society of General Internal Medicine Task Force on the Domain of General Internal Medicine," *JGIM,* 2004; 19:73

[18] Larson, 73

The Doctor's Visit—Jan Steen

(Courtesy, Wiki Commons)

CHAPTER 5

Devaluing Continuity of Care

Primary care involves the formation of long-term relationships between doctors and patients.

Traditionally, such relationships, once formed, were rarely broken save by the retirement of the physician or the relocation of the patient. Occasional patients were discharged from care by physicians for narcotic-seeking behavior or other similar circumstances.

However, the usual assumption was that a patient's doctor would be there for them both for outpatient appointments and hospitalizations. Perhaps the doctor's partner would cover and see the patient if the doctor were away. When patients referred to "my doctor," they meant this primary care physician who would direct all their care. Occasionally the patient might need to see a specialist recommended by their primary care doctor.

There was merit to this continuity. Multiple studies showed that, "continuity of care, which implies that individuals use their primary source of care over time for most of their health care needs, is associated with greater satisfaction, better compliance and lower hospitalization and emergency room use."[1]

It would be the advent of health insurance that would lead to the loss of continuity. For many years health insurance was limited to and supplied by Blue Cross or commercial insurance companies. The creation of Medicare and Medicaid added more insured patients, but the role of any of these insurers was to pay the bills rather than tell patients which doctor to see.

With the expansion of health insurance and the use of new technology and medications, health care costs rose.

To control costs and fend off calls for national health insurance, the Nixon administration began to promote the creation of Health Maintenance Organizations (HMOs). Nixon announced this, "new national health strategy" on February 18, 1971.[2] HMOs offered the alternative payment scheme of capitation, where doctors were paid a set fee for providing whatever care an individual patient needed that year. The Administration tried to encourage patients to join HMOs who received a set fee for each member. Since HMO payments were based on the number of "covered lives," a strong incentive was created to attract as many patients as possible. The Nixon, and later Reagan, administrations encouraged corporations to set up HMOs.

One question that was given short shrift in this new scheme was a patient's relationship with their doctor. Under the HMO model, patients could only see doctors employed by that HMO. So, if Dr. Brown, who Mrs. Smith had seen for twenty years, was not a member of her HMO, she could no longer see him. Instead, she was reassigned to a new doctor who knew nothing about her but was employed by the HMO. This began the trend of treating existing patient-doctor relationships as unimportant.

It is not patients who decided that these relationships were inconsequential. A 1991 study of Medicare patients found that over half had a relationship with their primary care doctor of over five years while 35.8% had a relationship of over ten years with the same physician.[3]

As the money devoted to health care grew, more companies sought profits by becoming health care insurers. The multiplicity of insurers was of little benefit to the patient as it rarely meant that patients had more choices. Instead, since most group insurance was provided through the workplace, patients had to accept whatever health care plan their employer chose that year.

When the choices were no longer mainly Blue Cross, the growing number of choices meant an increased chance that the insurance Mrs. Smith received from her employer would not include the possibility of seeing her long-time physician, Dr. Brown.

There was little incentive for anyone to prioritize the patient-physician relationship, and so they did not. Employers might try to keep employees happy by choosing a plan that would not force too many employees to change doctors. More often, especially as health insurance became an increasing proportion of the total cost of the employee, the choice would be made on the basis of which insurer costs the company the least.

Insurers now had multiple things to consider when choosing which doctors to cover. For HMOs such as Kaiser, the choice was easy. They would only cover doctors employed by Kaiser-Permanente. For other insurers having more doctors on their "panels" might please patients and allow them to attract more patients. On the other hand, the insurers might be able to pay less to the doctors by contracting with only certain medical groups and hospitals in exchange for lower charges. The insurers gained major power, for they could deprive a doctor of much of his patients and income by excluding them from those whose services they would pay for. Again, any relationships a patient might have, particularly with their primary care physician, was not a major factor for the insurers.

Cassell observed a philosophical basis for the change, noting, "The claim of twentieth-century medicine has been that medical science is the source of medicine's power. The importance of the individual physician has become subsidiary, as though any doctor with the knowledge and command of the technology is as good as any other doctor."[4]

This trend has continued up to today. When our primary care clinic contracts with an insurer, they could care less whether our doctors already have a relationship with their patients or what they refer to as their "covered lives."

The negotiation with insurers is particularly difficult for solo or small doctor practices that have no leverage with the insurer. However, even mid-sized doctor practices cannot negotiate on equal terms with the insurers. Most doctors try to sign enough contracts to be able to keep their existing patients, for such relationships remain of paramount importance to primary care doctors.

The result has been increasing fragmentation of care, with an increasing number of patients seeing multiple doctors. Barnett et al. looked at Medicare patients in 2000 vs. those in 2019. During that time, the number of patients with a PCP and the number of visits on average to the PCP were essentially unchanged. In contrast, specialty visits rose 20%, and the number of different specialists seen by patients on average increased by 34%. The proportion of patients seeing five or more physicians each year almost doubled.[5]

Ironically, even as the insurers increasingly broke the patient-physician continuity model, increasing evidence showed how continuity of care improved health in multiple ways. First, continuity of care reduced health care costs and hospitalizations. Gill and Mainous demonstrated in a population of Medicaid patients in Delaware that, "higher provider continuity was associated with a lower likelihood of hospitalization for any condition."[6] Another study surveyed over 12,000 Medicare patients. Those with longer relationships with their primary care physicians were hospitalized less and incurred less overall costs. Sustained patient-physician relationships resulted in the greatest satisfaction both for patients, their physicians and the physicians' staff.[7] Further, research showed that long-term pa-tient-physician bonds led to fewer broken appointments, decreased use of laboratory tests, decreased visits to emergency rooms and fewer hospitalizations. Not surprisingly, these relationships also led a patient to disclose more information to their doctors and led to increased compliance with patient instructions.[8] [9]

Discussing their study, Rosenblatt and others commented, "The fact that patients with a principal care physician have lower emergency department visit rates, even after socioeconomic factors and health status are controlled for, is powerful confirmation that having a regular physician matters."[10]

Hussey et al. studied over 300,000 Medicare patients with heart failure, chronic lung disease or diabetes. After adjustment for other factors, higher levels of continuity were associated with a lower risk of inpatient hospitalization, emergency room visits and risk of complications for these three conditions. Each further increase in a scale of continuity, based on what percentage of visits occurring with a single provider, resulted in a significant reduction in the cost of care for these three conditions.[11]

Continuity of care is especially important when patients have severe illnesses.[12] Studies document that it leads to improved physician and staff satisfaction, increased patient satisfaction and improved compliance with treatment by patients.[13] Notably, the evidence showed improved care for children as well as adults.[14] [15]

The evidence that continuity of care reduces emergency room use is striking. A Seattle study of 785 children found that those with the most continuity of care with a doctor had 35% fewer emergency room visits than those with the least continuity.[16] Another study found that patients who had seen their doctor three times during the year had a significantly lower chance of even a single ER visit and an even lower chance of multiple ER visits.[17] The authors commented, "In most cases, it is the patient rather than the physician who decides when to seek emergency care. When patients have a continuity relationship with their physician, it is likely that they will develop a sense of trust in the physician's knowledge and medical judgment...when the need for urgent care is questionable, patients with high continuity are more likely to seek the opinion of their physician before going to an ED (emergency department)."[18]

From the emergency room perspective, two-thirds of the emergency room directors surveyed cited the lack of a primary care provider as a major reason patients seek care in the ER.[19]

Another evaluation revealed that women with a usual source of care were much more likely to have received preventive care, including mammograms, breast exams and PAP smears.[20] Among women over fifty in the study, having a regular doctor tripled the likelihood of having had a mammogram in the prior year.[21]

Continuity of care was also valuable for children as evidence showed that mothers of children with a regular pediatrician were more likely to comply with medical regimens and keep follow-up appointments. Pediatrician continuity yielded, "higher staff and pediatrician satisfaction, better patient-provider relationships and greater efficacy."[22]

The Nationwide Children's Hospital Primary Care Network cared for over 120,000 children, mostly on Medicaid, across thirteen offices in Ohio. Before 2017 patients were assigned to the office rather than individual PCPs. The group then decided to link patients to particular PCPs and encourage follow-up with that PCP. After increasing the number of patients linked to a particular PCP from 0 to over 90%, they reported a 20.5% decrease in emergency room utilization, a higher frequency of patients keeping appointments and a higher percentage of patients receiving well-child visits.[23]

An analysis from California looked at multiple factors that could potentially affect getting preventive care, including demographics, financial status, and insurance status. The single most key factor in whether patients would get preventive care was having a regular established source of care.[24] A study of black and Hispanic women in New York City revealed that women with a regular site of care but no regular doctor were more likely to have received a breast exam, PAP and mammogram than those without a regular site of care. However, those with a regular physician had an even higher rate of having received these services than women who had a regular site of care but not a particular provider.[25] The authors concluded, "For uninsured minority women, this relationship between continuity of care and receipt of recent screening was especially important. For these traditionally underserved groups, better use of cancer screening was associated with greater levels of continuity."[26] The study emphasized, "the effectiveness of having a specific clinician over and above having a usual source of care."[27]

Increased continuity has also been demonstrated to result in improved diabetic control.[28]

Another analysis compared patients who felt connected to a single physician to those connected only to a specific practice. Patients who reported this one-on-one relationship with their primary care doctor were much more likely to receive recommended preventive care.[29]

Wasson and colleagues randomized 776 men older than fifty-five into either having a regular physician or not. Such a double-blind, randomized trial is the gold standard in medicine in trying to undercover the truth about any interventions. During the eighteen-month study period, those with continuity of care had fewer emergent admissions (20% vs. 39%) and fewer days in the hospital (15.5 vs. 25.5 days). Those who received continuity also perceived that their doctors, "were more knowledgeable, thorough and interested in patient education."[30] The study suggested that continuity of care resulted both in significant cost savings and improved patient satisfaction

Cabana and Jee reviewed all studies looking at continuity of care over a thirty-six-year time period, which showed eighteen studies that looked at the effect of "sustained continuity of care.[31] Four studies showed that such continuity was associated with increased patient satisfaction, seven showed decreased emergency room visits and hospitalizations, and five showed increased preventive care. No study showed any negative effect from long-term continuity of care.

Cabana and Jee noted that, "the association between sustained continuity of care and quality of care appears most consistent for patients with chronic conditions."[32] Since such patients tend to be sicker and have more emergency room visits and hospitalizations than the average, the effect of the long-term doctor-patient relationship is most pronounced vis-à-vis the patients that generate the most costs to the health care system.

Saultz and Lochner did another review of studies of continuity. Of the eighty-one separate care outcomes analyzed in forty studies, fifty-one were significantly improved by more continuity of care. Twenty studies looked at the effect of continuity of care on cost. Increased continuity for a patient with a regular physician was associated with significantly lower cost or utilization for thirty-five of forty-one cost variables.[33]

Other studies have evaluated the comprehensiveness of care offered by PCPs. This has been defined by the extent to which the PCP is able to manage a patient's conditions as opposed to the patient getting some of their care elsewhere. These studies suggest, "primary care practices providing a broader range of services have lower Medicare expenditure and emergency department utilization."[34] The studies also found that the most comprehensive practices had lower rates of hospitalization.[35]

There is an argument that if patients all had health insurance, having a primary care physician would have less impact on costs and use of preventive care. However, a Canadian study of over half a million people found that continuity of care still resulted in reduced use of emergency rooms and better preventive health care.[36]

Patients continue to value having a regular primary care physician. A study of patients in the United States and the United Kingdom in 2001 showed that far more of the patients in the United Kingdom had been with their doctor for over six years (69.8% of UK patients versus 8% of US patients). However, American patients valued continuity with a doctor even more than the British (92.4% of American patients versus 70.8% of the British). Both groups had a high level of trust in the regular doctor, with the trust being related to the length of time the patient had seen the doctor.[37] The American patients were asked how important it was to them to see the same doctor every time they had a health problem. Over 92% answered that it was important or very important.[38]

Fletcher et al. surveyed 225 patients at a University hospital clinic. They concluded that, "continuity of care was the highest priority" for these patients.[39]

To summarize, patients place a high value on continuity of care. It is associated with increased patient adherence to medical advice, improved health status, loyalty to a physician's practice and reduced malpractice claims.[40]

I have certain patients who only want to see me. If I am unavailable, they will opt to wait for several days rather than see one of my able partners. Many of my partners' patients have the same attitude. Even the ones who choose to see someone else for an acute issue would much rather see their PCP. The longer the relationship, the more important, in general, it is to the patient to be seen by their PCP. Primary care scheduling thus attempts to fill the schedule as much as possible while leaving sufficient slots so that patients with an acute problem can see their doctor when needed. Continuity of care continues to be highly valued by patients even as it has shown to improve many health care outcomes.

I had an example yesterday of how much cheaper and better it would be for patients to be able to see a primary care doctor. I have a longtime older gentleman with well-controlled HIV and diabetes who did very well until his longtime partner died a few years ago. Since then, it has been a struggle to control his extreme anxiety, despite medications and counseling.

He had an appointment with me on Monday. He called the on-call doctor Sunday night, asking if he should go to the emergency room. He called our nurse when the clinic opened Monday morning. Both suggested that he instead keep his appointment with me that afternoon. He then called the insurance company triage nurse who, not knowing the patient, suggested he go to the emergency room. There he had a workup costing several thousand dollars with imaging and extensive labs that revealed nothing.

In contrast, I have another patient with schizophrenia, HIV infection and cirrhosis of the liver. Our long-term relationship has allowed me to treat him for any disease exacerbations in my office. It has meant he has not seen an ER or hospital for over a decade. The only specialist he sees is periodic visits with a psychiatrist. Without a long-term PCP, this patient, statistically at least, would have cost the health care system and his insurer far more money.

No insurer or government program rewards doctors for having long-term relationships with patients. Instead, as we shall see in upcoming chapters, the insurers do almost everything else except this to try to reduce costs. Rosenblatt et al. concluded, "It is tempting to treat the physician as one industrial input in a production function that produces health care...the risk of this approach is that it may disrupt a component of medical care that is fragile and difficult to quantify, but valuable – the doctor-patient relationship...in disrupting a sustained relationship between one patient and one doctor, something of value is destroyed."[41]

Given the benefits of continuity of care, it is at times appalling how little attention is paid to it, particularly for the poorest patients. Our clinic experienced this with regard to the Oregon Medicaid population. A number of years ago the state decided that it might be more efficient and/or less costly to have intermediary coordinated care organizations (CCOs) manage the care of Medicaid patients in what is called the

Oregon Health Plan. Therefore, a number of private and semi-public entities were created. Some were affiliated with a particular hospital or health care system, such as Kaiser or Providence, and tried to manage Medicaid patients within their closed systems. For patients under these plans, any prior relationships with outside doctors were ignored. In Portland, there were two CCOs managing Medicaid patients that signed contracts with independent doctors, among others, letting the doctors see these patients.

The first, which I shall label Group A, was closely linked to a hospital. Group A offered good rates to the hospital for these patients while setting payments very low for primary care doctors. Group B, an outsider to Portland without the same links, paid hospitals less but paid primary care doctors almost double for that care.

After initially having contracts with both, in 2017, our clinic chose to continue with Group B, which paid us much more for taking care of the same patients. Most of these patients had long-term relationships with our doctors and opted for Group B when they realized it would allow them to continue care with us.

What happened next is debatable. The official version is that Group B was inefficient, perhaps paid outpatient doctors too much, and hence, when it ran into financial issues, was forced to give up caring for these Medicaid patients. Another version is that Group A had strong links with the powerful local hospital and influential politicians in the state legislature who made sure that Group A was paid more than group B, thus making sure that A would win the competition with B. Declaring that they had been paid less than the other CCOs, Group B pulled out of the Medicaid market in December 2018.[42]

For our story, the important detail is that our clinic now had 1100 plus Medicaid patients for whom we had provided long-term care but no contract with a Medicaid CCO. Group A initially said that they would contract with us, but then, after having sent us a draft contract, announced that they had changed their minds. Our many efforts to get them to change their minds were to no avail.

Our 1100 patients were forced to change doctors. Patients with AIDS, brittle diabetes mellitus, depression and a host of chronic conditions were arbitrarily reassigned by Group A, which had taken over. One complicated, hard-to-control diabetic was taken from their long-time internist and assigned to a naturopath. Our doctors, who specialized in taking care of AIDS patients, saw the patients turned over to nurse practitioners. Trying to reverse Group A's decision, one of our doctors wrote them, noting, "I have a patient with cognitive delay who functions at about an 8-year level. She has been seeing me for the past five years, and today came in with her mother, in absolute distress that she has to change physicians."[43] The physician went on to add, "Several of my patients have reported that they are being told that Fanno Creek Clinic did not want to see them. They tell me this information is coming from (Group A). This is absolutely not the case."[44]

Group A later claimed that the decision was because, "our network for primary care providers in the Metro area is currently closed to all new providers....CCOs are not required to contract with any willing provider"[45] I am unsure how we irritated Group A so much that they decided to blacklist us. We were told later that reassigning patients to clinics with whom they were aligned was a financial benefit to those entities, but I do not know the truth of this. I do know that pleas to Group A, the state government and the state legislature to help us continue our care of patients were ignored. Perhaps like so many, they considered primary care providers as interchangeable. To me, ripping patients away, against their will, from their long-term physician was disgraceful. At the time announcing the decision to the doctors and staff of our clinic, I wrote, "If it is possible for the administrators of an insurance company to feel shame, they should feel shame at this decision which destroys so many long-term doctor-patient relationships."[46]

I should note that our doctors could have and subsequently made more money by not having to care for these Medicaid patients. When they wanted to continue caring for them, it was because the doctor valued the relationship with the patient. They saw them as distinct human beings rather than, in the words of the insurers, "covered lives."

I should be over this by now, five years later. However, to paraphrase a line from the movie *The Magnificent Seven,* "Nobody takes my patients and tells me to run. Nobody." There are some things that are hard to forget or forgive.

Increasingly though, insurers and hospitals try to recruit patients directly. Dr. Richard Gunderman commented, "Hospital marketing may encourage patients to suppose that their relationship with the hospital is more important than their relationship with any particular physician...to position the hospital at medicine's center is to create an unbalanced system, one that will continually jar both patients and the health professionals who care for them."[47] Gunderman concluded, "The true core of good medicine is not an institution but a relationship – a relationship between two human beings. And the better that those two human beings know one another, the greater the potential that their relationship will prove effective and fulfilling for both."[48]

The relationship part of medicine falls outside the simple rules and game plans of the insurers and hospitals. Perhaps it is because it can't be quantified. Writing in *JAMA* almost a century ago, Dr. Francis Peabody commented, "The treatment of a disease may be entirely impersonal; the care of the patient must be completely personal. The significance of the intimate personal relationship between physician and patient cannot be too strongly emphasized, for in an extraordinary number of cases, both diagnosis and treatment are entirely dependent on it."[49]

94

The benefit to the patient of a doctor who knows them is something obvious to every patient and every primary care physician. Increasingly the powers that be don't care.

---

[1] Starfield, Contribution, 481

[2] Starr, 396

[3] Linda J. Weiss, Jan Blustein, "Faithful Patients: The Effect of Long Term Physician-Patient Relationships on the Costs and Use of Health Care by Older Americans," *American Journal Public Health,* December 1996; 86(2): 1742

[4] Cassell, 80

[5] Michael A. Barnett, Asaf Bitton, Jeff Souza, Bruce E. Landon, "Trends in Outpatient Care for Medicare Beneficiaries and Implications for Primary Care, 2000 to 2019," *Ann Int Med,* December 2021; 174(12): 1658

[6] James M. Gill, Arch G. Mainous, "The Role of Provider Continuity in Preventing Hospitalizations," *Arch Fam Med,* July/August 1998; 7: 352

[7] Weiss, 1742

[8] Marshall H. Becker, Robert H. Drachman, John P. Kirscht," A Field Experiment to Evaluate Various Outcomes of Continuity of Physician Care," *Am Journal Public Health,* November, 1974; 64(11): 1062

[9] Roger A. Rosenblatt and others, "The Effect of the Doctor-Patient Relationship on Emergency Room Use Among the Elderly," *Am Journal Public Health,* January 2000; 90(1): 100

[10] Rosenblatt, 100

[11] Peter S. Hussey, Eric C. Schneider, Robert S. Rudin, D. Steven Fox, Julie Lai, Craig Evan Pollack, "Continuity and the Costs of Care for Chronic Disease," *JAMA internal Medicine,* May 2014; 174(5): 742

[12] Naomi Breslau, "Continuity Reexamined: Differential Impact on Satisfaction with Medical Care for Disabled and Normal Children," *Medical Care,* April 1982; 20(4): 347

[13] Becker, 1069

[14] Breslau, 347

[15] Becker, 1069

[16] Dimitri A. Christakis, Jeffrey A. Wright, Thomas D. Koepsell, Scott Emerson, Frederick A. Connell, "Is Greater Continuity of Care Associated with Less Emergency Department Utilization," *Pediatrics,* April 1999; 103(4): 738

[17] James M. Gill, Arch G. Mainous, Musa Nserko, "The Effect of Continuity of Care on Emergency Department Use," *Arch Fam Med,* April 2000; 9: 333

[18] Gill, The Effect, 337

[19] Gary P. Young, Michele B. Wagner, Arthur L. Kellerman, Jack Ellis, Doug Bouley, 24 Hours in the ED Study group, "Ambulatory visits to Hospital Emergency Departments: Patterns and Reasons for Use," *JAMA,* August 14, 1996; 276(6): 464

[20] Susan Louise Ettner, "The timing of Preventive Services for Women and Children: The Effect of Having a Usual Source of Care," *Am J Public Health,* 1996; 86:1748

[21] Ettner, 1753

[22] Marshall H. Becker, Robert H. Drachman, John P. Kirscht, "Continuity of Pediatricians: New support for an Old Shibboleth," *Journal of Pediatrics,* April 1974; 84(4): 599

[23] Dane A. Snyder, Jonathan Schullen, Zeenath Ameen, Christina Toth, Alex R. Kemper, "Improving Patient-Provider Continuity in a Large Urban Academic-Primary Care Network," *Academic Pediatrics,* March 2022, 22(2): 305

[24] Andrew B. Bindman, Kevin Grumbach, Dennis Osmond, Karen Vranizen, Anita L. Stewart, "Primary Care and Receipt of Preventive Services," *JGIM,* 1996; 11:269

[25] Ann S. O'Malley, Jeanne Mandelblatt, Karen Gold, Kathleen A. Cagney, Jon Kerner, "Continuity of Care and the Use of Breast and Cervical Cancer Screening Services in a Multiethnic Community," *Arch Int Med,* July 14, 1997; 157: 1462

[26] O'Malley, 1467

[27] O'Malley, 1469

[28] Benjamin T. Dilger, Margaret C. Gill, Jill G. Lenhart, Gregory M. Garrison, "Visit Entropy Associated with Diabetic Control Outcomes," *J Am Board Fam Med,* 2019: 32: 739

[29] Steven J. Atlas, Richard W. Grant, Timothy G. Ferris, Yuchiao Chang, Michael J. Barry, "Patient-Physician Connectedness and Quality of Primary Care," *Ann Int Med,* March 3, 2009: 150(5): 325-6

[30] John H. Wasson and Others, "Continuity of Outpatient Medical Care in Elderly Men: A Randomized Trial," *JAMA,* November 2, 1984; 252(17): 2413

[31] Michael D. Cabana, Sandra H. Jee, "Does Continuity of Care Improve Patient Outcomes," *Journal Family Practice,* December, 2004; 53(12): 974

[32] Cabana, 978

[33] John G. Saultz, Jennifer Lochner, "Interpersonal Continuity of Care and Care Outcomes: A critical Review," *Ann Fam Med,* March-April, 2005; 3(2): 159

[34] Eugene C. Rich, Ann S. O'Malley, Claire Burkhart, Lisa Shang, Arkadipta Ghosh, Matthew J. Niedzwiecki, "Primary Care Practices Providing a Broader Range of Services have lower Medicare Expenditures and Emergency Department Utilization," *JGIM,* 2021; 36(9): 2796

[35] Ann S. O'Malley and others, "Practice-site-level measures of primary care comprehensiveness and their associations with patient outcomes," *Health Services Research,* 2021; 56: 371

[36] Verena H. Menac, Monica Sirski, Dhiwya Attawar, "Does Continuity of Care Matter in a Universally Insured Population," *Health Services Research,* April 2005; 40(2): 389

[37] Arch G. Mainous, Richard Baker, Margaret M. Love, Denis Perira Gray, James M. Gill, "Continuity of Care and Trust in One's Physician: Evidence from Primary Care in the United States and United Kingdom," *Fam Med,* January 2001;33(1): 22

[38] Mainous, 25

[39] Robert H. Fletcher and others, "Patients' Priorities for Medical Care," *Medical Care,* February 1983; 21(2): 234

[40] Saran, 251

[41] Rosenblatt, 101

[42] Jeff Heatherington, Press Release, December 18, 2017

[43] Angela Marshal-Olsen, Communication to Gina Johnson, May 3, 2018

[44] Marshall-Olsen

[45] JaNae Haymond, Communication to Lane Hickey, November 30, 2018

[46] Gregg Coodley, Communication to Fanno Creek Clinic, February 9, 2018

[47] Richard Gunderman, "Hospitalists and the Decline of Comprehensive Care," *NEJM*, 375(11): 1013

[48] Gunderman, 1013

[49] David Meltzer, "Hospitalists and the Doctor-Patient Relationship," *Journal of Legal Studies*, June 2011, 30(S2):594

(Courtesy, Wiki Commons)

CHAPTER 6

The Rise of the Hospitalists

She said, "You know I was diagnosed with cancer?" She had been my patient for nine years since my partner retired. Her husband, now deceased, had been my patient for years longer. I knew that this delightful eighty-one-year-old woman had been in the hospital. Yet I was taken aback when she asked if I had known about her cancer, for I had not known. No one at the hospital had communicated with me. The urologist who had done the biopsy hadn't phoned me with the results. We talked about how she was feeling dizzy and tired and about what else had happened, and what medications she was on now. A week later, I heard that she was back in the hospital. I didn't really know what had happened until she returned a few days later, accompanied by her daughter. She had gone to the hospital with severe abdominal pain but had been relatively quickly sent home. The nurse practitioners who provided her hospital care had never diagnosed the source of abdominal pain or had her seen by a cancer specialist. Instead, they wanted to refer her to palliative care and possibly hospice.

I had never seen this wonderful woman angry before. She felt awful and felt that her care had been awful. She had even erroneously been told that she had diabetes, and I had to explain that she didn't.

Her daughter related that her mom was told she had to be discharged, despite feeling so very ill, after being told that Medicare would not pay for a longer stay. She had been admitted on "observation status," thus formally still in the emergency room, a maneuver hospitals use to improve their profits.

Patients staying in the hospital under observation status are considered outpatients and can't stay very long unless their status is changed.

Of course, she was only on "observation status" because of how the nurse practitioner had coded her hospital admission. Medicare, whatever its faults, doesn't force elderly patients with cancer to leave the hospital when they still have horrible abdominal pain.

The patient was sent home on multiple medications, but when I saw her two days later, she had taken a total of two pills from a list of over a dozen prescriptions. She hadn't been able to swallow the other pills.. Those caring for her in the hospital noted her swallowing problem from a prior mouth cancer but failed to connect the dots as to how that meant she would not be able to take a bucketload of pills anymore.

In the office, she was in tears from the pain. She didn't want to go into hospice; she wanted to talk to an oncologist to see what options she had. She was so ill I would have readmitted her, except for her anger about how she was treated was such that she vowed never to go to that hospital ever again.

How did it come about that my patient could be admitted twice and her long-time doctor was never contacted by those seeing her in the hospital? How could her care have been so lacking? Yet this is just a particularly egregious example of a little-known but crucial change in American health care that has affected tens of thousands in the last two decades.

Traditional primary care practice involved the care of patients both in the office and when the patient was hospitalized. This was not always easy for the primary care physician (PCP). Since the number of their patients hospitalized at any point varied tremendously, they could not simply schedule a set time for this. Usually, caring for patients in the hospital involved adding time to the PCP's day, either before or after time in the office.

Nevertheless, such care was a source of satisfaction for most primary care doctors, who felt that it gave them the chance to use another aspect of their training and be able to follow patients throughout the course of their illness.

For patients, it was a given. Patients expected that their doctor would see them in the hospital. That was when they most needed the doctor who knew them the best.

The invention of hospitalists changed this. As with most changes in American medicine, the original impetus was financial. The first factor was a change in the payments to hospitals from Medicare that was implemented in 1982–83 under the Reagan administration. The rising cost of health care led Medicare to change hospitals' reimbursement from paying for each service provided to providing a set payment, depending on the diagnoses. Hospitals whose patients had less than the expected length of stay would earn the same for less cost. Where the patient stay exceeded the expected amount, hospitals would be providing extra services for free since they would not get additional reimbursement.

This change put tremendous pressure on hospitals to discharge patients as quickly as possible. Pressure was put on the primary care and specialty doctors caring for hospitalized patients to get them out as soon as possible.

Patients felt the impact of this pressure without understanding the reasons behind it. A whole new field was created for attorneys to sue for premature discharge, particularly if something went wrong.

The effect of this cannot be overstated. Traditionally hospitals had no incentive to discharge patients; now, they had every incentive. The Veterans Administration hospitals were traditionally those least concerned with money as it was felt that veterans deserved good treatment. As a medical student on an Internal Medicine rotation in 1983, I well remember the patient who stayed an extra week because his truck didn't work. My medical resident jokingly suggested an auto club consult. Nonetheless, we felt no pressure to discharge this older veteran. Such a stance would seem utterly bizarre to those in training or working at the hospital in 2021.

As part of their effort to reduce hospital stays, hospitals wrestled with how to get the primary care doctor to get the patient discharged as soon as possible. A primary care physician who rounded on her hospital patients in the evening after clinic meant, at times, a whole extra day in the hospital for the patient. Of course, the patients usually preferred this to being sent home before they really felt well.

The next development that affected hospital care was the spread of health maintenance organizations in the 1980s. Health maintenance organizations are essentially insurers that provide health services for a fixed annual fee. Health maintenance organizations began in the late 1920s in California, initially contracting with different municipal departments to arrange medical care for their employees for a fixed fee. HMOs were relatively insignificant in the United States until the Nixon administration pushed the concept to cut health care costs. In a White House discussion on February 17, 1971, Nixon supported the idea of HMOs, which Ehrlichman explained as, "All the incentives are towards less medical care, because the less care they give them, the more money they make."[1] The key development was passage of the Health Maintenance Organization Act of 1973, which required employers with twenty-five or more employees to offer an HMO option if the employer offers other healthcare options.[2] This "dual choice provision" expired in 1995. In the interim, once the Federal government had issued the basic regulations by 1977, HMOs grew rapidly over the next decades. Whether HMOs actually saved money in the long run is disputed.[3]

Since HMOs received a set fee regardless of their costs, they, too, had a strong incentive to try to reduce hospital costs. They began to explore mechanisms to do so, initially by avoiding hospitalizations. One randomized trial from Seattle showed that, "HMO patients had 40% lower admission rates (to hospitals)."[4]

Another cost-saving solution was to employ physicians whose only focus was on managing the hospitalized patients. Such hospitalists would only be at the hospital and thus could devote full effort to getting patients discharged as soon as possible.

This concept was remarked upon and amplified in a landmark *NEJM* article on August 15, 1996. In it, Robert M. Wachter and Lee Goldman from the UCSF Medical School argued that "we anticipate the rapid growth of a new breed of physicians we call 'hospitalists' – specialists in inpatient medicine – who would be responsible for managing the care of hospitalized patients."[5] They argued, "Because of cost pressures, managed care organizations will reward professionals who can provide efficient care."[6] Wachter and Goldman predicted that hospitalists, by focusing only on hospitalized patients, could reduce their costs.

Wachter and Goldman also argued that would be higher quality care. They gave the initial caveat that, "many physicians, though primarily serving outpatients, have exceptional skills in providing inpatient care." However, they went on to assert, "It seems unlikely, however, that high-value care can be delivered in the hospital by physicians who spend only a small fraction of their time in this setting."[7]

To bolster this claim, they cited studies that showed better outcomes for patients with certain diseases, such as AIDS, when cared for by those with more experience with such diseases.[8] I would argue that this can't be extrapolated in comparing care by hospitalists versus primary care doctors. For instance, in my clinic, three of us each take care of a large number of HIV-infected patients. Should one of these patients become admitted to the hospital, each of us would likely be more experienced in HIV care than the hospitalist of the day, who likely does not have this as a focus. Nevertheless, health maintenance organizations and hospitals were convinced that the hospitalist model would save them money. Soon hospitals hired large numbers of hospitalists.

The trend was increased by restrictions imposed on hours of residents following the death of Libby Zion, the daughter of a prominent journalist, which was attributed to overworked and tired residents. In July 2003, the Accreditation Council for Graduate Medical Education limited residents and fellows to working no more than eighty hours a week.[9] Residents and fellows had served as an inexpensive workforce for hospitals. With their work hours reduced, hospitals felt even more of a need to hire other in-hospital physicians. i.e., hospitalists.

By 2006 it had become the fasting growing medical specialty, with over 20,000 hospitalists in the United States.[10] The consequence was a rapid drop in the number of hospitalized patients cared for in the hospital by their PCP from 1996 to 2006.[11]

In their 1996 article, Wachter and Goldman argued that primary care doctors who wanted to continue to follow their own patients in the hospital would be able to do so, stating, "to date, most systems employing hospitalists have not required that inpatient physicians manage the care of all hospitalized patients."[12]

Yet such flexibility did not survive.[13] Hospitals, convinced that the hospitalist model was the key to reduced costs, frowned on deviations from it. Primary care doctors who wanted to continue to follow their own patients were strongly discouraged from doing so.

The primary care clinic where I work was the last one in Portland to give up rounding on our patients at our local hospital. By then, nurses would be telling our patients that their doctor was not going to see them. One of my partners witnessed a nurse telling his patient this while he was standing a few feet away.

Traditionally the medical residents followed patients admitted by physicians in the community. Within twenty-four hours of the incident mentioned above, one of our doctors had admitted a patient that the residents agreed to follow. Late in the day, they changed their minds, leaving the doctor to scramble to see and admit the patient. Apparently, the residents' focus was changing to support the hospitalists at the hospital rather than outside physicians.

Shortly thereafter, on January 25, 2011, we met with the hospital administrators. We asked whether we could have some patients followed by the hospitalists while we continued to be responsible for others. The message was this wasn't possible. We would need to use the hospitalists entirely if we wanted to continue to be on the health plan affiliated with that hospital. I replied on January 25 that, "I didn't like being threatened with the semi-explicit threat that we would be kicked off...health plans etc. if we didn't accede to the hospitalists' timeline."[14] The hospital administrator replied on January 26 that, "the intent was to work collaboratively with you and your team...I'm sorry there was an impression of some type of threat."[15] Yet by February 11, we had surrendered to the inevitable; all of our patients admitted to that hospital were under the care of the hospitalists starting April 1.[16]

We tried to admit and follow our patients at another hospital in the city starting April 15. Yet again we were swimming against the tide. By the end of 2011, our group now used the hospitalists at both of the hospitals.[17]

Wachter and Goldman concluded, "The medical community must continually reevaluate the new approach to ensure that any possible discontinuity in care is outweighed by improved clinical outcomes, lower costs, better education for physicians, and greater satisfaction on the part of patients."[18]

Many physicians pushed back against the arguments for hospitalists. In a letter to the *NEJM*, pediatrician David Epstein wrote, "I do not agree that separating patients from the doctor who knows them best, at perhaps the patient's moment of greatest need is desirable. Nor is it clear that such separations save money."[19]

Dr. William Nakashima wrote, "Under the system they propose, patients who have been seeing their own physicians for years would be cared for by strangers. Patients ill enough to be in the hospital are those who need their regular physicians the most. This is especially true if the patients have incurable diseases...It is sad, but the most important part of medicine, the relationship between the doctor and patient, is being forgotten."[20] Family physician Sanford Guttler noted how hospitalized patients, "are often worried and not themselves. Their families are confused and unfamiliar with the many intensivists and surgeons they encounter."[21]

Eric J. Cassell, a Clinical Professor of Public Health at Cornell Medical School, wrote, "The difficulty in caring for hospitalized patients argues for better training of primary care physicians ...rather than the creation of a new specialty."[22] He also concluded, "It is understandable that the call for 'hospitalists' might arise in response to demands for greater efficiency and lower cost, but will it make for better medicine, now or in the future. It is bad enough to be a lemming but is it necessary to help find a faster route to the sea?"[23]

Yet these physicians wrote in terms of what was best for patients. The driving factor of the change to hospitalists, regardless of the rhetoric, was what would save money for hospitals and managed care groups, not what was best for patients.

Professor Tim Hoff, an expert in health care systems, argued that some primary care physicians' acquiescence in this change was the result of low payments to PCPs for their hospital work, combined with a lower volume of patients hospitalized driven by incentives to keep patients out of hospitals.[24] Hoff quotes an anonymous internist as saying, "I don't work in the hospital anymore, which is a change from how it used to be. But it's a necessity. I can make more money coming into the office and seeing patients all morning than I can going to the hospital to see my one or two patients there."[25] Hoff concluded, "The field of primary care has contributed to its own continuing demise, handing over more sophisticated work to others with little but a whimper."[26]

I would disagree based on my experience that the power of the hospitals in making this change overran any objections.

Another driving factor in the growth of hospitalists involves their role in easing the work for surgeons and other procedurally based physicians. By providing coverage for inpatients of these doctors, the hospitalists allow them more time to focus on their main source of income, procedures. Pham et al. wrote, "Hospitals offer or expand hospitalist services to attract and align with the interests of high revenue admitters, such as proceduralists."[27] Pham et al. continued, "Procedure-based physicians (such as surgeons)...generate greater revenues and therefore greater influence with hospital management. These specialists reportedly perceive that hospitalists offer more efficient consultations and reduce the time the specialist spends on medical management."[28]

We have noticed this experience with patients we refer to a large orthopedic clinic. These surgeons used to ask the primary care doctor if the patient was safe for surgery, figuring the PCP knew them best. Now they have the patient cleared for surgery by the hospitalist or by their nurse practitioner, whose knowledge of the patient comes from a single preoperative screening visit.

It is indisputable that the average length of hospital stay has fallen, although this trend began before the use of hospitalists. The average length of hospital stays in the United States dropped by an average of three days from 1970 to 2005.[29]

The change to hospitalists may have saved money for hospitals. It certainly had several negative consequences. In place of patients seeing their regular doctor every day, they would meet a new doctor. Since hospitalists worked shifts, patients would sometimes be followed by a new doctor every day.

Wachter and Goldman argued that "high-quality providers and systems will develop protocols based on contact by telephone, e-mail and fax to guarantee continuity of care at admission, hospitalization, and discharge."[30] They also argued that primary care doctors could make "social visits" to their hospitalized patients.

The reality turned out to be different. Communication with the primary care doctor became a low, even forgotten priority. As a medical resident from 1985 to 88, I would have been roasted over the coals if I had failed to talk to patients' regular doctors daily while they were in the hospital and on admission and discharge.

Yet the hospitalists feel no such pressure. They must assume that the primary care doctor has nothing to add to the care of the patient since they almost never contact them once the patient is admitted, during the hospital stay or at discharge. Nor does the emergency room usually bother to involve the primary care doctors in the admission process.

Dr. Fred Lafferty described the process, "Hospital emergency rooms are a time-consuming and financial disaster for the patient. He or she is greeted by a receptionist, secondly by a nurse, and finally, after more waiting, by a doctor...We are now up to eight to ten hours in the emergency room. In the meantime, no attempt is made to call the primary physician who may have valuable information that would often eliminate the need for admission. If admission is recommended, the patient is admitted to the hospitalist, who starts from scratch since he rarely calls the primary physician."[31]

Dr. Howard Beckman reported his experience in a 2009 article in the *Annals of Internal Medicine*, commenting, "I am seldom informed of a patient's arrival in the emergency department or consulted to discuss their impressions of the patient's ambulatory course into the decision-making process...patients erroneously assume that I have been part of the admission conversations. My belief that hospitalist care would result in 'abandoning my patients' has largely been validated."[32]

Our group's experience is that often patients are told that their primary care doctor has been contacted and agrees with the plan. When patients report this to me, I don't want to embarrass my hospitalist colleagues by telling patients that this is a total lie and that no one talked to me.

Other primary care physicians who have written about the problem report similar experiences. Frederick Barken commented in his 2011 book about primary care, "What hospitalists have not done, however, is improve doctor-doctor communication on a patient's discharge from the hospital back to the care of his primary physician."[33]

I am contacted about once or twice a year about a patient of mine in the hospital. Our hospitalists have limited access to our outpatient chart, so I must conclude that they feel like there is nothing to be gleaned from it. My experience doesn't differ from that of my partners and most primary care doctors in our city. The rare times I am contacted is when the hospitalists want me to convince my elderly patient to do something they don't want to do, such as go on hospice or change their care status to do not resuscitate.

Studies have documented that this is more than simply my experience. Transition post-discharge is particularly problematic. Pham quoted one hospitalist who stated, "once they are out the (hospital) door, they're not my responsibility."[34]

Kripalani and colleagues, in an analysis of 73 studies, reported that, "direct communication between hospital physicians and primary care physicians occurred infrequently," which translated that it occurred in only 3–20% of admissions.[35] The authors also noted that discharge summaries, which should be available immediately after discharge, were available in only 12–34% of post-discharge visits. Even when available, discharge summaries frequently lacked information such as test results, the hospital course, and discharge medications. The authors wrote, "Poor information transfer and discontinuity are associated with lower quality of care on follow up, as well as adverse clinical outcomes," citing a variety of reports demonstrating this.[36]

Another study looked at how often the primary care doctor had the discharge summary when the doctor saw the patient after hospitalization. In this study, the discharge summary was available in only 12.2% of post-hospital visits. In those few cases where the primary care physician had this information, there were fewer readmissions to the hospital.[37]

Moore et al. looked at the likelihood of errors due to discontinuity of care. They found that 49% of patients experienced at least one error in the handoff from hospitalists to primary care doctors.[38]

The problem may be less for physicians in closed systems, such as Kaiser, who share information systems. One doctor commented, "For people who don't have connectivity, the chances of medication screwups...the likelihood of harm happening (is greater)."[39]

A decade ago, Berwick and Hackbarth estimated that failures in care coordination, "when patients fall through the slats in fragmented care," cost $25–45 billion in wasteful spending in 2011.[40] I have no reason to believe that this number has gone down, for communication has not improved.

After making the case that it was too hard time wise for primary care doctors to also care for their patients in the hospital, the notion that doctors would have time just to make "social visits" was even more unrealistic. This might work in an academic medical center where a salaried doctor might only have to walk down the hall, but it is nonsense in the real world.

There is a negative effect on patients who may feel abandoned by their regular doctor when hospitalized or bewildered by the array of well-meaning hospital doctors who are constantly changing. Barken wrote, "In adopting the hospitalist model of specialty care, we have improved the overall efficiency of care at the expense of patient comfort. Chronically ill, fragile, elderly patients have lost the continuity, comfort and intimacy of the relationship they had with one doctor."[41] Hoff added, "The absence of PCPs from the hospital medicine scene can worsen negative dynamics already endemic to our health care system... it further fragments care for all patients in a system where it is already hard to know whom to trust."[42]

There are other negative effects on patient care. The hospitalists will frequently change the patients' medications in the hospital. As mentioned, the primary care doctor doesn't know about these changes unless he or she can manage to find the discharge summary, often not done for several days after the patient leaves.

I have had many patients who have decided on their own to return to their old pre-hospital medication list. Many pick and choose some of the new medications and some of the old. How is this good medical care?

Clearing up confusion by doing medication reconciliation between what is written on the discharge paperwork and what is actually being taken is another task that is dumped on the primary care doctor.

Another issue is the hospitalist assumption that the complicated dosing regimens possible in the hospital can be easily replicated after discharge. Instead, there is a huge body of literature showing that compliance with medications was inversely proportional to the number of times a day a patient had to take pills.

For there is a foreseeable consequence that doctors who don't practice outpatient primary care will not understand as much how to make it work as those who do.

Another problem is hospital tests where the results are still pending at the patients' discharge. Research indicated that 41% of patients had test results still pending at discharge. The primary care physicians were unaware of over 60% of these pending tests, leading to the likelihood that critical issues would be lost in the transition from hospitalist to PCP.[43]

In a follow-up article ten years later, Wachter celebrated the rapid growth of hospitalists while admitting, "I expected stronger evidence by now of the field's salutary impact on safety and quality."[44] Indeed hospitalists have become the fastest-growing specialty in internal medicine. At least in the early years, up to 90% of hospitalists were generalists, most from internal medicine and secondarily from family medicine and pediatrics.[45] Thus, these were doctors who might earlier have become primary care physicians.

The clearest benefit of hospitalists was in reducing the length of stay of patients, thus reducing hospital costs and increasing profitability. A study at Tufts New England Medical center showed that a six-week period of use of hospitalists reduced length of stay, increasing hospital profitability, if annualized, by 1.3 million dollars.[46] Many studies confirmed that hospitalists were able to reduce patients' average length of stay.[47]

Limited studies show the effects of hospital care by hospitalists vs. PCPs. Wachter noted that in a study after a year of using this model at UCSF, there were, "impressive cost-saving with no adverse impact on quality and patient satisfaction." [48] Another study looked at 2858 hospitals from 2007 to 2015, concluding that hospitals employing hospitalists had a shorter average length of stay than hospitals that did not use hospitalists.[49] Lindenauer and colleagues reported a retrospective study of 76,229 patients hospitalized from 2002 to 2005, which showed a small reduction in length of stay in patients managed by hospitalists versus primary care doctors, but no change in the inpatient mortality or overall patient cost.[50]

Other studies have given far more negative results. A study of 650,651 older adults hospitalized in 2013 used the Medicare database to look at outcomes. Reflecting the change by 2013,

59.7% were cared for by hospitalists versus only 14.2% cared for by PCPs. The study found that hospital stays were 12% longer for patients under PCPs. However, PCPs were more likely to discharge the patient home rather than to rehab or other facilities. Most shocking, at thirty days out from the hospitalization, 10.8% of those cared for by hospitalists had died compared to 8.6% of those under the care of their primary care doctor.[51] After pointing out that primary care doctors had a better outcome than other covering doctors, the authors concluded, "Our results suggest that longitudinal contact with a patient may translate into meaningful differences in care patterns and patient outcomes."[52] In plain English, being cared for by your regular physician in the hospital may be better than any other option. If I were a patient and had a choice (which most patients don't), I would certainly choose the option that would reduce my chance of death by about 20%.

This was just one study, but I was not able to find any studies of comparable size rebutting their findings.

Cost savings for hospitals are not necessarily savings for the entire health care system. A huge study that looked at the costs of care after hospital discharge included 5% of Medicare patients with medical hospitalizations from 2001 to 2006. This encompassed 205,190 admissions at 4657 American hospitals. The study showed that hospitalist care cut the length of stay by 0.64 days, reducing hospital charges by $282. However, Medicare costs in the thirty days after discharge were $332 higher for patients cared for by hospitalists.[53] Thus the hospitalists reduced hospital costs but increased the overall cost of care for Medicare.

Patients cared for by hospitalists were less likely to be discharged home than those covered by primary care doctors, instead having more nursing facility use after discharge. Hospitalists discharged 5.5% fewer patients home compared to PCPs. This translated into 120,000 patients fewer discharged home as a consequence of the use of hospitalists.[54]

The study authors concluded that the, "decrease in length of stay by hospitalists may be obtained at a cost of increased discharges to other health care facilities, such as skilled nursing facilities."[55] The hospitalists' patients were also significantly more likely to return to the emergency room or be readmitted to the hospital than patients cared for by PCPs. Tellingly, patients cared for by hospitalists had fewer visits with their PCP after discharge than those where the PCP managed all the care.[56]

Two other studies of patients with upper gastrointestinal bleeding and strokes, respectively, showed higher readmission rates among patients cared for by hospitalists. [57] [58] In the latter study, the shorter length of stay among patients managed by hospitalists was also unfortunately paired with a, "significantly higher odds of discharge to an inpatient rehabilitation facility," rather than to home.[59] The authors concluded that earlier studies that did not show a higher readmission rate may have looked at particularly motivated hospitalists rather than care when large numbers of hospitalists were practicing.[60]

Another analysis found that readmission rates were not particularly changed by the style of hospitalist practice.[61] This suggests that it was inherent to separating the hospital care of patients from their regular doctors.

A few weeks ago, I had two patients whose speedy discharge may have been more profitable for the hospital, but not better care and probably more expensive in the long run. One was a seventy-year-old gentleman who presented with melena, dark stools suggestive of bleeding, critically severe anemia and uncontrolled heart failure. I asked the hospitalist for cardiology and gastroenterology to see the patient. The gastroenterology physician assistant saw the patient and decided his evaluation could wait until his scheduled colonoscopy three and a half months later. Cardiology was not consulted. The patient was discharged in two days, temporarily feeling better after a blood transfusion. Since the cause of his bleeding was not diagnosed, he was soon readmitted with uncontrolled heart failure and anemia.

A second patient was a ninety-six-year-old woman admitted with severe anemia and chest pain who underwent drainage of bloody fluid from her pleura, the lining of the lung. The fluid was non-diagnostic, but she was sent home quickly anyway. When I saw her a few days after discharge, her pleura was again full of her fluid and her hematocrit was down to a third of normal. She, too, was soon readmitted.

In both cases, the emphasis was on holding down the length of stay to make money for the hospital. In the long run, both patients will cost the health care system more than if their management was still under their primary care doctor.[62]

The patient whose story I related at the start of the chapter didn't benefit from the superior skills in inpatient care of the hospitalists. She didn't feel well cared for. Nor was this a case of an impoverished inner-city hospital that could not afford better, but instead, one of the most profitable hospitals in the state. A primary care doctor who cared for such a long-time patient may not have saved the hospital money in this situation, but they certainly could have done a better job caring for the patient and letting the patient feel cared for.

I would consider this a clear case of poor care by the hospitalist physicians, except that this severely ill elderly patient wasn't cared for by a doctor. While well-intentioned, the nurse practitioners entrusted with her inpatient care were out of their league.

Dr. Wachter probably did not anticipate this, but many hospitalists taking care of hospitalized patients are now nurse practitioners. This practice started almost twenty years ago. Despite the rapid growth of hospitalist physicians, the numbers were not sufficient to cover all the needs for hospitalists. Nurse practitioners began to be employed to fill the gap, with evidence suggesting that over half of hospital systems have nurse practitioners acting as hospitalists.[63] Of course, it is cheaper for hospitals to employ nurse practitioners as hospitalists than physicians.

Nurse practitioners have an average of six to seven years of training compared to eleven to sixteen for physicians.[64] Nurse practitioners have to spend 500 hours of clinical training before licensure. Reviewing the differences between the fields, one nurse wrote, "The amount of clinical experience is really what sets doctors apart from nurse practitioners during school...Ultimately, by the time a physician is practicing independently, they have thousands of hours of clinical training behind them."[65] One estimate from a physician involved in health education is that physicians have had 21,000 hours of clinical training by the time they start to practice.[66]

A recent survey found that almost three-quarters of the nurse practitioners working as hospitalists were certified in primary care. For three out of four, on-the-job training was the most common qualification to be a hospitalist.[67]

There is limited data comparing nurse practitioners as hospitalists to other practitioners.[68] [69] [70] One study comparing nurse practitioners to medical residents, doctors in training, showed that the resident teams had a shorter length of stay and less direct patient costs and higher patient satisfaction.[71] Another study of 381 patients at a Midwest hospital reported that outcomes of patients cared for by nurse practitioners under a medical director were comparable to those of medical residents. However, in this study, half of the patients initially assigned to the nurse practitioners ended up being admitted to the medical residents at the request of the attending physicians and nurse practitioners, leading this data to be less than convincing.[72]

There have been no studies that compared nurse practitioner hospitalist teams to primary care physicians in the care of hospitalized patients. However, for hospitals, the main and perhaps only statistic that matters is shortening the length of stay, thus saving them money.

If the rationale for hospitalists is really to get doctors whose focus on inpatient care gives them special expertise and increased experience over primary care doctors to improve patient care, the use of nurse practitioners does not achieve this. If the primary purpose is to save money and shorten hospital stays, nurse practitioners may well be able to do this, although the evidence for this, as shown above, is sparse.

Few things are more morally troubling than the value of patients being discounted. Yet this happens frequently when older patients are admitted to the hospital, and their primary care doctor is not there to advocate for them. Being ill, they are not at their best, physically or mentally. Yet all too often, a hospitalist who has known them for an hour or a day suggests that they should be referred to palliative care or hospice.

I am not against either of these services conceptually. I am against patients being railroaded into them because a doctor concludes, based on brief acquaintance, that the patient's quality of life is so poor that further medical services are not worth spending on them. Unfortunately, socioeconomic factors sometimes play a role in this estimation of the patients' worth, a fact I learned during the olden days when I rounded on patients in the hospital. If you are an elderly patient being admitted to a hospital, you will likely get much better care if you are white, well-educated and well-off, especially when you don't have your PCP there to be your advocate.

Thus has hospice become a verb. To be "hospiced" means being referred to hospice as quickly as possible with the inevitable consequences of a quick death by ramping up the morphine. Unfortunately, some, although not all, of the hospices, assume that since the patient has accepted hospice, the only goal is pain control, no matter the result. Families are surprised when their parent goes from simply being ill to going on hospice because they have a life expectancy of less than six months to being dead in a day or two. The latter is easily accomplished when the morphine is turned up enough.

Six months ago, I saw an eighty-eight-year-old patient of mine and his wife. He had been admitted to another of our local hospitals with a worsening of his chronic congestive heart failure. He was persuaded by the hospital team that his prognosis was so bad, given his heart failure, that he should go on hospice. I saw him back in clinic after discharge. He noted that his breathing was okay, while his main complaint was chronic low back pain from a prior compression fracture.

The patient, his wife and I had a long discussion about what kind of further care he wanted. He did not want heroic measures like electric shock and intubation if his heart stopped. However, neither was he ready to die. He repeated several times during our discussion that the hospital nurses and doctors pushed hospice on him while saying, "We are not here to save you. We are here to kill you."[73]

While I am skeptical that this was the exact language that was used, this was the clear message the patient took away. He came to this office visit wanting my opinion, saying that he didn't trust all these strangers who were pushing him so aggressively onto hospice. I spent a lot of time trying to find out what he really wanted. Afterward, I assured him that I would follow his desire to continue medical treatment of his heart disease and give medicines for his back but avoid either heroics or letting him be rushed on to large doses of morphine that would eliminate what was mild-moderate back pain at the cost of his life. In the end, I put him on the lowest dose of oral tramadol, one of the weakest narcotic pain killers, with a plan to reevaluate his pain and breathing in two weeks. He returned two weeks later feeling good with minimal pain and no complaints of shortness of breath. He was off all narcotics. Now, more than six months later, he is stable and enjoying living at home with his wife

It is not that primary care doctors are saints always able to choose the path of wisdom. What I brought to the encounter was simply a willingness to listen and a long-time relationship with the patient that encouraged him to be honest about what he felt.

These end-of-life issues have been noted by others. Writing in the *New England Journal of Medicine*, Dr. Richard Gunderman observed, "Who is better equipped to abide by an incapacitated patient's preferences or offer counseling on end-of-life care: a physician with whom the patient is well acquainted or one the patient has only just met?"[74]

The realities of the hospital make the death with dignity movement irrelevant. For those patients following the death dignity rules, the reasonable steps of consulting more than one doctor as well as sometimes a mental health evaluation is well thought out and logical. Every day euthanasia that occurs with patients on hospice requires no such steps. I cannot remember a hospitalist ever referring a depressed patient who wanted to die to have a mental health evaluation before sending them to hospice. Indeed, I would argue that it would be logical to have any patient who opts for what will be a quick death through hospice to have a mental health evaluation beforehand. This could help separate out those who are depressed from those who have had time to make a thoughtful decision to end their life.

I don't want to tar all hospitalists or hospices as thoughtless. However, I usually refuse hospital referrals to hospice. Instead, I try to meet personally with my patients and hopefully their families after discharge home. I want to see a patient that someone else wants to refer to hospice to see if that is really what the patient wants. My advantage in those situations is only in knowing the patients for years. Longitudinal knowledge about patients was one of the advantages when primary care doctors followed their own patients in the hospital.

Still, the lack of conversation between the hospitalists and the PCP can cause the opposite problem. A family physician told me, "I had people who got coded (resuscitated) who were DNR (do not resuscitate)...because there weren't good communications."[75] He concluded, "There are so many ways for things to go haywire if the communications are bad."[76]

There are still more negative consequences of the use of hospitalists. Formerly primary care doctors rounding on hospitalized patients would run into and interact with doctors from other practices as well as specialists. This opportunity has disappeared. Huff quoted one internist still doing hospital rounding as saying, "If I didn't go the hospital, there would be weeks go by where I wouldn't interact with a specialist in a professional setting....When you're referring one of your patients to a specialist, you want to know what this person is like."[77] A family physician for a large hospital-owned medical group explained the breakdown in communications between PCPs and specialists, "In the old days, you would talk to them while you were rounding (seeing hospital patients)...You knew all the specialists you were referring to...the biggest thing that's happening in primary care compared to the old days is not having phone calls or personal communications."[78]

Since we gave up rounding at the hospital, I almost never see any physicians outside of my colleagues. I may talk on the phone with a specialist but have no idea what they are like, what they look like or how they interact with patients. I think the experience is similar for my partners. This isolation makes the job harder and less fulfilling.

Others have remarked about other possible negative consequences for PCPs of giving up inpatient care to hospitalists. Physicians have suggested that this will weaken their ability to care for sick patients as outpatients. Some have suggested that this will make the job more monotonous. It has been suggested that patients will feel less connected to their primary care doctor when that doctor does not take the trouble to follow them in the hospital.[79] Gunderman noted, "It's likely to become increasingly difficult for community physicians to really mean it when they promise patients to always be there for them."[80]

The one benefit for primary care physicians that has been suggested is that giving up inpatient work will improve the lifestyle for doctors, with more predictable and limited hours. This lifestyle enhancement is most important for newer doctors and those who may want to work part-time. In my own group, the older physicians did indeed feel more aggrieved by the change than did our younger colleagues, many of whom worked part-time. Yet again, the driving factor was the hospital, not the doctors.

Another rationale given for the use of hospitalists was that it would free up primary care doctors to see more outpatients, thus effectively increasing the supply of primary care physicians.[81] A review of data from 2008 reported that PCPs who relinquished hospital work to hospitalists saw an extra 8.8 office visits a week compared to PCPs not using hospitalists.[82] However, other factors, such as the advent of electronic medical records, have resulted in almost all primary care doctors seeing fewer patients than they did in the past, even when they also managed patients in the hospital.

Moreover, the huge number of doctors becoming hospitalists has largely been at the expense of the number of doctors going into primary care rather than any reduction in the number of specialists. A 2008 survey revealed that 85% of hospitalists were trained in general internal medicine and thus would have become primary care doctors if the hospitalist option were not there.[83] The growth of hospitalists has contributed to the decrease in the number of primary care doctors and the overall primary care visits available to patients.

What do patients want? In one of the few surveys of patients, some, "two-thirds said that they would prefer care by their own physician to that of a hospitalist if they were hospitalized for a general medical condition while 25% report no preference and only 9% prefer a hospitalist."[84]

A more recent study compared hospital care of frequently hospitalized patients by their PCP to the now-standard care of hospitalists. The results showed patients felt positive about being cared for by their PCP, felt cared for by their PCP, had shared trust with their PCP, appreciated the longitudinal continuity with their PCP and preferred their PCP to be involved with their hospitalization. In contrast, those cared for by hospitalists questioned whether their PCP was contacted during the hospitalization, with one woman stating, "I don't know for sure that they are calling him and letting him know or if he is getting the reports or any of that."[85] A clear majority of patients wanted their PCP to be involved during their hospitalization, yet the majority of patients cared for by hospitalists did not have interaction with their PCP during their hospitalization. My own experience and that of others confirms that there is only rarely communication from hospitalists during my patients' admissions.

Clearly, patients would prefer to be cared for by their regular doctor if hospitalized. This is not today's reality. I suspect that there weren't more studies asking patients' opinions about the change because no one cared about their opinions compared to saving money.

In conclusion, the switch to hospitalists has been good for hospitals, saving them money and increasing profitability. It is not clear that it has reduced overall health care costs and may have increased them. There is evidence that it has led to more readmissions and emergency room visits post-discharge. Communication between hospitalists and PCPs has been poor, with negative consequences for patients' care. It is, at best, a mixed blessing for PCPs, reducing their hospital workload in exchange for decreased job satisfaction, increased isolation and a further decline in the prestige of the field. It has greatly contributed to the decreased number of PCPs. It is not what patients would choose. For primary care, it is yet another factor in severing the bond between doctor and patient. Yet if the genie cannot be put back in the bottle, perhaps he can be redirected. In my last chapter, I will outline ways that this situation can be improved, so no more patients ask, "You knew I had cancer. Right?"

---

[1] Richard Nixon, Transcript of Taped Conversation between President Richard Nixon and John D. Ehrlichman, 1971, https://en.wikisource.org/wiki

[2] Joseph L. Dorsey, "The Health Maintenance Organization Act of 1973 (P.L.93-222) and Prepaid Group Practice plans," *Medical Care*, January 1975; 13(1): 1

[3] Jaeun Shin, Sangho Moon, "Do HMO Plans Reduce Expenditures in the Private Sector," *Economic Inquiry*, January 2007; 45(1): 82

[4] Sheldon Greenfield and others, "Variations in Resource Utilization Among Medical Specialties and Systems of Care: Results from the Medical Outcomes Study," *JAMA*, March 25, 1992; 267(12): 1629

[5] Robert M. Wachter, Lee Goldman, "The Emerging Role of 'Hospitalists' in the American Health Care System," *NEJM*, 335(7): 514

[6] Wachter, Emerging Role, 514

[7] Wachter, Emerging Role, 514

[8] Valerie E. Stone, George R. Seage, Thomas Hertz, Arnold M. Epstein, "The Relation Between Hospital Experience and Mortality for Patients with AIDS," *JAMA*, 268(19): 2655

[9] Ibrahim, 367

[10] Robert M. Wachter, "The State of Hospital Medicine in 2008," *Med Clinics North America*, 2008; 92: 265

[11] Gulshan Sharma, Kathlyn E. Fletcher, Doug Zhang, Yong-Fang Kuo, Jean L. Freeman, James S. Goodwin, "Continuity of Outpatient and Inpatient Care by Primary Care Physicians for Hospitalized Older Adults," *JAMA*, April22/29, 2009; 301(16): 1671

[12] Wachter, Emerging Role. 516

[13] C. Kilgore, "Some Internists Bid Farewell to Rounds," *Internal Medicine News*, March 1, 1995; 1:3

[14] Gregg Coodley, Communication to Bill Sherer, January 25, 2011

[15] Janice Burger, Communication to Gregg Coodley, January 26, 2011

[16] Gregg Coodley, Communication to Fanno Creek Clinic Providers, February 11, 2011

[17] Gregg Coodley, Communication to Fanno Creek Clinic Providers, October 6, 2011

[18] Wachter, Emerging Role, 516

[19] David Epstein, "The Role of 'Hospitalists' in the Health Care System," *NEJM*, February 6, 1997; 336(6): 444

[20] William F. Nakasahima, "The Role of 'Hospitalists' in the Health Care System," *NEJM*, February 6, 1997; 336(6): 445

[21] Sanford Guttler, "The Role of 'Hospitalists' in the Health care System," *NEJM*, February 6, 1997; 336(6): 445

[22] Cassell, 130

[23] Cassell, 131

[24] Hoff, 19

[25] Hoff, 67

[26] Hoff, 1

[27] Hoangmai H. Pham, Joy M. Grossman, Genna Cohen, Thomas Bodenheimer, "Hospitalists and Care Transitions: The Divorce of Inpatient and Outpatient Care," *Health Affairs*, 2008; 27(5): 1317

[28] Pham, 1320

[29] Hoff, 66

[30] Robert M. Wachter, Lee Goldman, "The Role of 'Hospitalists' in the Health Care Systems," *NEJM*, February 6, 1997; 336(6): 445-6

[31] Lafferty, 19-20

[32] Howard Beckman, "Three Degrees of Separation," *Ann Int Med*, December 15, 2009; 151: 890-1

[33] Barken,

[34] Pham, 1321

[35] Sunil Kripalani, Frank LeFevre, Christopher O. Phillips, Mark V. Williams, Preetha Basaviah, David W. Baker, "Deficits in communications Between Hospital Based and Primary Care Physicians: Implications for Patient Safety and Continuity of Care," *JAMA*, February 28, 2007; 297(8): 831

[36] Kripalani, 838

[37] Carl van Walraven, Ratika Seth, Peter C. Austin, Andreas Laupacis, "Effect of Discharge Summary Availability During Post Discharge Visits on Hospital Readmissions," *JGIM*, March 2002; 17: 186

[38] Carlton Moore, Juan Wisnivesky, Stephen Williams, Thomas McGinn, "Medical Errors Related to Discontinuity of Care from an Inpatient to Outpatient Setting," *JGIM*, August 2003; 18:646

[39] Anonymous, June 24, 2021

[40] Donald M. Berwick, Andrew D. Hackbarth, "Eliminating Waste in US Health Care," *JAMA*, April 11, 2011; 307(14):1514

[41] Barken,

[42] Hoff, 81

[43] Christopher L. Roy and others, "Patient Safety Concerns Arising from Test Results that Return After Hospital Discharge," *Ann Int Med*, July 19, 2005; 143: 121

[44] Robert M. Wachter, "Reflections: The Hospitalist Movement a Decade later," *Journal Hospital Medicine*, July/August, 2006; 1(4): 251

[45] Hoff, 18

[46] Douglas Gregory, Walter Baigelman, Ira B. Wilson, "Hospital Economics of the Hospitalist," *Health Services Research*, June 2003; 38(3): 905

[47] Wachter, The State, 267

[48] Robert M. Wachter, Patricia Katz, Jonathan Showstack, Andrew B. Bindman, Lee Goldman, "Reorganizing an academic medical service: Impact on cost, quality, patient satisfaction and education," *JAMA*, 1998; 279(19): 1560

[49] Khanhuyen P. Vinh, Stephen L. Walston, Jeff Szychowski, S. Robert Hernandez, "The Effect of Hospitalists on Average Length of Stay," *Journal of Healthcare Management*, May-June 2019; 64(3): 169

[50] Peter K. Lindenauer, Michael B. Rothberg, Penelope P. Pekow, Christopher Kenwood, Evan M. Benjamin, Andrew D. Auerbach, "Outcomes of Care by Hospitalists, General Internists and Family Physicians," *NEJM*, December 20, 2007; 357(25): 2589

[51] Jennifer P. Stevens, David J. Nyweide, Sha Maresh, Laura A. Hatfield, Michael D. Howell, Bruce E. Landon, "Comparison of Hospital Resource Use and Outcomes Among Hospitalists, PCPs and other Generalists," *JAMA Internal Medicine*, 2017; 177(12): 1781

[52] Stevens, 1785

[53] Yong-Fang Kuo, James S. Goodwin, "Association of Hospitalist Care with Medical Utilization After Discharge: Evidence of a Cost Shift from a Cohort Study," *Ann Int Med*, August 2, 2011; 152

[54] Kuo, 152

[55] Kuo, 158

[56] Kuo, 152

[57] JT Go and others, "Do hospitalists affect clinical outcomes and efficiency for patients with acute upper gastrointestinal hemorrhage," *Journal Hospital Medicine*, 2010; 5:133

[58] Bret T. Howrey, Yong-Fang Kuo, James S. Goodwin, "Association of care by hospitalists on discharge destination and 30 day outcomes following acute ischemic stroke," *Medical Care*, August 2011,; 49(8): 701

[59] Howrey, 701

[60] Howrey, 706

[61] James S. Goodwin, Yu-Li Lin, Siddhartha Singh, Yong-Fang Kuo, "Variation in Length of Stay and Outcomes among Hospitalized Patients Attributable to Hospitals and Hospitalists," *JGIM*, 201; 28(3): 370

[62] Gregg Coodley, Communication February 7, 2022

[63] Sharon E. Bryant, "Filling the gaps: Preparing nurse practitioners for hospitalist practice," *Journal of the American Association of Nurse Practitioners*, January 2018; 30(1): 4

[64] Julie Monroe, "Nurse Practitioner versus Doctor: In Depth Career Comparison," *Nursing Process.org, 2021*

[65] Monroe

[66] Charles Bentz, Personal Communication to Gregg Coodley, March 31, 2021

[67] Louise Kalan, Tracy A. Klein, "Characteristics and perceptions of the US nurse practitioner hospital workforce," *J Am Assoc Nurse Practitioners*, November 16, 2021.doi: 10.1097/JXX.000000000000531

[68] Michael C. Iannuzzi, James C, Iannuzzi, Andrew Holtsbery, Stuart M. Wright, Stephen J. Kohl, "Comparing Hospitalist-Midlevel Practitioner Team performance on Length of Stay and Direct Patient Care Cost," *J Grad Med Educ*, March 2015; 7(1): 65

[69] Mathilde H. Piero and others, "Outcomes-based trial of an inpatient nurse practitioner service for general medical patients," *Journal Evaluation Clinical Practice*, 2001; 7(1): 21

[70] Marie J. Cowan and others, "The Effect of a Multidisciplinary Hospitalist/ Physician and Advance Practice Nurse Collaboration in Hospital Costs," *Journal Nursing Administration*, February 2006; 36(2): 79

[71] Iannuzzi, 65

[72] Piero, 21

[73] Gregg Coodley, Conversation with Patient , June 8, 2021

[74] Gunderman, 1012

[75] Anonymous, to Gregg Coodley, June 24, 2021

[76] Anonymous, to Gregg Coodley, June 24, 2021

[77] Hoff, 74

[78] Anonymous, to Gregg Coodley, June 24, 2021

[79] Hoff, 77-80

[80] Gunderman, 1012

[81] David O. Meltzer, "Hospitalists and Primary Care," *JGIM*, 2015; 30(5): 541-2

[82] Jeongyoung Park, Karen Jones, "Use of Hospitalists and Office Based Primary Care Physicians Productivity," *JGIM*, August 2014; 30(5): 572

[83] Park, 572

[84] Meltzer, Hospitalists, 604

[85] Erin Yildirim Rieger and others, *BMJ Open*, 2021:11:e053784. Doi: 10:1136/bmjopen-2021-053784

(Courtesy, Wiki Commons)

CHAPTER 7

The Insurers Take Over Doctoring

In the days of yore, medical decisions would be made by doctors and patients. Health insurance companies would not be involved in deciding which tests a patient needed or what therapies should be prescribed.

At some point, insurers began to be more involved in the process through the mechanism of denying payment for what were deemed unnecessary services. At this stage, the insurers could discourage procedures or tests by refusing to pay, but they never would have assumed themselves capable of recommending what tests, treatments or other interventions physicians should do.

Now, however, insurers feel themselves quite capable of deciding the course of treatment for patients. Indeed, they act like they need to be parents to primary care doctors, who are either too childish or ignorant to know what needs to be done. Thus, every day a primary care doctor might receive a dozen or more recommendations as to the best treatment for their patients. This might be reminders as to why medication A is not recommended for patients over sixty-five or why diabetics need to be prescribed medications to lower their cholesterol. Doctors will be instructed as to why this patient needs a mammogram or colonoscopy. The worst companies ask the doctors to reply to justify themselves if they are not implementing the insurers' recommendations.

The problem goes beyond presuming the primary care doctor incapable of managing the patient. The blizzard of recommendations can take up hours of each day. Of course, the insurer will not be paying the doctor for their time in looking at this but will feel aggrieved if the doctor doesn't follow their recommendations.

On Monday, March 22, 2021, I received in the mail eight recommendations from a company called Prime Therapeutics, who did not identify at whose bequest they sent these.[1] There was also one from United Healthcare, two from Aetna Active Health Management, and one from Healthnet. I also received recommendations electronically from other companies that day.

Beyond the sheer volume, the suggestions are often irrelevant or ridiculous, given the actual situations of the patients. Of the ones I received on March 22, there were multiple that didn't make sense for anyone who actually knew the patient. I was reminded that Mrs. B was overdue for a mammogram. Mrs. B had a prior bilateral mastectomy, so she didn't actually need a mammogram. I was told that Mrs. M should not be taking a beta-blocker since I had noted earlier that she had mild, stable heart failure. Yet Mrs. M had refused to come in for many months due to the Covid pandemic, so I hadn't had time to discuss whether to change this medicine she had been on for two decades. At least this insurer covered themselves by stating, "this report does not take into account patient-specific variables that may factor into your prescribing decisions."[2] It was suggested that Mr. H should have his blood pressure medicine adjusted. However, Mr. H was undergoing chemotherapy for non-Hodgkins lymphoma. His mildly elevated blood pressure was not the key issue at the moment as he tried to tolerate the nausea and loss of appetite induced by the chemotherapy.[3] Cholesterol-lowering therapy was suggested for a diabetic who had already not been able to tolerate multiple drugs for this purpose.

The list goes on. It was noted that Mr. N was non-adherent to diabetes medications. Actually, he no longer needed them since he had lost so much weight. I was reminded that Mr. C was non-compliant with his diabetes and cholesterol medications since he had not picked up his refills. Unfortunately, this was because alcohol had taken such a toll on him after many years that he was too confused to take any medications regularly. I was warned that Mr. V, one of the city's smartest attorneys, was on two agents that could impair his thinking. I wonder how many more cases he could win without these since he was almost uniformly successful in his practice.

The guidelines about the need to be careful about the use of drugs in the elderly has been particularly misused. It has changed a reasonable list of drugs to be careful of in older patients due to increased risk of confusion, etc., to a list of drugs that should be prohibited. Doctors prescribing any of the drugs on the list are questioned as if they have committed a sin and are forced to justify their behavior. I just received an e-mail titled "Retrospective Drug Utilization Review" from United Healthcare questioning the prescription of Digoxin for a sixty-eight-year-old man with atrial fibrillation and reduced cardiac ejection fraction. It didn't matter that digoxin, derived from the foxglove plant, has been used for centuries or that this was exactly one of the situations for which its use is recommended or that the patient had already been on it for several years. The letter stated, "The attached report identifies your patients with potential clinical concerns that require your attention," before adding the disclaimer, "this report does not take into account patient-specific variables that may factor into your prescribing decisions."[4] Yet the report assumes that the prescription was improper; the burden of proof is on the primary care doc to show why it is not.

Another letter told me that Mr. C had received prescriptions for three medications that affected the central nervous system. One was Paxil which he had taken for years for depression. He had debilitating peripheral neuropathy, leg pain secondary to diabetes and HIV infection. He had received hydrocodone/acetaminophen, which he took only a couple of times a week despite the pain since he was afraid of addiction. When hospitalized, his pain medicine was switched to Tramadol, a weaker narcotic. The insurance company note admitted, "This is an automated alert that may not take into account all of the patient's history."[5] I have taken care of this delightful patient for two decades. I know his history by heart. This communication did not add anything to his care.

One pharmacy chain wrote expressing concerns that an older patient had received prescriptions (non-narcotics) from several different doctors.[6] Should I have had to write back saying this is what happens when a patient sees a neurologist, gastroenterologist, endocrinologist, orthopedist, psychiatrist, cardiologist and a PCP? I would have preferred that this patient have fewer complex problems and see fewer specialists, but this wasn't going to happen.

Within the mass of suggestions, there were a few that were reasonable, informing me of patients that might have forgotten to refill a medication or could benefit from a colonoscopy.

Yet the majority of suggestions were irrelevant. The individuality of patients is forgotten as those putting together the suggestions for the insurers take the diagnoses reported in claims data and merge this with the cookbook list of what patients in this category need.

Another bit of craziness is when the insurer chides the doctor for doing something that is the result of the insurer's actions. I recently received a letter telling me that my prescription of glimepiride for a seventy-year-old woman with diabetes was questionable due to its possible side effects on the elderly.[7] Yet why is she on that drug? She is also taking another inexpensive drug, Metformin, while her other conditions made use of another inexpensive agent, pioglitazone, inadvisable. I had wanted to give her a newer agent called Jardiance, but she could not afford what it cost, given how little the insurer would cover of it. Thus, I am giving her samples of

Jardiance while still needing to give her more inexpensive medicine to control her diabetes.

I recently received a letter from an insurer's Medication Therapy Management Program suggesting that my patient could have her medications evaluated by a clinical pharmacist.[8] The assumption, of course, is that the PCP doesn't understand why he prescribed the medications for this delightful eighty-seven-year-old who is a long-time patient of mine. In this case, the insurer just offered the service. To make sure I got the message, they faxed it three times the same day, at 8:34 a.m., ten a.m. and ten p.m. I hope that this was an automated process, rather than some poor office worker forced to stay late into the night to harass the doctors.

We have been part of a different Med Advantage insurance, where doctors were financially penalized if they didn't get their patients to call the clinical pharmacist.

Frequently the insurers will chide PCPs for the use of what someone has said are "questionable" inexpensive drugs but are unwilling to cover enough of the cost of newer, more expensive agents to make this a feasible option for patients.

All of this is insulting to the primary care doctor, who is treated like an ignoramus who needs to be taught the right way to practice. Perhaps it makes the insurer feel like they are looking out for the patient. One recent document stated that , "Prime Therapeutics Guided Health program offers valuable insights that may enhance the care you provide to your patients."[9] The company communication went on to proclaim, "Prime Therapeutics LLC (Prime) is an independent pharmacy benefit management company dedicated to providing innovative, clinically based, cost-effective pharmacy solutions."[10] At least they are modest in their claim to virtue.

The insurance company intervention goes beyond simply letters. Many of the insurers have decided to hire nurse practitioners to make home visits to patients. For example, on March 29, 2021, I received a letter from HouseCalls, an organization hired in this case by United Healthcare. The letter told me how one of HouseCalls advanced practice clinicians had done a home visit to Mr. D ten days earlier. The letter noted, "During their visit, the clinician completed a physical exam, encouraged your patient to get appropriate preventive screenings, and discussed the importance of talking with you and following your treatment plan."[11] The communication goes on to say, "The HouseCalls visit isn't intended to replace the care you provide."[12] Yet when our office calls patients such as this to remind them to schedule a checkup, our staff is often told that they already had one, compliments of the insurance company.

The minions the insurers hire don't have access to our patient charts. Thus, we frequently get advice to do things that have already been done. House Calls sent me a letter about their recommendations for one of my patients, following a home care visit, in June 2021.[13] It suggested providing a flu shot, pneumonia vaccination, tetanus shot and education to quit smoking. The immunizations had all been done while I have talked to the patient, who has many complex chronic conditions, every three months for a decade, trying to get him to stop smoking. The HouseCalls visit was a complete waste of health care resources, and the letter to me a waste of my time. A letter about another patient I had been seeing for two decades for diabetes and other conditions suggested that I measure a hemoglobin A1C, a measure of diabetic control. If they had been able to look in the patient's chart, they would have found fifty or so hemoglobin A1C results, usually one every three months, that have been normal for years.[14]

I received a letter from Regence BlueCross that they, in collaboration with a company called Signify Health, had sent a physician to conduct a "comprehensive health assessment" on one of my Medicare Advantage patients. The letter commented, "The clinicians performing these assessments had the advantage of seeing the patient in his or her own home, with caregivers, and with access to medications and supplies the patient is currently using. The clinician also had the advantage of an extended period of time to spend with your patient with no acute issue to address, along with special training in diagnosing chronic conditions."[15] The insurance administrator added a cursory, "This assessment is not intended to replace the evaluation and clinical care that you provide to your patients."[16]

The insurer thus is willing to pay for an extended home physician visit. Ironically, this physician included in his recommendations screening for osteoporosis. Yet this is not something that this insurance plan will cover for men except in very limited circumstances. How is this helpful to me or to the patient? Moreover, this visit was to a very healthy, ambulatory sixty-five-year-old, which is the wrong prioritization if the insurer wants to cut costs.

We will discuss the real reason it is financially beneficial for the insurers to pay for this in Chapter 14. Moreover, if the patient decides not to come in for another physical with their PCP, the continuity of care between physician and patient is weakened, which has been shown to lead to worse patient outcomes. What is superficially beneficial for the insurer is not so good for the patient or the doctor.

Financially this also hurts the PCP. For if the patient doesn't come in to see the PCP, this is lost revenue as surely as if they had changed to another doctor. Actually, it is worse since the PCP is still responsible for doing the prescription refills, referrals and all the other administrative tasks that come with being the patient's physician. There is just no payment for these services.

Again, as the evidence for continuity of care presented earlier shows, the best, least expensive care will be delivered when the patient sees their regular doctor. Thus this type of care may not even be beneficial for the insurance company.

Today I received another letter from Providence Medicare Advantage Plans telling me that Mr. X, who has Providence

Medicare, was assigned a "Dual Plus Care Manager" to, "manage and monitor your patient's Individualized Care Plan (ICP)."[17] This ICP was written by this care manager without any consultation with me, the PCP, although I am supposed to review it and send any changes to the "Care Management Team."

I took care of X's mother in the early 1990s and starting seeing him shortly after that. After twenty-plus years taking care of him, I don't need a care manager to tell me that X is fighting eviction. X and I have been discussing this for years. As X grew older, he found fewer and fewer employers who wanted to hire an age sixty-plus worker and subsequently became increasingly financially strapped.

If the insurance company really wanted to help X, they could give him insurance for free or reduce his medical costs. Hiring a Care Manager, in this case, doesn't help anyone, although it seems to make the insurers feel good.

CMS and the insurers have taken another step to managing medical care. Medicare, Med Advantage and even some commercial plans don't pay for screening labs. Let's suppose a doctor wants to make sure a patient doesn't have diabetes. She might want to check blood sugar or hemoglobin A1C, a test of sugar over a three-month period. However, the above powers that be won't pay for these tests as a part of a physical or a wellness exam or the diagnosis codes under screening for diabetes or even under a family history of diabetes.

The tests will be paid for if the doctor knows that the patient already has a history of elevated sugar or diabetes, but not to find out if this is the case. Doctors can only get the tests paid for if there is some other symptom or disease that justifies the test.

The same policy applies to screening for high cholesterol or thyroid disease, or prostate cancer.

At the same time, simple, inexpensive blood tests for screening aren't covered, the government has mandated that insurance must pay for screening mammograms or colonoscopies. Thus a $2500 colonoscopy to screen for colon cancer is covered, but a $2 test to screen for diabetes is not, nor is a $10 test to screen for prostate cancer.

Such policies are frankly indefensible, penny wise and pound foolish. Yet obviously, CMS and the insurers know better than the PCPs how to best provide for the health of patients.

No one ever proclaimed openly that insurers or their hired minions, such as pharmacy benefit management companies, should be instructing physicians how to practice. The insurers simply take advantage of their financial power to shovel the paperwork at the actual primary care doctors. Nor do insurers ever ask the PCP if they thought having another physician or nurse practitioner evaluate the patient was of any benefit.

Even as they want to manage the details of patient care, the insurance companies are forcing doctors into an unwanted role to act as an insurer. Let me explain what I mean. New insurance contracts, at least for primary care doctors, insist that doctors accept downside risk. This means that the primary care doctor is responsible for trying to keep patients out of the hospital. If too many are hospitalized, or their costs are too high, anything above a certain amount will have to be paid back from the PCP to the insurance company. Yet isn't insurance designed to charge patients, based on statistical analysis, enough premiums to cover the cost of the sicker patients who will cost more than they pay? The new formula makes the PCP responsible for any excess, forcing them to be the insurer and letting the insurance company off the hook.

Perhaps PCPs employed by hospitals and large companies can do this since their employer would cover any excess costs. For a solo PCP or even a moderate-size group of PCPs, this is impossible since they don't have the deep pockets to cover this. This seems like a good formula to drive the last remaining solo or small groups of practitioners out of business.

140

Moreover, the whole premise is absurd. Even as the PCPs were forced to give up control of patients in the hospital, somehow they are supposed to manage in-hospital costs by some sort of telepathy, or perhaps mind control on the hospitalist. They can't control hospital costs or what specialists the patient is referred to in the hospital. Without control of the most expensive part of patient care, how is the PCP supposed to control costs enough to be able to take the risk that patients might prove so ill and sick that their costs exceed what is budgeted?

I regret to say that CMS is part of this weird charade. We looked at one of their new programs that was supposed to generate more income for the PCP. The PCP would have to agree to be paid half of the current Medicare fee for all patient visits for fifteen months. At that time, CMS would calculate how much the patient has cost. If there is a surplus, doctors will receive this. If there is a deficit, the PCP would be responsible for paying this back. What kind of moron does CMS think would agree to be paid half as much and then risk having to owe more money to CMS? Maybe this works for hospital-owned groups where they have the resources to play this kind of Russian roulette. If independents are forced to accept such arrangements, more and more will give up primary care.

I have never heard a clamor from patients for doctors to be guided more by their insurance company. Nor do patients want the PCPs to be responsible for excess costs. They expect that is what insurance is for. Most patients don't want their doctors to be acting on behalf of their insurance company. They want the doctors to be acting at their behest.

---

[1] Prime Therapeutics, Communication to Gregg Coodley, March 22, 2021

[2] United Healthcare, Retrospective Drug Utilization Review, Communication to Gregg Coodley, March 22, 2021

[3] Aetna Active Health Management, Communication to Gregg Coodley, March 22, 2021

[4] United Healthcare, Retrospective Drug Utilization Review, Communication to Gregg Coodley, March 30, 2021

[5] Moda Health, Request for Prescription Change or Information, Communication to Gregg Coodley, April 2, 2021

[6] Express Scripts Clinical Team, Communication to Gregg Coodley, April 19, 2021

[7] United Healthcare, Communication to Gregg Coodley, March 31, 2021

[8] United Healthcare Clinical Engagement Services Team, Communication to Gregg Coodley, April 26, 2021

[9] Prime Therapeutics

[10] Prime Therapeutics

[11] Sidney Gottlieb, HouseCalls Plan of Care Report to Gregg Coodley, March 29, 2021

[12] Gottlieb

[13] HouseCalls, Communication to Gregg Coodley, June 17, 2021, 4

[14] HouseCalls, Communication to Gregg Coodley, June 17, 2021

[15] Cheryl Pegus, Regence Blue Cross, Communication to Gregg Coodley, January 27, 2021

[16] Pegus

[17] Providence Medicare Advantage Plans, Communication To Gregg Coodley, April 8, 2021

Paperwork.

(Courtesy, Wiki Commons)

CHAPTER 8

The Administrative Burden: Credentialling

Once upon a time, anyone could declare themselves a doctor and begin to practice. Medical training consisted of an apprenticeship with an established doctor until the physician was ready to practice. Over time, the process changed to include attending one of a host of medical schools of very uneven training. The result was that many practicing physicians were poorly trained and as likely to harm as help patients.

Following a landmark study of the issue by Abraham Flexner, more uniform training and regulation was implemented, forcing many marginal medical schools to close. The new pattern consisted of four years of medical training, followed by an internship where the new graduate would practice medicine. Longer periods of post-graduate training, residencies, soon followed to give additional skills to the graduates and allow them to specialize as surgeons, internists, or pediatricians. At the end of residencies and fellowships, doctors take exams to certify their competency in their specialty. Finally, to be able to practice in a state, the physician needed to acquire licensure in the state. The state medical boards would regulate this and investigate physicians accused of malpractice or malfeasance.

Licensure stood as the final step for many years. Hospitals, however, could decide which physicians had "privileges" to admit and follow patients at their hospital. It was in the hospitals' interests to have as many physicians as possible use their facility, so one would think that this approval was usually easily given. However, hospitals used the requirements to further the interest of the wealthiest doctors. Starr wrote, "Blacks and foreign-born doctors, particularly Italians and Slavs, were almost completely unrepresented on hospital staffs...when doctors from lower-status ethnic backgrounds obtained positions, they did so at the lower levels of the system."[1] Discrimination extended to post-graduate medical training, which had become a growing part of training in the 1900s. A hospital administrator in Rhode Island commented in 1940 about the selection process for interns (first-year post-graduate doctors), "In the earlier day, we had competitive examinations, but we had to discontinue those. The person who did best on the examination might not show up well in the intern situation. He might lack tact...and more likely, the persons that did best on the written examinations would be Jewish."[2]

Hospital privileges are no longer denied, at least overtly, due to prejudice. However, the requirement for privileges remains a powerful tool, which could be effectively used to exclude those seen as too outspoken or likely to challenge the existing order.

However, for many years if you could get over the hurdles of getting in and completing medical school, completing a post-graduate residency, passing medical board exams and getting a state license and hospital privileges, you were able to practice medicine.

The insurance companies decided that state licensure, board certification, and even hospital privileges were insufficient. Thus, insurers decreed that physicians who wanted to see patients with their insurance had to be "credentialed" with that insurer. Each insurer established its own credentialing process, which usually had to be repeated annually.

Who gained from this process? For insurance companies, it offered a way to control physicians. Rather than allow patients to see any physician in a specialty, insurers would credential only those who would agree to contracts for their services that were favorable to the insurer. By controlling whether a physician was able to see patients on their plan, insurers gained enormous control over physician behavior. The assumption of such power helped lead the insurers to feel that they had the right to govern more aspects of physician behavior. Insurers also could retaliate against physicians who challenged them by simply refusing to credential them.

I know of one excellent physician who was cut off by several insurers after the state board wanted him to take steps to monitor his practice following a surgical complication. I think the real crime for the insurers was when he challenged them in court for cutting him off their panels. Thus, even when the board limitations had been satisfied, they refused to let him see their patients for a decade afterward. I think he was one of the best physicians in his field, and felt comfortable sending my family members to him. Of course, I am only a doctor, not an insurer.

Insurance companies justified their credentialing requirements by saying they wanted to assure the best quality care for patients. In essence, they would duplicate the role of the state medical board. There has been little or no evidence that such credentialing requirements, of which patients are unaware, has done anything to improve the quality of medical care or has helped patients.

How about physicians? The practical effect has been to create another large administrative burden for physicians, which is entirely uncompensated. At our practice of twenty physicians, we deal with a dozen insurers who each want each doctor to be re-credentialed every year. We have an employee whose only job is doing the paperwork for this credentialing.

A few years ago, we spoke to our state legislators about ways to reduce this administrative burden. We suggested that state licensure could serve as sufficient credentialing. If this weren't sufficient, credentialing could be for more than one year, particularly for doctors who had had no complaints or suits against them. At the very least, all the insurers could accept a single credentialing form to reduce the work of having to do marginally different forms for each one.

Our efforts were squashed like the proverbial bug. The power the credentialing gave the insurance companies is such that they rejected any effort to even streamline it. Legislators who had been sympathetic to the ideas of reducing the administrative burden quickly abandoned any interest in doing so after hearing from the lobbyists of the insurers.

Of course, the insurers claimed that they had been working for four years to develop a common credentialing form but were still in the process of doing so. In my testimony to the legislature, I remarked than it took less time to develop the atomic bomb.. I guess getting a good form is a more complicated task.

Licensure has generally been less controversial, but not without issues There is a negative ramification of licensing. Many states ask physicians seeking licenses about their mental health history. A recent study suggested that physicians, despite having higher rates of depression, burnout and suicide than the general population, rarely seek mental health treatment.[3] Physicians cite the negative effects on licensing as a reason to avoid such treatment.[4] One study of 181 residents and fellows at a large academic medical center found that 61% felt that they would have benefited from mental health treatment, yet only a quarter sought treatment. Half cited concern for their ability to obtain licensure as the reason for avoiding this care.[5]

Studies have found that most doctors find the burden of licensing and credentialling to be frustrating. The 2019 Medical Group Management Association survey of 400 group practices reported that 78% found the burden of credentialling for Medicare and Medicaid to be moderately-extremely burdensome.[6]

There also has been a dramatic increase in licensing fees over the last twenty years, in some cases tripling. This is a small but characteristic way in which overhead costs for primary care have increased.[7]

There is a case to be made for licensure to prevent continued practice by doctors who impair rather than aid their patients' health. To the duty of disciplining doctors for negligence or criminal behavior, licensure boards are now confronting how to discipline doctors who spread misinformation. Since January 2021, eight physicians have been sanctioned for spreading misinformation about the coronavirus. Dr. Kristine Lawson, head of the California Medical Board, commented, "Doctors who are out in the public domain, making broad statements about discredited treatments, our processes weren't designed for that."[8] The backlash has been dramatic, with Lawson getting threatened while some states have restricted the powers of the state medical boards.

There is much less justification for the repeated credentialing required by insurers and hospitals. Doctors also have to pay annual fees for "hospital privileges" at each hospital to practice there. Many times, this is required in order to get on the insurance panels that use these hospitals, even if the doctor never sets foot in the building. I suppose physicians should be grateful that getting re-credentialed on every insurer every year only costs our time and money.

---

[1] Starr, 167

[2] Oswald Hall, "The Stages of a Medical Career," *American Journal of Sociology,* March 1948, 327

[3] Daniel Saddawi-Konefka, Ariel Brown, Isabella Eisenhart, Katherine Hicks, Eileen Barrett, Jessica A. Gold, "Consistency Between State Medical License Application and Recommendations Regarding Physician Mental Health," *JAMA,* May 18, 2021;325(19): 2017

[4] Alexandra L. Aaronson, Katherine Backes, Gaurava Agarwal, Joshua L. Goldstein, Joan Anzia, "Mental Health during Residency Training: Assessing the Barriers to Seeking Care," *Acad Psychiatry*, 2018; 42(4): 469

[5] Aaronson, 469

[6] Medical Group Management Association, "Annual Regulatory Burden Report," October, 2019;
https://www.mgma.com/Resources/Governement-Programs/mgma-Annual-Regulatory-Burden-Report

[7] Lafferty, 14

[8] Darius Tahir, "Medical Boards get pushback as they try to punish doctors for Covid misinformation," *Politico*, February 1, 2022

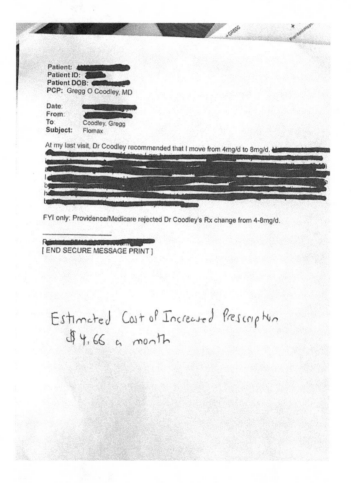

Patient:
Patient ID:
Patient DOB:
PCP: Gregg O Coodley, MD

Date:
From:
To: Coodley, Gregg
Subject: Flomax

At my last visit, Dr Coodley recommended that I move from 4mg/d to 8mg/d. ████████████████

FYI only: Providence/Medicare rejected Dr Coodley's Rx change from 4-8mg/d.

[END SECURE MESSAGE PRINT]

Estimated Cost of Increased Prescription
$4.66 a month

Increasing the dose of the generic medication Tamsulosin from 0.4 mg once daily to two daily for this patient was rejected by Insurance, saving the insurer $4.66 a month.

(Courtesy, Fanno Creek Clinic)

CHAPTER 9

Insurers as Doctors: Prior Authorizations

There once was a day when physicians could choose what medications were best for their patients. The best physicians, then and now, would discuss with the patient why they were recommending this drug, its potential benefits and potential side effects. If there was agreement, the doctor would write the prescription, the patient would take it to the pharmacy, and the medicine would be given to the patient.

Over time, the development of new expensive medications made pharmaceuticals an increasing cost for both patients and insurance companies.

Insurers struck on two ways to limit costs of medications. To limit the skyrocketing cost of medications, they would require physicians to get their approval in order for the companies to pay for the medications. The second concept was to make those involved in the health care of the patient, from hospitals to primary care doctors, financially responsible for the costs. In these "risk-based plans," hospitals and primary care doctors would make more money if the total cost of the patients' care were below a certain level and less if it exceeded that cost. This financial risk created incentives for doctors to avoid prescribing expensive drugs. We will discuss this more in later chapters.

Let us return to "prior authorizations (PAs)," the process by which insurance companies refuse to pay for certain medications unless doctors go through a lengthy written explanation of why the drug is the best choice. Insurers and their employees sometimes try to justify this as them being concerned about patient safety. The national medical director for pharmaceutical policy for Aetna commented in a 2014 interview, "We're trying to make sure this is the right thing for the patient. And if there's something about the patient that is a safety issue or that suggests there's a different way to go for treating that patient, to ensure those things are being considered."[1]

Prior authorizations can take several forms. In the first, the drug can't be prescribed without approval. Physicians may have to show that patients have failed other drugs. The definition of failure is vague. Another process is limiting the quantity of the drug the patient can get before the physician has to go through the whole process once more. Finally, another approach creates classes of drugs that only certain specialists can prescribe.

Even if one was naïve enough to assume that it really wasn't all about money, the assumption still is that the insurer knows better than the physician what is best for the patient.

There is at least some rationality in requiring consideration of alternatives when doctors prescribe very expensive medications. Yet insurance companies already have large monetary disincentives in place to discourage the use of the most expensive agents. Most insurers establish various "tiers" of drugs for which patients have different co-pays. For example, for some drugs, the patient may only have a $5 co-pay, whereas for others, they may be responsible for paying half the cost of a medication that costs a few thousand dollars a month. This is a very efficient market mechanism to encourage patients and doctors to choose cheaper alternatives. One disadvantage is that neither doctors nor patients know in advance how much a particular drug will cost the patient. Frequently, patients call back to say that the drops for their ears or diabetes medicine is several hundred dollars, which they cannot afford. The doctor must then find a cheaper alternative, again not knowing how much any drug will cost the patient. Since each insurer negotiates different prices for different drugs with the pharmaceutical companies, there is no real way to know the cost of alternatives. Our office then has to spend time calling the pharmacy and asking how much different choices would cost the patient before the doctor prescribes this alternative.

There has been a substantial increase in the number of drugs where the insurers ask for prior authorizations. A Kaiser Family Foundation study looked at when Medicare started paying for drugs in 2006. At the time, 8% of brand name medications required prior authorizations, while 18% were subject to some form of utilization management.[2]

By 2013, 21% of brand name medications covered under Medicare Part D required prior authorizations, while 35% were governed by utilization management rules.[3] Thus the number of drugs requiring prior authorizations almost tripled in seven years while those needing other special permissions doubled. By 2019 some 24% of the brand name medications required prior authorizations.[4] The percentages were higher for new drugs. In 2016 67% of anti-depressants and drugs for autoimmune disease, multiple sclerosis and chronic myeloid leukemia required prior authorizations.[5]

What lacks any conceivable rationale other than a desire for control is when the insurer asks doctors to send in prior authorizations for inexpensive generic drugs. Earlier this week, a patient called to let me know that his insurer had denied my prescription to increase his tamsulosin 0.4 mg daily from one to two. Tamsulosin, originally marketed under the brand name Flomax, is often the first choice of therapy for men with benign prostatic hypertrophy (BPH), where the en-larged prostate causes urinary frequency, urgency and diffi-culty urinating. BPH is almost invariably the result for any man who lives long enough. The added cost for three months of another pill daily of Tamsulosin, if one walked into a pharmacy and paid cash, is about $14.[6] This works out to $4.66 a month. Thus, the insurance refused to pay for an increased drug cost, by doubling the dose, of $4.66. Instead, I would be required to write a lengthy message to the insurer discussing the patient's condition and what other drugs he had tried previously for this condition. In this case, any other drugs I could try would mostly be far more expensive than the Tamsulosin.

Every time doctors want patients to get drugs requiring PAs, she would be forced to write a justification for it to the insurer. Every time she did that, she would be taking time away from seeing patients. The administrative time for doing PAs clearly translates to a loss of revenue.

Even for the insurer, this is crazy. They are almost always going to give approval after an appeal for a drug this cheap. So, the effort of the doctor and of the insurance company employee who had to read the prior authorization is a loss of time for both. Unless their staff is all slave labor, it will cost the insurer more time to review the paperwork than the $4.66 a month they would save by denying this medicine.

Could it be any worse? Of course, it can always get worse. Yesterday I received a prior approval request for 81 mg of aspirin for a long-time Medicaid patient of mine. In Oregon, Medicaid patients are managed by private companies, theoretically, to improve their care.

Another PA was for insulin glargine, a long-acting insulin usually known as "Lantus" that has been on the market since 2000. In 2018 there were over twenty-four million prescriptions for it in the United States, making it the twenty-sixth most prescribed drug.[7] Diabetics who depend on insulin don't really have a choice to go without it. The insurer's letter stated that they would pay for it for, "the maximum thirty days temporary supply that we are required to cover unless you obtain a formulary exception from us."[8] So we had to write another prior authorization letter about why this insulin dependent diabetic patient would still need insulin after 30 days.

This week I have received prior authorization requests that needed to be filled out for albuterol, the usual first choice for asthma that goes for $18.27 a month.[9] Almost any other asthma drug used today will be ten to thirty times as much, but somehow the insurer needed justification why they should pay $18 to save the patient a trip to the ER or hospitalization.

A similar story was reported in Minnesota by family physician Randy Rice when he tried to refill Ventolin, a type of albuterol. The patient had been on it for years, and it had been a preferred drug but now required a prior authorization. Rice noted, "They wouldn't tell me what the preferred drug was." [10] He wrote prescriptions for two other brands of the albuterol inhaler, which were both denied. Rice commented, "The patient, who has severe asthma, went home that weekend without his rescue inhaler and could have ended up in the ER or hospital."[11] On Monday, he found that the approved drug was Xopenex which was newer and more expensive.

Sometimes the prior authorization is requested even when there is an easy solution. A partner told me of having to write a prior authorization for venlafaxine extended-release, a generic anti-depressant. It turns out the electronic prescription she wrote was for capsules of venlafaxine extended-release, which required a prior authorization, whereas no PA was required for identical strength venlafaxine tablets.[12]

Sometimes the prior authorizations are justified as an attempt to prevent prescription of potentially dangerous drugs to elderly patients. In 1997 the Beers criteria was developed as a consensus statement about medications and classes of medications that generally should be avoided in elderly patients given their increased toxicity. Yet what started as general guidelines became hard and fast rules that could be violated only by asking special permission of the insurers.

I recently received a pharmacy request for a prior authorization in order to refill a patient's prescription for Lorazepam, an inexpensive anti-anxiety drug. You can find this online for $6.90 for a one-month supply.[13] My sixty-five-year-old patient had been on for it for years, starting when her husband developed a debilitating chronic illness that made her the caregiver for him and her then young children. Her husband had died, and her children had grown, but now, after twenty years of her taking it, the insurer questioned why she should receive this medicine. After all, she is now sixty-five, and six dollars is six dollars.

Other primary care docs have had similar problems with prior authorizations for generics. Rhode Island Internist Yul Ejnes commented that although the request is usually approved, "the benefits manager puts us through the process of getting prior authority supposedly just to let us know that the medication may be dangerous."[14] Dr. Damon Raskin, a California internist, commented, "It may be that even though it's a generic, it may not be on the payer's formulary, or maybe they got a better deal on some other drug. They don't give reasons; they just wanted us to fill out the paperwork."[15]

All too frequently, the situation would be the epitome of Kafkaesque. Walgreen recently told one of my partners that Mrs. K's Symbicort inhaler (a combination of budesonide/formoterol) is not covered by her insurance. The doctor asked the nurse to send in a script for generic budesonide. This was turned down also, but among the acceptable alternatives listed was Symbicort.[16]

What about savings on more expensive drugs? The most expensive drugs are usually newly approved agents for which there is no alternative. Then there are drugs for HIV. Until the last few years, these antiretrovirals, which can cost over $2000 a month, were almost never challenged. I think the insurers were afraid of any backlash they would get. They must be less afraid of a backlash; insurers are now beginning to refuse to cover certain antiretrovirals unless the doctor does the prior authorization. Insurer refusal to pay for certain chemotherapy for cancer patients has also increased in recent years.

I find the push to make patients switch antiretrovirals against HIV particularly problematic. When a person is well controlled on a regimen, I try to keep them on this regimen. This saves the other HIV drugs for use should the patient's regimen stop working. Forcing the patient to change to a new regimen risks the new agent being either: 1) harder to tolerate due to side effects; or 2) less effective. And even if the new agent is well tolerated and effective, the forced switch means that the new agent will no longer be available should the regimen fail.

Recently an insurer refused to fill a prescription for Selzentry, a drug for HIV, for my patient. The decision was made by the insurer consultant, an otolaryngologist, or ear, neck and throat physician, who stated that it would only be approved as part of, "an optimized background antiretroviral regimen."[17] They refused our staff's appeal. I had to call the Prior Authorization department and explain multiple times to the staff there that he had been taking the drug for over a decade and that it was part of an optimized background antiretroviral regimen since his HIV had been completely suppressed on it for at least the five years I had been seeing him.

For a primary care doctor, one of the most insulting things about the PA process is the requirement that only certain specialists are given leeway to prescribe certain drugs. I have taken care of thousands of patients with elevated cholesterol. If they fail or don't tolerate standard therapy, the statins, there is a very effective new albeit expensive alternative, Praluent. Yet the insurers will never approve my prescription for this drug. Instead, I must refer the patient to an endocrinologist or cardiologist who can prescribe the drug. This is a waste of health care dollars and a literal slap in the face to the PCP, who is presumed too ignorant to be trusted to prescribe this medicine. I suppose what might be even more demeaning is when the patient is seen by the physician assistant for the endo-crinologist or the cardiologist, and the prescription is accepted because he or she is part of the specialist team. Failure to authorize the agent when there are no good alternatives means that the patient has not gotten optimal care.

We have just been talking money so far. Policymakers discuss the excessive cost of prescription drugs. They rarely discuss the insurance company's refusal to pay for drugs. They don't discuss the patient annoyance about the prior authoriza-tion process and the patient rage, such as when their insurer refuses to pay for their long-time treatment for their rheuma-toid arthritis.

The burden falls disproportionately on the poorer and the elderly since Medicare and Medicaid, which receive lower per-patient payments than commercial insurance, have a stronger incentive to avoid expensive drugs.

The cost of physician time is astonishing. A 2010 American Medical Association survey found that physicians spend an average of twenty hours a week on prior authorizations, work-ing out to over 868 million hours annually spent by physicians. The total costs for physicians were around $69 billion annually in hours subtracted from revenue-generating patient care.[18]

A repeat AMA survey published in 2017 wasn't that differ-ent, with physicians and practices spending 853 hours annu-ally as the average physician did thirty-seven prior authoriza-tion requests a week. Ninety percent of physicians surveyed reported that the PA process delayed patient access to neces-sary care.[19]

The number of staff involved in this process is also crazy. A large Indiana orthopedics group reported in a 2014 article that they had six full-time employees just dealing with prior authorizations at an annual cost of $180,000.[20] A solo PCP in Iowa reported having to do eighteen to thirty-six prior authorizations a week, each taking twenty to sixty minutes.[21]

In a 2018 survey, 1000 practicing physicians reported

completing a mean of thirty-one prior authorizations each week, requiring about fifteen hours of time.[22] A more recent 2019 article changed the estimate slightly to sixteen hours of physician time plus fifty-five hours of their staff time each week for an annual cost of $31 billion.[23] Whether $31 or $69 billion a year, the cost is too high for a process whose benefit is marginal for everyone but the insurer. A survey of physicians found that 75% reported that the process was a high or very high burden on their staff.[24]

The latest estimate is that PAs cost $93.3 billion annually, divided into $6.0 billion for payer administration, $24.8 billion for manufacturers supporting patient access, $26.7 billion for physicians navigating utilization management and $35.8 billion for payers in drug cost-sharing. The authors concluded, "All stakeholders in the US pharmaceutical system would benefit from a de-escalation of utilization management."[25]

Studies have also shown that the biggest component of physician time spent interacting with health plans had to do with prior authorizations. The data also indicated that PCPS spent far more time dealing with these problems than specialists.[26]

A 2019 survey of 400 practices found that the prior authorizations were the most burdensome of all the administrative issues doctors deal with. Eighty-three percent reported that prior authorization requirements were very or extremely burdensome.[27] One practice commented, "Prior authorization has been out of control for years, and it is only getting worse. The insurance companies walk away with record profits and no accountability except to their shareholders. All of the burden is placed upon the providers/medical offices who continue to see declining reimbursement and increasing overhead costs."[28]

The burden is the worst in January and February, where prior authorization requests are reported to rise 55% due to formulary modifications and patients switching plans.[29]

Many of the prior authorizations are for patients' current long-time medications, which don't change with the calendar year. The 2016 AMA survey of physicians found that 80% reported that they are sometimes, often or always required to repeat PAs for prescription medication when a patient is stable.[30]

Another negative aspect is that the process delays care. In a review of prior authorizations, Larry Jones and colleagues wrote, "Different payors process and adjudicate PAs differently, increasing the amount of paperwork and frustration felt by clinicians and patients."[31]

Anders Gilberg, Senior VP, Medical Group Management Association, commented in May 2021, "A physician might have contracts with twenty to thirty health plans, each with their own payment rules, their own rules on how to get services and how to get things approved."[32]

The fact that each insurer has different drugs for which they require prior authorizations as well as different processes for asking for a prior authorization greatly adds to aggravation for no discernible benefit for the health care system as a whole. The 2016 AMA survey of physicians found that 90% reported that the PA process often or sometimes delayed access to necessary care.[33] Requirements for PAs can be different for different plans within the same insurance company.[34]

In many cases, the insurer will eventually grant authorization. Of the 8.1 million Medicare Part D prior authorization requests for medications in 2017, 35% were initially rejected, but then 73% of these were ultimately granted after the doctor appealed for reconsideration.[35] Thus, the whole process resulted in only about 10% of drugs eventually being refused, suggesting first that many of the denials were not correct. It also says that tremendous work and effort is being asked of physicians to block a small proportion of prescriptions.

Primary care physicians have also noted cases where the specialist sends the patient back to the PCP to obtain a prior authorization. Internist Jeffrey Kagan commented, "I'm not sure how much is true rules of the insurance company and how much avoidance of extra work by the specialists. A similar dump by some specialists is to send patients back for pain meds so the specialists don't have to prescribe them."[36]

Those requiring prior authorizations, such as the insurers or their minions, the pharmacy benefit managers (PBMs), don't worry about the cost to physicians. Medical analyst Randy Vogenberg commented, "The PBMs job is all about managing money and not paying out what they determine to be unnecessary costs. If it means more costs on the medical side, that's unfortunate, but they say, 'that's not our job.'"[37]

Another area where prior authorizations have expanded is for Medicaid, driven by rapid growth in Medicaid spending on medications. Such restrictions may have unintended consequences. Some of these that have been noted include "lower use of essential therapies; declines in health; substitution of less effective, more toxic or more expensive medications for non-reimbursed agents; or increased use of more costly physician or institutional care."[38]

Analysis showed, for example, that "arbitrary limits on the number of Medicaid prescriptions reimbursed for chronically ill elderly and disabled people resulted in a 35% reduction in the use of clinically essential drugs (such as insulin)."[39] However, the consequence was, "a 200% increase in the use of services (such as nursing homes and emergency mental health services) whose costs exceeded the cost of the drugs."[40]

Prior authorizations may reduce drug utilization.[41] However, the reduction may include necessary as well as unnecessary drugs. Studies have found that over a third of medications initially blocked by prior authorization mandates are never picked up by patients.[42]

Moreover, just as reduced hospital lengths of stay don't necessarily lead to overall reduced health care costs, the reduction in spending on drugs may not lead to overall health care savings

Research showed that prior authorization mandates for medicines to treat diabetes, depression, schizophrenia and bipolar disorder are associated with worsening disease status, increased hospitalizations and higher net medical costs.[43]

In a study of schizophrenics, a state cap on the number of prescriptions of any drug for Medicaid patients to a maximum of three in a month reduced the use of anti-psychotic and other mental health medications by 15-49%. However, it also resulted in increased visits to community mental health centers and emergency rooms, the latter averaging 1.2-1.4 episodes per patient per month. The estimated average increase in mental health costs during the cap ($1530) was seventeen times as much as the savings in reduced drug costs. When the cap was removed, the use of medications and mental health services reverted to baseline levels.[44] Soumerai et al. concluded, "The limit on drug benefits increased patients' agitation or exacerbated schizophrenic symptoms, thereby increasing the use of expensive acute care services."[45]

The same study also revealed another flaw in three-drug limits. A middle-aged woman with schizophrenia was admitted on an emergency basis to the hospital. Previously her regimen included an anti-psychotic drug, a drug for Parkinsonism, a heart drug and insulin. She had opted to get her other three drugs refilled rather than her insulin, which resulted in her hospitalization with diabetic ketoacidosis.[46]

Nevertheless, capping the number of drugs that Medicaid patients could receive was a popular strategy, with fourteen states implementing such caps by 1984.[47]

Seabury and colleagues did another analysis of the effect of formulary restrictions on Medicaid patients with schizophrenia. Compared to those without restrictions, schizophrenic patients facing formulary restrictions were more likely to be hospitalized and had 16% higher total costs. Similar results were found in bipolar patients. The authors also estimated that these policies led to increased incarceration of these patients, with increased incarceration costs estimated to be $362 million nationwide in 2008.[48]

Bergeson studied patients with type II diabetes mellitus where the doctor prescribed a diabetes medicine that required a prior authorization. Those patients who did not get the medicine had significantly higher overall medical costs over the subsequent twelve months. Thus, the plan denial of the medications was counterproductive. Patients whose expensive medication was denied did enough worse as to result in higher overall costs compared to those receiving the medicine.[49]

Bloom and Jacobs looked at the effect in West Virginia of a prior authorization requirement for cimetidine which is used to treat peptic ulcer disease. The PA program reduced cimetidine use 84% but was followed by an increase in hospitalizations for peptic ulcer disease.[50]

Prior authorization restrictions can have other unanticipated consequences. Pregabalin (brand name Lyrica) is a treatment for neuropathic pain, such as diabetic peripheral neuropathy or postherpetic pain following shingles. However, due to its high costs, many insurers were reluctant to authorize it and required prior authorizations. An evaluation compared outcomes for patients in four states where the Medicaid program required prior authorizations for Lyrica versus four states without such requirements. In the states with prior authorizations, there was less use of Lyrica. However, instead, there was increased use of narcotics as an alternative pain medication as well as higher overall disease-specific health care costs.[51]

The problem still persists today, even after a generic version of Lyrica has become available. Insurers often still want prior authorizations for Lyrica. At the same time, the national effort to reduce narcotic use has led to increased use of prior authorizations for narcotic pain medications. What do the insurers suggest? They suggest patients try acetaminophen, the chemical form of Tylenol. This is a good place to start but not very helpful or sufficient for the very many patients with chronic severe back problems or painful neuropathies. Perhaps those making the decisions for the insurers have either never had chronic pain or have the good fortune to be able to get whatever treatment is necessary.

In many cases, insurers exclude entire categories of effective drugs from reimbursement without a PA. For example, all benzodiazepines may be excluded. While these anti-anxiety agents can be overused, they are actually far safer than some of the alternative drugs they replaced, such as barbiturates, for anxiety. Harvard professor Stephen Soumerai concluded, "Rigid policies that target essential classes of medications with heterogeneous patient responses and side effects could reduce appropriate care, adversely affect health status, and cause shifts to other drugs or more expensive types of care."[52]

One of the most problematic effects is when patients are forced to switch from a drug they are using safely and effectively to a new agent, which costs the insurer less. This is like playing Russian Roulette. Every time a patient tries a new agent, there is always the risk that it may give significant side effects and/or be ineffective. So, a patient whose depression is well controlled on drug A is changed to drug B, which they may stop due to intolerance, or it simply won't be as effective.

It is not simply wasted doctor time and money or worse patient outcomes that are problematic with prior authorizations, for the entire process is driven by what many would consider corruption. For the pharmacy benefit managers don't decide which drugs to include based on which are better for patients or even their average costs.

Instead, the pharmacy benefit managers retain a percentage of whatever rebates they can negotiate with pharmaceutical companies. Thus, they can and will choose to put a drug on the preferred formulary for which they get a large kickback rather than the drug whose outside price is really the least.

There are no transparency requirements for the PBMs to disclose how much kickback they receive for each drug they put on the formulary. Since this distorts the formulary from simply including the medicines with the lowest average wholesale price, it makes it even harder for physicians to know which drugs will need a prior authorization.

Policymakers don't usually worry about the cost or aggravation to primary care doctors, whose offices are responsible for handling the vast majority of these appeals. After all, doctors, even those in primary care, make a lot of money. Yet money is never the factor that makes a primary care doctor decide to retire early. It is the aggravation of doing senseless work again and again.

Nor does anyone seem to care when patients are denied the best treatment. After all, the insurers know best.

---

[1] Jeffrey Bendix, "The Prior Authorization Predicament," *Medical Economics*, July 10, 2014, 34

[2] Bendix, 35

[3] Bendix, 35

[4] Jack S. Resneck, "Refocusing Medication Prior Authorization on Its Intended Purpose," *JAMA*, February 25, 2020; 323(8): 703

[5] Resneck, 704

[6] Drugs.com, March 26, 2021

[7] Agency for Healthcare Research Quality, Medical Expenditure Panel Survey (MEPS), 2008-2018, Rockville, MD, ClinCalc Drug Stats Database version 21.1, ClinCalc.com

[8] Healthnet Medicare Programs, Patient Transition Fill, Communication to Gregg Coodley, March 22, 2021

[9] Goodrx.com

[10] Howard Bell, "The Prior Authorization Burden," *Minnesota Medicine*, November-December, 2014, 19

166

[11] Bell, 19

[12] Christine Oliver, Communication to Gregg Coodley, May 5, 2021

[13] Goodrx.com

[14] Bendix, 35

[15] Bendix, 35

[16] Walgreens, Communication to Fanno Creek Clinic, April 9, 2021

[17] OptumRX, Communication to Gregg Coodley, July 3, 2021

[18] Bendix, 29

[19] J. Collins Corder, "Streamlining the Insurance Prior Authorization debacle," *Missouri Medicine,* July/august 2018; 115(4): 313

[20] Bendix, 32

[21] Bendix, 32

[22] Resneck, 703

[23] Laney K. Jones, Irene G. Ladd, Christina Gregor, Michael A. Evans, Jove Graham, Michael R. Gionfriddo, "Understanding the medication prior-authorization process: A case study of patients and clinical staff from a large rural integrated health delivery system,: *Am J Health Syst Pharm,* April 1, 2019; 76(7): 454

[24] Jones, 454

[25] Scott Howell, Perry T. Vin, James C. Robinson, "Quantifying the Economic Burden of Drug Utilization Management on Payers, Manufacturers, Physicians and Patients," *Health Affairs,* August 2021; 40(8): 1206

[26] Lawrence P. Casalino and others, "What Does it Cost Physician Practices to Interact with Health Insurance Plans," *Health Affairs,* 2009, 28(4), w537

[27] Medical Group Management Association, Report 2019, 5

[28] Medical Group Management Association, Report 2019, 5

[29] Resneck, 703

[30] American Medical Association 2016 Prior Authorization Physician Survey, American Medical Association, 2017, 2

[31] Jones, 454

[32] Todd Shyrock, "Permission Denied: Why Prior Authorizations Aren't going away," *Medical Economics*, May 2021, 19

[33] American Medical Association, Prior Auth, 2

[34] Laney K. Jones, Ilene G. Ladd, Michael R. Gionfriddo, Christina Gregor, Michael A. Evans, Jove Graham, "Medications requiring prior authorization across health insurance plans," *Am J Health -Syst Pharm*, 2020: 77: 644

[35] Resneck, 703

[36] Bendix, 35

[37] Bendix, 30

[38] Stephen B. Soumerai, "Benefits and Risks of Increasing Restrictions on Access to Costly Drugs in Medicaid," *Health Affairs*, January/February 2004; 23(1): 136

[39] Soumerai, Benefits, 136

[40] Soumerai, Benefits, 136

[41] Jones, 453

[42] Resneck, 703

[43] Resneck, 703

[44] Stephen B. Soumerai, Thomas J. McLaughlin, Dennis Ross-Degnan, Christina S. Casteris, Paola Bollini, "Effects of Limiting Medicaid drug-Reimbursement Benefits on the Use of Psychotropic Agents and Acute Mental Health Services by Patients with Schizophrenia," *NEJM*, September 8, 1994; 331(10): 650

[45] Soumerai, Effects of Limiting, 654

[46] Soumerai, Effects of Limiting, 654

[47] Stephen B. Soumerai, Jerry Avorn, Dennis Ross-Degnan, Steven Gortmaker, "Payment Restrictions for Prescription Drugs Under Medicaid: Effects on Therapy, Cost and Equity," *NEJM*, August 27, 1987; 317(9): 555

[48] Seth A. Seabury, Dana P. Goldman, Iftekhar Kaisekar, John J. Sheehan, Kimberly Laubmeier, Darius N. Lakdawalla, "Formulary Restrictions on Atypical Antipsychotics: Impact on Cost for Patients with Schizophrenia and Bipolar Disorder in Medicaid," *Am J Managed Care*, February 2014; 20(2): e52

[49] Joette Gdovin Bergeson, Karen Worley, Anthony Louder, Melea Ward, John Graham, "Retrospective Data Base Analysis of the Impact of Prior Authorization for Type 2 Diabetes Medications on Health Care Costs in a Medicare Advantage Prescription Drug Plan Population," *J Manag Care Pharm,* June 2013; 19(5): 374

[50] BS Bloom, J. Jacobs, "Cost Effects of Restricting Cost Effective Therapy," *Medical Care*, 1985: 23(7): 872

[51] Jay M. Margolis and others, "Effect of a Medicaid Prior Authorization Policy for Pregabalin," *Am J Managed Care*, 2009; 15(10): e95

[52] Soumerai, Benefits and Risks, 144

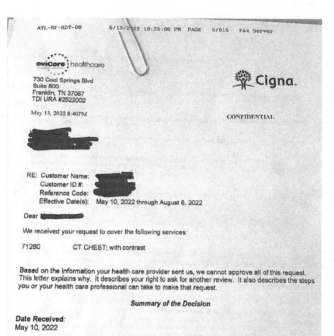

Referral for chest CT rejected by the insurer.

(Courtesy, Fanno Creek Clinic)

CHAPTER 10

Insurers as Doctors: Referrals

Managed care brought a change to the process of referrals from primary care doctors. Previously there had been no formal process for a primary care doctor to refer a patient to a specialist. Often the primary care doctor would send a letter to the specialist giving the reason for the referral, and the specialist, after seeing the patient, would write back with their thoughts and proposed treatment.

This changed with the advent of managed care and health maintenance organizations. Now patients needed to get the authorization of the primary care doctor, who would need to get the blessing of the insurance company. Barken aptly wrote, "As a primary care physician, I was recast as a 'gatekeeper,' the person at the turnstile of a veritable health care amusement park."[1]

Patients pushed back against this scheme, leading to the abandonment of portions of it. Primary care physicians were unhappy in the role, while specialists resented patients being unable to see them without permission.[2] Bodenheimer et al. noted, "The gatekeeper role focuses the attention of physicians and patients on activities that both perceive as negative: the PCP as judge, meeting or denying the patient's requests, and the PCP as drudge, everlastingly mired in the tedious process of obtaining authorization for referrals."[3]

Moreover, there was little evidence that the gatekeeper function actually reduced costs. Bodenheimer and colleagues noted, "Evidence on the effect of gatekeeper systems on health care costs is scanty."[4]

Still, much of the process has continued. For many insurances, patients need to get their PCP to send a referral to the insurance company before they can be referred to a specialist or for complicated imaging.

The key aspect of specialist referrals to the insurer is that the specialist has to be credentialed with their plan and in network. The paperwork involved in the referrals is such that physicians must hire staff to handle these referrals. Our clinic has two full-time referral coordinators who do nothing else. They still need extra help from the other front office staff at times due to the number of referrals.

Yet all this effort is a waste of time for both doctor and insurer. If a specialist is in network, referrals are always approved. I cannot remember a single instance in the last thirty years when a specialist referral to a doctor in the insurer's network was ever turned down. If approval is 100% of the time, what utility is there for anyone in having to go through this time-consuming, expensive process?

One of the newer concepts in health care is the idea of shared risk plans, most popular so far with some of the private Medicare Advantage plans. Under this concept, there is a bucket of money for each patient based on funding from Medicare (or it could be via a commercial insurer). If the cost of the patient's care can be held below this amount, a portion of the surplus is distributed to the primary care doctor. The idea is to incentivize the primary care doctor to reduce the costs by making fewer referrals, choosing cheaper drugs, etc. These plans, by including this incentive, may result in primary care doctors making fewer referrals.

Ironically, the Stark laws were enacted to prevent doctors from gaining financially from making referrals, prohibiting specialists, hospitals or anyone else from paying, in any way, for referrals from the primary care doctor. However, paying doctors not to refer, which is, in essence, what the risk-sharing plans do, is considered okay.

Perhaps the societal objective of reducing health care costs means that this unbalanced treatment is worthwhile. However, it begs the question of whether it will result in fewer than the ideal number of referrals. It also creates an ethical dilemma for physicians. Most physicians try to refer when they think it appropriate without being deterred by any financial considerations. Still, it does create uneasiness. When I refer a patient to a specialist under the risk-sharing plans, I cannot completely forget about the possible financial loss. If I think the patient doesn't need to see a specialist, I worry whether I am being affected subconsciously by the monetary considerations.

Thus, the risk-sharing plans create ethical issues for primary care doctors, yet another aspect taking away from the satisfaction of primary care practice.

There is another aspect of referrals that is disheartening to the primary care doctor. An elderly patient may be declining. Family or friends suggest that they see a specialist. Yet it may be a condition, such as dementia, that can be no better managed by a specialist than a PCP, for the treatments are few and marginally effective. It contributes to the PCP's sense of not being valued when the assumption is the specialist is the only one that can give the best treatment to the patients.

I saw an eighty-four-year-old patient I had been managing for about two decades. She has chronic atrial fibrillation, an irregular heart rhythm, and congestive heart failure. I had seen her through her breast cancer and was finally able to persuade her to quit smoking. I had seen her husband for years until he passed away.

The patient complains of fatigue at each visit but has never wanted to accept my suggestions to increase her heart medications to better control her symptoms. She feels like she is stable, which is true.

Recently her granddaughter, hearing her complaints, insisted that she should see a cardiologist. The patient was referred to the cardiologist at her insistence, where she saw a nurse practitioner. The nurse practitioner sent her back without any major change in her management.

The episode was confirmation of how patients or their families now see specialists as "special" compared to their "regular" primary care doctor.

One of the suggestions for reform is to transform PCPs from gatekeepers to coordinators of care. Bodenheimer suggested that financial incentives could help implement this, with increased payment copayments for uncoordinated specialty visits, increased fees to PCPs to take care of complex patients and avoiding PCPs benefiting financially from not referring. Bodenheimer suggested giving PCPs extra payments for coordinating the care of complex patients while reducing specialist incentives for excess services by paying them by salary or capitation.

Some insurers do require higher patient copayments to see specialists. However, no real financial incentives have been created to pay PCPs for the management of complex patients. Instead, insurers pay for "care managers" who send treatment plan suggestions to the PCP. Since most of this is irrelevant or obvious, and the PCP is already overwhelmed by the volume of suggestions from the insurers, the value of such "care managers" is zero or perhaps a negative. Indeed, it feels that the insurer is spending money for this "care management" that should go to the PCP who is actually caring for the complex patient.

Finally, the risk-sharing plans put the PCP on the hook for total costs of care, incentivizing them to refer less, a concept directly contrary to Bodenheimer's suggestions.

Insurers also demand referrals for diagnostic imaging tests. The insurance companies increasingly require doctors to get authorization from them before ordering some of the more expensive imaging tests, such as CT (computerized tomography) scans or MRI (magnetic resonance imaging). Barken wrote, "The primary care physician operates within a system of rationing by roadblock."[5] Yet the situation is worse than when he practiced because now there are financial penalties beyond the bureaucracy that the PCP confronts in pursuing imaging.

Under the risk-sharing plans ordering these tests creates the same dilemma as specialist referrals. Ordering fewer tests may result in surplus money, a part of which will go back to the doctor. Again, it is noteworthy that while it was and is thought improper for doctors to make money from referring patients for imaging, it is considered kosher to pay them, indirectly, for not ordering the tests.

For medical imaging, both when risk-sharing is involved, and when it is not, insurers require physicians to get their approval before patients can get the MRI or CT or other expensive studies.

At a minimum, this involves extensive paperwork for the office staff. My clinic has the equivalent of another full-time person just to get approvals for this imaging.

Yet sometimes all their work is insufficient. The insurers have hired outside firms to make final decisions about these tests. You can be sure that these firms received the work by assuring the insurers that they could reduce the overall costs by making sure fewer tests were approved.

When these companies refuse to accept the paperwork as sufficient justification for the test, the primary care doctor must call them personally. After many minutes repeating the same information, such as case number, their name and the patient's name to multiple people, the physician may be fortunate enough, or not, to reach a physician employed by the firm for what is called a "peer-to-peer consultation." The primary care doctor must then convince this physician that a test is needed. Last week it took a prolonged discussion for me to get approval for a follow-up CT scan of the lungs for my patient with lung cancer.

Like the doctor who worked for the coal company in the

old one-company town, the doctor working for the firm has a strong incentive to deny the test. If they approve everything, their firm won't be saving the insurer any money, and the insurer may dispense with their services.

Every time I do these peer-to-peer consultations, I vow I will not do them again. One is passed from person to person, often with extended wait times, before eventually ending up with a doctor. I say to myself that it is not worth the aggravation just to get a test approved. Yet when the situation arises again, I am back, feeling that my job is to advocate for my patient. It is another of those things that can make a primary care physician wonder if the job is worth it.

Then there are insurance company rules that don't make much sense medically. Dr. Linda Girgis explained, "With certain insurance companies, every time I order an MRI of the lower back, they want the patient to have had a plain x-ray first. Why? ...If I am looking for a herniated disc, a plain x-ray will not show it, but rather an MRI is needed. I know this, but sometimes the only way to get the patient to get the test is to do it anyway."[6]

Thus, the process can actually increase costs for the insurer if the doctor does the plain x-ray and then the MRI compared to the MRI alone.

There is yet another aggravating aspect of referrals. Many insurances will balk if the PCP orders an expensive test, such as a knee MRI, but will readily approve it if ordered by the orthopedist.

Thus do the insurers further demean the primary care doctor, assuming that for some things, only a specialist is competent. It just adds further insult to injury when the patient arrives at the specialist's office to be seen by their physician assistant.

The burden in terms of time and money for the PCP and their practice to do referrals is substantial. A national analysis estimated that primary care practices spend 19.8 hours of work per physician on referrals.[7] Again, this is simply unpaid work that the doctors have to do to satisfy the insurers.

One of the biggest harms that the "gatekeeper" role generated was a decline in trust in their PCPs by patients. A patient survey found that 94% of patients valued their PCP as the first contact for medical problems, and 89% valued their role as coordinator of referrals. Depending on the issue, 75–91% of patients preferred to seek care initially from their PCP rather than a specialist.[8] This data shows that patients prefer to have their primary care doctor coordinate their care rather than just seeing a bunch of specialists on their own without such coordination.

At the same time, patients want to be able to see a specialist when they think they need to. Almost a quarter of the patients in the study reported that either their PCP or medical group put up barriers toward their seeing a specialist. The result is unhappiness with the PCP. As the study's authors concluded, "Patients who had difficulty obtaining referrals were more likely to report low trust, low confidence and low satisfaction with their primary care physician."[9]

One of the new innovations aimed at reducing cost is the accountable care organization (ACO) which binds many clinics and doctors to share risks on different insurance plans. Since ACOs are accountable for all of their patients' expenditures, they benefit from controlling and reducing referrals. Many ACOs already offer lower copayments for referral to specialists within the ACO, while others urge PCPs to refer only to such specialists. The question is whether PCPs' duties to patients are corrupted when they receive either directions to or financial benefit from keeping referrals within the ACO.[10]

I believe that trust would be further weakened if patients understood the financial incentives dangled before PCPs to reduce referrals. In the gatekeeper role of the 1990s, the PCP clearly could be seen as the barrier to getting the referral. The pay-for-performance, risk-sharing models of the current age offer even greater financial benefits to doctors who can keep costs down. Avoiding referrals to specialists is a crucial component of the cost-cutting strategy that PCPs in these models have been encouraged to follow. I believe that there is only less rebellion by patients against this aspect of the plans because it is more hidden from their view.

Specialty referrals often generate additional costs and testing. Barken summed it up well, writing, "Special doctors order special tests. It is self-affirming. A proliferation of procedures ensues, in which the specialist attempts to add some value through his contribution to the case. If I have obtained a chest X-ray, then the pulmonologist will perform a CT scan of the patient's chest."[11]

A further problem is all the times the specialist's office doesn't give feedback about the results of the consultation. We have a staff person who spends their time trying to retrieve this clinical information.

While the PCP faces financial penalties for referrals, the specialist is at no financial risk for any test or service they provide.

The primary care doctor can lose on both ends. She may be balked at ordering tests or proper drugs. She is forced to refer to a specialist to do this. Even as the insurers want PCPs to refer less, they create situations where the PCP cannot do anything else. When PCPs discourage referrals, they risk losing the trust of their patients.

Sometimes it is not hard to see why no one wants to become a primary care doctor.

---

[1] Barken, 2

[2] Thomas Bodenheimer, Bernard Lo, Lawrence Casalino, "Primary Care Physicians Should be Coordinators, Not Gatekeepers," *JAMA*, June 2, 1999; 281(21): 2045

[3] Bodenheimer, Primary Care Physicians should be Coordinators, 2046

[4] Bodenheimer, Primary Care Physicians should be Coordinators, 2047

[5] Barken, 15

[6] Shyrock, 18

[7] Casalino, What Does it Cost, w537

[8] Kevin Grumbach and others, "Resolving the Gatekeeper Conundrum: What Patients Value in Primary Care and Referrals to Specialists," *JAMA*, July 21, 1999; 281(3): 261

[9] Grumbach, Resolving the Gatekeeper, 261

[10] Matthew DeCamp, Lisa Soleymani Lehmann, "Guiding Choice – Ethically Influencing Referrals in ACOs" *NEJM*, January 15, 2015; 372(3): 205

[11] Barken, 80

Paperwork.

(Courtesy, Wiki Commons)

CHAPTER 11
Primary Care: Drowning in Trivia

Paperwork for all doctors has increased over the years, a fact that is no surprise to any physician practicing in the United States. Jerome Kassirer wrote in the *New England Journal* in 1998, "Physicians' time is increasingly consumed by paperwork that they view as intrusive and valueless."[1]

In the subsequent two decades, the burden of such "paperwork" has increased exponentially.

However, primary care, for a number of reasons, has to take care of far more than their specialist colleagues. I will list some of these tasks that make up a typical work day for a PCP.

All nursing home patients need their orders reviewed and signed off on every ninety days. All home health plans need to be approved. All physical therapy, for which the primary care has sent in a referral, needs the doctor to sign approval of the plan, repeatedly if extended therapy is needed. Barken described this as being, "the medical police, or MPs, obligated by local, state and federal government to supervise nonphysician health professionals, as though our rubber-stamp approval could prevent some unscrupulous occupational therapist from robbing Medicare blind. When the visiting nurse attends a patient in her home, I must sign a form that verifies the nurse truly was there, guarantees that the nursing services were warranted and proper and verifies that the nurse rightfully deserves payment."[2]

When I ask for physical therapy or speech therapy, or wound care to see and treat a home-bound patient, I must sign off for each service they propose, even though they each have a much better understanding of what their discipline can offer to a particular patient. I must verify that the patient is home-bound.

All FMLA (Family Medical Leave Act) paperwork, whether for a patient or their family member, falls to the primary care doctor, as does any paperwork about applications for disability. In Oregon, physicians sign off forms for medical marijuana. We fill out disabled driving permits. We are asked to write notes excusing patients from jury duty, for time off work and return to work notes.

Dealing with patients' psychosocial issues is an important part of primary care. It can be very satisfying to talk to patients about family relationships or life stresses. Filling out the paperwork that is associated with it in the twenty-first century is not enjoyable or satisfying. It is also something that specialists can escape to a large degree. We have many patients who return with forms that need to be completed who were told by a specialist to "have your PCP do it."

For patients in nursing homes, we are contacted and must grant written absolution every time a medication is missed for a patient or if the patient refuses that medication. We are contacted if the resident falls or is constipated, or can't sleep. In signing these forms, we assume the risk for any bad outcome and remove it from the nursing facility and its staff. Barken beautifully described this, writing, "Like a hot potato, the primary care doctor, as guarantor of record, is handed responsibility for any adverse outcome...the primary care physician today is a general liability sink, carrying an obligation as the guarantor of a good day."[3]

We are expected to get POLST (orders about resuscitation) and advanced directive forms done in cooperation with the patient. Some insurances now penalize the physician if she can't persuade the patient to fill out the form.

We are contacted by pharmacy management companies if

a patient stops taking a prescribed medication or if they take a medication that seems contraindicated now they have turned sixty-five. We need to explain how they have been on the medication successfully for twenty years without any side effects.

Patients expect us to retrieve all test and visit results, including those done by specialist physicians, or if the patient is seen in the emergency room or free-standing urgent care.

If we are fortunate, we will receive copies of every consult note, emergency room note and test for each patient. Much more commonly, we need to track down the results. We need to review these and decide which ones require further action. We then need to contact patients to follow up on these. I will have at least sixty of these documents requiring review each day.

Coordination of care has been recognized as an increasingly important part of the PCP's day. Two studies reported that two groups of primary care doctors spent 13% and 14% of their day on uncompensated care coordination.[4] Another analysis reported, "Nearly one-half of a primary care physician's workday is spent on activities outside the examination room, predominantly focused on follow-up and documentation of care for patients not physically present."[5]

There have been attempts by CMS to try to offer some reimbursement for this care coordination. Yet the efforts to garner this revenue may be more trouble than it's worth. For example, CMS offered a patient management fee a few years ago. However, the doctor could only bill if she spent more than fifteen minutes on this encounter.

I don't do fifteen-minute coordination for most patients. Instead, I do dozens of three- five-minute tasks, from reviewing their physical therapy plan or recent lab results. Thus, I could not ask for payment for any of these. Even for those rare times when I had the time to spend more than fifteen minutes at a time doing tasks for a single patient, the reimbursement of $10-20 that was offered was not worth the time of having to generate another claim to Medicare.

The medical home concept was based on the idea that doctors would receive higher fees which would include this care coordination. I've been told that our group is paid more by certain insurances. I don't think it is a huge difference.

We review the results of x-rays and lab tests done on each patient. Each one requires a letter, electronic message or phone call to the patient regarding the results. Or a message to the patient, plus a message to the nurse or referral coordinator about what needs to be done. We often will send an e-mail and call the patient to make sure the message has been received and understood. If they don't understand our comments, we will spend time explaining them again. One of the hallmarks of medicine today is that many patients expect results right away.

For the primary care physician, there is a challenge in finding out the optimal time spent on a phone or electronic communication with patients. Unlike lawyers, PCPs can't bill for their minutes of phone consultation. Hoff quoted a PCP as saying, "Patients don't understand. If I don't get them in the office, I don't get paid. It's that simple. They all want me to call them with these test results or to answer a question they have that might keep them out of the office, but that's time I spend that has no reimbursement associated with it."[6]

Such direct patient communication is another component of the PCP's day.

For many years we cleared patients as commercial truck drivers or as pilots. We do pre-employment exams or fill out forms telling the employer that the patient can safely work or participate in sports or other activities. It is hard not to feel that the major purpose is to shift the liability for any bad events off the shoulders of those asking for the forms.

When patients are sick or have other issues, they ask us to write letters to the airlines or cruise lines or tour companies so that they get their money back.

We fill out the death certificates for patients. Yesterday I received a request asking me to fill out another form to offer more clarification about a middle-aged patient who had died at home in bed of unknown causes. I had written as much on the death certificate. I answered the state's new questions the same, "Cause Unknown." Did the author of the letter imagine that I had somehow learned information about an event that happened six months ago? People die, sometimes for reasons we don't really know (in the absence of an autopsy). Asking me to answer the same question again is just repeating the work.

We manage patients' preventive care, even if they have not seen us for an extended period. We remind them to get their mammograms or a diabetic eye exam, or flu shot.

We do preoperative exams. We fill out forms for dentists saying that the patient is okay for the dental procedure. We do preoperative evaluations before cataract surgeries, although Medicare assumes that this will be done by the Ophthalmologist as part of their fee for the surgery. In this case, we want to make sure the patient will be safe even if the government says that this is not our responsibility.

If we work with a physician's assistant, we are responsible for signing off on their work as well as doing their supervision. We sign unsigned nurse notes on the computer, usually documenting that a message was left for a patient.

We fill out forms for pharmaceutical companies' drug assistance programs so patients can get otherwise unaffordable medications. We may sign forms to get samples for patients.

Today I received a letter from Pfizer saying they needed to check if the signature I had signed on the sample request form was really me.[7] Apparently, this is to comply with the Federal Prescription Drug Marketing Act. Still, it is a lot of trouble for what amounted to fourteen tablets, a one-week supply of medication.

Yesterday a lab worried that an insurer would not pay for

a prostate antigen test, a screen for cancer in men. Their note said the gender was wrong even though their own note listed the patient as male. The patient has always been male. We had to respond to point out that they had the correct gender listed on the form they sent us.

I received a letter informing me that my patient had received two diuretic medications for high blood pressure at the same pharmacy.[8] This was because I had switched him from one to the other, which is often more effective. Somehow the company writing missed that the prescriptions were at different times, suggesting that one replaced the other. Did I benefit from this missive about something I already knew and understood? I think not.

Each day at work, we wonder what new form of idiotic request we will get. If it didn't waste so much time, we could make a game of what was the most ludicrous letter or request received that day. Yet, no matter how stupid, we need to answer lest our patients be denied something.

I need not mention the referral authorization, drug authorization and credentialing outlined in the last chapters.

There is another time-intensive task confronting doctors. We, or rather our staff of billers, submit bills to insurers. Many of these claims are rejected and need to be rewritten. For payment delay generates huge amounts of money with which the insurers can make more money. Therefore, insurers often will do whatever they legally can to delay payment and force editing of the claims or submission of charts in order to benefit from this "float."

Insurers require a medical condition to be listed to justify every lab or imaging test ordered. Periodically different insurers will reject billing claims for a variety of simple, inexpensive lab tests, such as complete blood counts. Then the primary care doctor and/or his staff have to go back to supply a specific reason for each test. The insurer may only have to reimburse doctors $2 for the test, but the doctor is given the choice of writing off multiple low-cost tests or having to supply more documentation for each one.

Many insurers have decided to not pay for any routine testing during physicals or wellness exams. Thus, ordering a blood sugar to screen for diabetes in a patient will only be paid if the test is actually positive, i.e., the sugar is high. Otherwise, the doctor either needs to not do the screening or eat the costs of the test. Of course, maybe the insurer, such as United Healthcare, are more hard-pressed financially than their billions in annual profits suggest and can't afford to pay for screening for diabetes or high cholesterol or prostate cancer.

We fill out forms documenting that patients have certain high complexity conditions so that their Medicare plan can get more money from the government. We will discuss this further in chapter 14. We fill out forms documenting for the insurers that patients have had the "quality of care" tests they demand.

Studies have documented the huge burden physicians shoulder in interacting with insurers. In a 2009 report, physicians spent three hours a week interacting with health plans while their staff spent much more, an estimated 29.8 hours a week. The study estimated that, "the national time cost to practices of interactions with plans is at least $23 to $31 billion a year."[9]

The burden was higher for primary care doctors, with practices spending an average of $64,859 per physician a year interacting with health plans, nearly a third of the income of the average PCP at that time.[10] Shanafelt and colleagues concluded, "The current burden of documentation related to the clinical encounter required to meet billing requirements, quality reporting, and separate justification for each test ordered individually is unsustainable."[11] Internist Louise McHarris observed, "This kind of stuff is such a colossal time sink. An incredible amount of time and resources are wasted on paperwork."[12] Gaffney et al. noted how American physicians spend far more time documenting in the electronic health record than doctors in other countries, resulting in outpatient visit notes approximately four times that of doctors elsewhere.[13] A large portion of this is driven by billing considerations rather than American doctors being more thoughtful about medical issues.

The burden of paperwork can have negative consequences on patient care. Beasley and colleagues talked about the negative impact of "information chaos" in primary care. They listed the five factors, beginning, "Information overload occurs when there is too much data, e.g., written, verbal and non-verbal physician's memory for the clinician to organize, synthesize, draw conclusion from, or act on....EHRs may make the situation worse by encouraging electronic copying and pasting, adding irrelevant information through use of templates, and the mixing of data needed for billing and legal protection with that needed for clinical care."[14] Additional factors can be lack of necessary information, erroneous information, information conflict, when data seems to conflict, and information scatter, defined as having the information located in multiple places.

Beasley et al. noted that one consequence of the information chaos might be "impaired situation awareness," which could be missing patient cues or other important data and decreased ability to integrate the various bits of information and decide what is important.[15] Another consequence is "increased mental workload," which shows up as increased stress and unhappiness among PCPs. The two problems can interact to worsen each other. Beasley noted, "Among PCPs, the higher mental workload has been positively associated with a higher perceived probability of medical error."[16]

It is worth noting that this paperwork burden and associated time commitment is not a universal feature of modern medicine or intrinsic to health care. A study comparing the United States and Canada showed that Canadian doctors spent a quarter of the time that American doctors did interacting with insurance. One difference is that Canadian physicians interact with a single payer while Americans have to interact with multiple insurers. The study showed that US doctors' nursing staff spent over twenty hours a week interacting with insurers, nearly ten times that of their Canadian counterparts. If the administrative costs for American physicians were similar to Canadian physicians in terms of interaction with insurance, this would save an estimated $27.6 billion dollars a year.[17]

We do medication reconciliation to make sure the medications listed in the chart are the ones the patient is actually taking. This is mandatory after every hospital discharge or discharge from a rehab facility. We do it on many other visits to make sure mistakes are not made or treatment based on false assumptions. We often ask patients to bring in all their medication bottles and review these to see if things are missing or if they are taking things we thought they stopped.

Nowadays, many patients can visualize the details of the chart via a patient portal, an online method of access into the patient chart. If patients think something needs to be corrected, they don't call their cardiologist or orthopedist to fix it. Instead, they call their primary care physician. Yesterday I received a note from a patient telling me about an incorrect diagnosis in her husband's chart. He is not my patient. So, I needed to look up who his doctor was and pass along the information. Sometimes the corrections are important. Sometimes it might be to note that they were taking a multivitamin three days a week instead of four. Yet the primary care doctor has to take time to correct the chart and let the patient know that it has been done.

We need to respond to every patient message via the portal as well as their phone calls and even occasional faxes and letters.

We may need to consult with the specialist as to their thoughts on the patient. We need to talk to their staff to expedite getting patients an appointment.

We need to request old notes on the patient. We need to make copies of relevant parts of the chart if they have a relative who is a nurse who they want to review their treatment.

None of these tasks are impossible. None takes hours by itself. Together they take hours. Most of this does not fall under the rubric of direct patient care. None of it is paid for.

A 2016 analysis looked at how doctors spend their workdays. For every hour doctors spend in direct clinical face-to-face time with patients, they spend another two hours working on the electronic health record and other desk work. In addition, many physicians spend another one to two hours outside office hours every night doing additional computer and clerical work.[18]

For all the publicity about electronic medical records and quality guidelines, both add to rather than reduce the work of the PCP. What helps more than anything is having good nurses who can help shoulder this burden. We are very fortunate at our practice to have some great nurses, some of whom have been with us for two decades. I can't imagine being able to deal with this morass of tasks, not to mention being able to provide optimal patient care, without them.

This paperwork is a huge issue for both older and younger PCPs. A seasoned family physician commented, "The dissatisfiers for the newer docs is the time it takes to do things in the EMR, all the paperwork...you feel like you are not doing much for the patient."[19]

There are other well-meaning programs that add to the workload of PCPs without generating the benefits intended. Most EMRs have automated health maintenance reminder systems that pop reminders of what is due at every visit. A study of doctors reported that 75% did not observe or pay attention to these alerts. Most ignored them when they did notice them.[20]

CMS has tried to compensate for this by creating some

payments to physicians for particularly lengthy and complicated paperwork on a patient. They have launched initiatives to look at how to reduce paperwork. But for the hundred tasks a day that each take two to five minutes, there is no recompense.

For of course under direct patient care, we need to write notes of every visit with every patient. Billing requirements have meant that these now need to include more and more details. For example, I saw a patient with long-standing atrial fibrillation. It was not enough to list this in my assessment and plan. Billing kicked the note back to me to ask if the atrial fibrillation was constant or intermittent. By my writing atrial fibrillation instead of chronic atrial fibrillation in the patient chart, the diagnosis code would become atrial fibrillation, unspecified. Such a code is no longer acceptable to the insurer, so the visit would not be paid. The chart would go back to the primary care physician to fix.

The reality is that almost all primary care physicians see fewer patients a day since the advent of the electronic medical record due to the quantity of data the insurer requires with each visit. More complicated lengthier charts mean fewer patients seen and less time available. Hoff quoted one family physician as saying, "I would guess now that for every hour we see a patient, we're probably doing fifteen to twenty minutes work with lab data, x-ray data, calling the patient, calling the family. This adds 25% to your day."[21]

A 2019 survey of physician practices found that 86% reported that the overall regulatory burden on their practice had increased in the past year, while 96% argued that a reduction on this burden would allow them to reallocate resources toward patient care.[22] The list of administrative issues that over 50% of practices found very or extremely burdensome included prior authorizations, Medicare quality payment programs, audits and appeals, lack of EHR interoperability, Medicare Advantage chart audits and translation and interpretation requirements.[23]

Sinsky and colleagues eloquently concluded, "We agree that not all time spent on the EHR (Electronic Health Record) is frivolous, but we do believe that the two to three hours that physicians of multiple specialties, ages and settings are required to spend on computer and desk work for every hour of direct clinical face time is out of balance. Rather than ask physicians to do the wrong work more efficiently, we suggest first asking whether the work adds value to patients."[24]

The paperwork (now mainly but not completely done electronically) required has had a negative effect on primary care physicians. Does this matter to patients?

A study of 2620 patients in the Boston area found that patients whose doctors reported being very satisfied with their work had higher overall satisfaction with their health care.[25]

Kassirer wrote about this too, stating, "Cranky doctors are not likely to provide outstanding medical care. Payers, insurers and legislators must recognize this predicament and stop pretending that doctor discontent doesn't matter."[26]

I have outlined the paperwork on a typical day for a PCP. The same tasks, albeit for different patients, will be there every day for the 250 average work days each year for the 40 years a PCP might work. A PCP might have 10,000 days filled with these tasks to look forward to over their career.

The nation, the government and insurers need to ask whether they would rather have all this paperwork done or for PCPs to see patients. So far, the answer has been the former.

---

[1] Jerome P. Kassirer, "Doctor Discontent," *NEJM*, 339(21): 1543

[2] Barken, 22

[3] Barken, 23

[4] Thomas Bodenheimer, "Coordinating Care: A Perilous Journey Through the Healthcare System," *NEJM*, March 6, 2008; 358(10): 1069

[5] Andrew Gottschalk, Susan A. Flocke, "Time Spent in Face-to-Face Care and Work Outside the Examination Room," *Ann Fam Medicine,* November/December 2005; 3(6): 488

[6] Hoff, 29

[7] Pfizer, Communication to Gregg Coodley, April 5, 2021

[8] CVS Caremark Clinical Services, Communication to Gregg Coodley, April 18, 2021

[9] Casalino, What Does it Cost, w533

[10] Casalino, What Does it Cost, w539

[11] Shanafelt, Addressing Physician Burnout, 901

[12] Louise McHarris, Interview with Gregg Coodley, July 22, 2021

[13] Adam Gaffney and others, "Medical Documentation Burden Among US Office-Based Physicians in 2019: A National Study," *JAMA Internal Medicine,* May 2022; 182(5): 564-566

[14] John W. Beasley and others, "Information Chaos in Primary Care: Implications for Physician Performance and Patient Safety," *J Am Board Fam Med,* November 2011; 24(6): 3

[15] Beasley, 4

[16] Beasley, 4

[17] Dante Morra, Sean Nicholson, Wendy Levinson, David N. Gans, Terry Hammons, Lawrence P. Casalino, "U.S. Physician Practices versus Canadians: Spending Nearly Four Times As Much Money Interacting with Payers," *Health Affairs,* August 2011; 30(8): 1443

[18] Christine Sinsky and others, "Allocation of Physician Time in Ambulatory Practice: A Time and Motion Study in 4 Specialties," *Ann Int Med,* 2016; 165: 753

[19] Anonymous, Interview with Gregg Coodley, June 24, 2021

[20] Kenneth Schelbase, Thomas P. Koepsell, Thomas E. Norris, "Providers' Reactions to an Automated Health Maintenance Reminder System Incorporated into the Patient's Electronic Medical Record," *J Am Board Fam Pract,* 2003: 16: 312

[21] Hoff, 50

[22] Medical Group Management Association Report, 2019, 4

[23] Medical Group Management Association Report, 2019, 8

[24] Christine Sinsky, Michael Tutty, Lacey Colligan, "Allocation of Physician Time in Ambulatory Practice," *Ann Int* Med, May 2, 2017; 166(9): 683

[25] Jennifer S. Haas, E. Francis Cook, Ann Louise Puopolo, Helen R. Burstin, Paul D. Cleary, Troyen A. Brenan, "Is the Professional Satisfaction of General Internists Associated With Patient Satisfaction?" *JGIM*, 2000: 15: 122

[26] Kassirer, 1544

Daily Hours Needed by PCPs to meet quality measures (2020) – 8.6
   hours

Annual Cost to each PCP to meet quality measures – $50,408

Quality Measures in National Quality Measure Clearinghouse –
   >2500

Percent of Quality Measures Found to be Valid – 37%

"Future generations of physicians might be taught that it doesn't count if you can't count it, and they may be paid on this basis. Thus, they may not understand that most aspects of the quality of medical care are not measured and that medicine is not just a science but an art."

   -   Dr. Lawrence P. Casalino (1999)

"Rules, being general entities, always involve a certain misfit between themselves and the situation."

   -   Dr. Eric Cassell
       Doctoring: The Nature of Primary Care Medicine

CHAPTER 12
The Lure of Quality

The big mantra these days in primary care is "quality of care," or "quality improvement," or "value-based care." At first glance, this seems unobjectionable. Quality of care and quality improvement, like value-based care, sounds good. After all, who could object to quality or value?

The rub is how it is defined. For the government and the insurers, quality means completing a defined set of goals for patients. Some of these are straightforward, such as annual mammograms or diabetic eye exams. Others are more obscure, such as whether patients called back when a pharmacist employed by the insurer called them to discuss their medications. Yet as Dr. Cassell noted, "Rules, being general entities, always involve a certain misfit between themselves and the situation."[1]

The first problem with the quality measures is that they assume primary care physicians have unlimited time to follow and implement guideline recommendations. This is not the case. A study looked at how much time it would take for a PCP to meet the recommendations for ten common chronic diseases in a panel of 2500 patients. The researchers found that this would take 3.5 hours a day, or 828 hours a year, to provide care meeting these guidelines assuming the diseases are well controlled. Achieving this when the disease was not well controlled tripled the time required to 10.6 hours a day (2484 hours a year). Thus, it would take every hour or more the PCP worked to meet guidelines just for ten diseases, leaving no time to respond to the patients' acute complaints or any other chronic diseases the patient might have.[2]

Another study looked at how much of the physicians' time would be required to provide all the services recommended by the US Preventive Services Task Force (USPSTF) to an average patient panel. Yarnall et al. estimated that 7. 4 hours per working day or 1773 hours a year would be required from the PCP.[3] They concluded, "It is not feasible for physicians to deliver all of the services recommended by the USPSTF to a representative panel of patients."[4]

Yarnall et al. concluded, "The addition of even small interventions that require little physician time adds significantly to physician workload when these interventions are administered to a large number of eligible patients...In all likelihood, any new screening test a patient receives from a physician will be performed at the expense of some other currently provided service."[5]

Privett and Guerrier reevaluated the quality measures in 2020 to see if there had been any improvement in the time needed to meet them. They found meeting the US Preventive Services Task Force recommendations in primary care would require 8.6 physician hours per working day. Compared to 2003, there were fewer measures, but they required 1.2 more physician hours per day.[6] Again meeting the measures would take more than the full workday, even if primary care doctors did nothing else.

How do the preventive care mandates actually work in the care PCPs provide to patients? A study among family medicine doctors found that 58% of all visits (4.6 hours a day) were for acute medical illnesses.[7] This was not time spent trying to meet quality measures. If half the PCP's day is spent dealing with a patient's current issues, all the guidelines called for would be impossible for PCPs to meet in actual practice.

The evidence reveals that PCPs' attempts to meet these measures run into practical problems. A recent study looked at the prescription of statins, cholesterol-lowering drugs that are recommended under the guidelines for patients at elevated risk of cardiovascular events. The analysis found that prescribing fell the longer the day went on, which the authors attributed to clinicians falling behind or becoming fatigued and hence having less time and energy to try to meet the guidelines.[8]

The second problem is the cost of compliance with these measures. To deal with these measures costs American physicians and their staff an average of 785 hours a year. The estimated cost of compliance is $40,069 dollars per physician a year or over $15.4 billion dollars a year. The study's authors wrote, "81% of practices reported that they spent as much or more time dealing with these external quality measures than three years before. Yet only 27% of the practices felt that the measures were moderately or very representative of the quality of care."[9]

These results were based on both specialty and primary care. The burden was greater for primary care. Primary care doctors and their staff spend 19.1 hours a week dealing with quality measures, translating to an annual cost of $50,468, compared to 15.4 hours and $40,069 for physicians and their staff as a whole.[10]

Third, there is no single set of quality measures. Different external entities use different quality measurements, further complicating the tasks for physicians. State and regional agencies were reported to use 1367 measures of physician quality, of which only 20% were used by more than one program. A study of insurers found that they looked at 546 measures, which rarely were the same between insurers or identical to some 1700 measures used by the federal government.[11]

Many measures have been made public, leading patients to evaluate doctors based on their compliance with measures that may have very little to do with the quality of primary care delivered. In another study, the authors noted the rapid growth of quality measures, noting that they, "are used to provide public information for patients as well as a basis for financial 'pay for performance' incentives to physicians."[12] The authors note that over 159 measures of outpatient doctor care are now publicly available.

Fourth, sometimes the quality measures may be too rigid to fit actual patients. Boyd et al. noted, "Most CPGs (Clinical Practice Guidelines) do not modify or discuss the applicability of their recommendations for older patients with multiple comorbidities."[13] Since each guideline existed separately, Boyd et al. pointed out that the result of trying to do all of them might be to put an elderly patient on multiple drugs with an increased risk of side effects and adverse interactions.[14] They concluded, "Current pay-for-performance standards can create financial incentives for physicians to focus on certain diseases...These initiatives perpetuate the single-disease approach to care and fail to reward physicians for addressing the complex issues that confront patients with several chronic diseases."[15]

The measurements do not take into account patient refusal. Patients don't all blindly follow a physician's recommendations. Moreover, the quality recommendations/requirements do not allow for nuances. It is not clear that a diabetic who has successfully controlled her disease with diet absolutely needs a statin. The studies showing benefits in diabetics were mainly in a sicker population. Clearly, a diabetic who has been poorly controlled for years, with diabetic kidney disease and vision loss, is at much more cardiac risk than the well-controlled woman mentioned above. The quality requirements do not take into account these gradations.

They do not take into account patient realities that make the measurements absurd, such as requiring the doctor to order a mammogram on a woman with a bilateral mastectomy or a colonoscopy on a patient whose colon has been resected previously.

In fact, there is evidence that patients may be over-screened to meet quality measures. Studies have shown many very elderly women in poor health receive mammograms while many women who have undergone hysterectomies receive continued PAP smears.[16]

Fifth, it is questionable whether we are measuring quality improvements or just documentation of them. Dr. Lisa Rosenbaum recently wrote in the *NEJM*, "As reimbursement models shift towards value-based payment, QI (quality improvement) is no longer just about being better, but about documenting improvement to maximize payment. An entire industry has arisen to support the optimization and demonstration of performance."[17]

Sixth, the creation of all these quality measures has been an expensive enterprise, costing CMS $1.3 billion from 2008 to 2018. The thirty-five organizations that received this money as grants to develop and maintain quality measures certainly benefited from the program. Five of these organizations shared $872.9 million among them.[18]

The result is that the National Quality Measure Clearinghouse now lists more than 2500 quality measures.[19]

The issues previously mentioned all would become apparent in the MIPS program. The Merit-based Incentive Payment System (MIPS), implemented in January 2017, is a huge pay-for-performance Medicare initiative aimed at promoting quality. Including over 300,000 physicians, MIPS offers more money to physicians meeting markers for quality and cost of care. In an article published May 14, 2021, Khullar and colleagues wrote, "It is unclear whether MIPs accurately captures quality or effectively incentivizes improvements in health care delivery, but there is growing concern that the program increases administrative burden for clinicians and medical practices."[20] Khullar et al. calculated that the mean per physician cost to practices of participating in MIPs was $12,811, with physicians and their staff spending over 200 hours annually on MIPS-related activities.[21] Thus a huge amount of administrative work is created for primary care doctors to meet the quality goals.

Reviewing the data for MIPS, Hockenberry suggested that the cost of quality compliance was 13% of all Medicare payments for physicians. He noted that since this was equivalent to a 13% pay cut for primary care, CMS should consider whether the quality measurements would be worth paying PCPs 13% more. He concluded, "The lingering question is whether CMS can continue to raise the cost of compliance without being explicit about who is paying for what portions of the burden."[22]

In a survey of over 400 physician practices, 87% of those responding felt that the MIPS payment adjustments do not cover the time and resources needed.[23] In an earlier analysis, over three-quarters of practices said that Medicare Quality Payment Program requirements were very or extremely burdensome.[24] Over three quarters also felt that CMS feedback on either cost measure performance or quality measure performance did not help either reduce costs or improve quality.[25]

So, we find a huge amount of money spent chasing the rigid definitions of quality, as painted in a paint-by-numbers formula. Primary care doctors, in a different study, worried that, "administrative burdens were leading to the diversion of clinical resources away from patient-centered care and negatively impacting patient and clinician satisfaction."[26]

In fact, as Frakt and Jha wrote in the *Annals of Internal Medicine*, a similar earlier program, the Medicare Value-Based Payment Modifier(VM), "had no beneficial effect on the quality of or spending on care."[27] Roberts and colleagues, who studied the above program, concluded that, "Incentives to improve quality and lower spending in the MIPS may be somewhat stronger or weaker than those in the VM, but share many features that make them weak overall...incentives to decrease spending are weak because spending measures are given little weight in overall performance scores."[28]

Observers have noted the irony of trying to reduce spending by creating expensive programs that create massive administrative costs.[29]

A seventh problem is that for all the effort spent to meet quality measures, doubts have been raised about the validity and worth of many of these. MacLean et al. evaluated the validity of the measures in the MIPS Quality Payment Program.[30] They found only 37% of the ambulatory medicine criteria were found to be valid, suggesting that two-thirds of work toward quality in this program was at best misguided. MacLean et al. concluded that 35% of measures were invalid and 28% of uncertain validity.[31] Invalid measures included those with inadequate evidence to support them. For example, MIPs measure 181 "Elder Maltreatment Screen and Follow-up," required completion of a specific Maltreatment Screening tool and a documented follow-up plan for all patients sixty-five years or older. MacLean and colleagues pointed out that the US Preventive Services Task Force found insufficient evidence to warrant such routine screening, much less mandate using a specific tool. The authors concluded, "The use of flawed measures is not only frustrating to physicians but also potentially harmful to patients. Moreover, such activities introduce inefficiencies and administrative costs into a health system widely regarded as too expensive."[32]

A Government Accounting Office analysis found that CMS didn't have an effective strategy to evaluate whether the quality measures actually improve health outcomes.[33]

Value-based care, care theoretically based on delivering the highest quality, also may have built-in biases. There is strong evidence that MIPS has a greater negative impact on smaller practices, rural practices, independent practices and those serving poorer patients while offering the most financial benefit to large hospital-based practices with better information systems and existing resources. Roberts et al. concluded, "Inadequate risk adjustment for clinical and sociological features may lead to sustained transfers of payments away from practices serving poorer and sicker patients for reasons not related to the quality of efficiency of care."[34]

Colla et al. reviewed two large studies of physicians participating in MIPS in 2017 and 2019. They concluded that, "system-affiliated practices are more likely to be rewarded by pay-for-performance programs than independent practices."[35] Independent practices were far more likely to have negative adjustments to their payments than those owned by hospitals. Colla et al. also stated, "Primary care clinicians who serve medically and socially complex populations have greater pro-cess and operational challenges...Yet instead of adjusting reim-bursement to reflect the differential cost of caring for these populations, it appears that MIPS may further disadvantage safety net clinicians."[36]

A 2022 study also found that risk adjustments inadequately adjust for the differences in patient populations, meaning that those caring for the poorer and sicker patients may be unfairly penalized for their higher costs.[37]

The quantification of quality is, at best, a blunt instrument, for individual patient circumstances and desires affect the results. The insurer finds a primary care physician at fault if too many of his patients are not also taking cholesterol-lowering drugs called statins. Yet, many patients refuse to take the statins, having heard too much about the possible side effects.

Another set of quality measures looks at the use of medications found to cause more confusion in the elderly among patients over sixty-five. Doctors are penalized if they have patients on any of these medications. Yet the risks of confusion are very different in an eighty-five-year-old with severe de-mentia and a healthy woman who just turned sixty-five. Many patients have been on these agents for a decade or more. Are they really that much more likely to cause a severe side effect because the patient has reached the age of Medicare eligibility? The quality measurements are clearly an imprecise measure since patients vary so much. Yet declaring them the be all and end all ignores these differences. Here the Federal government bears some responsibility. The private Medicare Advantage plans are graded in part on how many of their patients meet these requirements. Thus, they lean hard on the doctors to achieve them. In fact, they offer substantial bonuses if doctors get their patients to meet these thresholds.

Yet flawed measures can lead to flawed approaches to treatment. In a *NEJM* article, MacLean et al. gave an example of a flawed measure, writing, "MIPS measure 236, 'Controlling High Blood Pressure,' for instance, requires that blood pressure of 140/90 or lower be achieved in the clinic setting for all patients. Forcing blood pressure down to this threshold could harm frail elderly adults and patients with certain coexisting conditions."[38]

Even worse, the criteria of whether this goal is achieved is often flawed. Blood pressure control is based on the last clinic-reported BP of the year. A patient could be counted as meeting it if one out of ten measurements is under the threshold, as long as it is the last one counted. Alternatively, a patient could fall below the goal should their pressure be up at their December visit.

From an economic or game-playing analysis, the proper strategy would be to have the patient in until a blood pressure below the threshold is achieved, then make sure they have no more visits or at least blood pressure measurements until the end of the year.

Somehow guidelines became mandates on which physicians were judged and paid. Blind adherence to guidelines can cause patients harm under the wrong circumstances. Reviewing such harm, Shah and Cifu wrote, "CDS (Clinical Decision Support) tools should be designed and used to supplement clinical judgment...even the best technology is no substitute for independent clinical judgment informed by medical knowledge and experience."[39]

From a practical basis, one of the biggest challenges in meeting quality goals is to get adequate data as to where the gaps are. One huge insurance company that we deal with is always hounding us to complete the measures for our patients. However, they are so far behind updating their own quality databases that we frequently receive requests to complete measures that we implemented and sent documentation to them three months earlier.

Since this insurer is either too cheap to hire enough data entry people to keep up or too inefficient, they persist in sending us outdated requests, further adding to the administrative burden of completing the measures.

Another problem that has been identified in programs that assess doctors on quality is that small physician practices may not have sufficient patients to draw conclusions. Nyweide et al. commented, "It is unlikely that individual primary care physicians annually see a sufficient number of eligible patients to produce statistically reliable performance measurements on common quality and cost measures."[40] Thus an alternate strategy is to aggregate all the doctors in a group. When this was done, Nyweide et al. still found, "Roughly 65% of all primary care physicians active in the Medicare program work in practices with insufficient numbers of beneficiaries to reliably differentiate the practice's performance from national quality and cost benchmarks."[41] The authors concluded, "The results from this study call into question the wisdom of pay-for-performance programs and quality reporting initiatives that focus on differentiating the value of care delivered to the Medicare population by primary care physicians."[42]

An alternative strategy has been suggested that urges focusing on a small number of the measures that have the most impact. Meltzer and Chung looked at thirteen common quality indicators. In terms of additional net health benefit, almost half came from a single indicator, control of blood pressure in diabetics, while seven of the thirteen accounted for 93% of the benefits.[43] Prioritizing these seven and ignoring the other half would generate over 90% of any benefit to health.

For the primary care doctor, using these quality measurements is logical when they clearly benefit the patient, such as screening at-risk patients for colon or breast cancer. Primary care doctors are frustrated when they can see that a particular quality measurement is irrelevant or even counterproductive for the patient. Yet they are hounded to do them. Dr. Lawrence Casalino commented, "Insofar as physicians view quality management as micromanagement-primarily as a requirement to comply with externally imposed standards, rather than as a way to improve care – their morale and their sense of professionalism may suffer."[44]

A telling commentary came early in the Covid pandemic when CMS announced delaying or suspending quality reporting measurements so that, in the words of CMS Administrator Seema Verma, "the healthcare delivery system can direct its time and resources toward caring for patients."[45] Rosenbaum commented that physicians could have said, "Seriously? Why isn't the essence of quality devoting our time and resources to caring for patients all the time?"[46]

Moreover, by necessity, even the enormous number of quality measures assess only a few things. Doctors do not get even a pat on the back for the successful management of patients. Most PCPs have complicated patients where good primary care controls their pain and treats their depression to improve the patients' quality of life. Yet this, what I would view as high-quality care, isn't measured by any quality measure.

Eisenberg, in an analysis of physicians' practice patterns, also questioned whether asking for uniform care from physicians was always a good thing. He wrote, "The mere presence of variation among providers is not necessarily to be bemoaned. Since patients' preferences are clearly not all the same, it may be that variation serves at least one useful purpose; it may enable patients to seek care from doctors whose practice styles are consistent with their preferences."[47]

Casalino noted, "Although paying for high quality is an innovation with obvious potential benefits, it may also lead to the misallocation of both organizational resources and physicians' time."[48] Casalino quoted the medical director of a large California HMO as stating, "Everybody's doing what they are required to do in responding to the quality measurements that are being used. Every ounce of energy is being diverted to responding to these; not one ounce of energy is going to any other aspect of quality."[49]

As we discuss later, the administrative cost of meeting things such as quality measurements is one of the factors leading to the closure of smaller practices. Rosenbaum wrote, "Truly unquantifiable is a loss to society as consummate community physicians become a dying breed."[50] She quoted health policy expert Dr. Rishi Wadhera as saying, "Community doctors want to practice medicine. They don't want to practice quality measurement."[51]

After a lifetime of practice, Barken could similarly write, "As long as all the right boxes are checked, why should the doctor deal with the complex social issues of aging that have no easy answers, for which they are not properly reimbursed, and which are not even 'on the test.'"[52] Cassell commented, "Differences in patients, physicians and context makes individual decisions as essential as ever."[53]

Even experts in the field have started to cast doubt on what the volume of quality measures actually accomplished. Frakt and Jha admitted, "We also must make a concerted effort to rethink our quality strategy with fewer, more patient-centered measures."[54]

Casalino observed that as quality measures, "are linked to

physicians' pay and organizational budgets, they begin to define what is important and what is real. Future generations of physicians might be taught that it doesn't count if you can't count it, and they may be paid on that basis. Thus, they might not even understand that most aspects of the quality of medical care are not measured, and that medicine is not just a science but an art."[55]

Casalino wrote this in 1999. Twenty years later, physician pay, at least under MIPS and similar programs, is tied only to what can be counted. In Chapter 14, I will explore more details about using quality as an alternative payment basis for primary care doctors.

Every primary care doctor has patients where the PCP's care helped save patients from bad outcomes and even saved money for the insurers. Thus, the harping on a fixed set of quality measurements and monetarily penalizing the PCP for not meeting goals that she knows are absurd for her particular patient is discouraging. The skilled primary care doctor knows that so much of what they do such as their listening, their obsessive worrying about patients, and their compassion, are not measured or apparently valued.

---

[1] Cassell, 158

[2] Truls Ostbye, Kimberly S. H. Yarnall, Katrina M. Krause, Kathryn I. Pollak, Margaret Gradison, J. Lloyd Michener, "Is There Time for Management of Patients with Chronic Diseases in Primary Care?" *Ann Fam Med*, May/June 2005; 3(3): 209

[3] Kimberly S.H. Yarnall, Kathryn I. Pollak, Truls Ostbye, Katrina M. Krause, J. Lloyd Michener, "Primary Care: Is there Enough Time for Prevention?" *Am J Public Health*, April 2003; 93(4): 635

[4] Yarnall, 637

[5] Yarnall, 637-638

[6] Natalie Privett, Shanice Guerrier, "Estimation of the Time Needed to Deliver the 2020 USPSTF Preventive Care Recommendations in Primary Care," *Am J Public Health*, January, 2021, 11(1): 145

[7] KC Strange, SJ Zyzanski, CR Jaen, "Illuminating the 'Black Box': A description of 4454 patient visits to 138 family physicians," *J Fam Pract* 1998; 46:

[8] Allison J. Hare, Srinath Adusumali, Saehwan Park, Mitesh S. Patel, "Assessment of Primary Care Appointment Times and Appropriate Prescribing of Statins for At-Risk Patients," *JAMA Network Open*, 2021; 4(5) e219050.doi.10.1001/jamaworkopen.2021.9050

[9] Lawrence P. Casalino and others, "US Physician Practices Spend More Than $15.4 billion Annually to Report Quality Measures," *Health Affairs*, March 2016; 35(3): 402

[10] Casalino, US Physician Practices, 405

[11] Casalino, US Physician Practices, 402

[12] Casalino, US Physician Practices, 401

[13] Cynthia M. Boyd, Jonathan Darer, Chad Boult, Linda P. Fried, Lisa Bout, Albert W. Wu, "Clinical Practice Guidelines and Quality of Care for Older Patients with Multiple Comorbid Diseases: Implications for Pay for Performance," *JAMA*, 2005; 294: 716

[14] Boyd, 716

[15] Boyd, 722

[16] Louise C. Walter, Paul Heineken, "Pitfalls of Converting Practice Guidelines into Quality Measures," *JAMA,* September 15,2004: 292(11): 1302

[17] Lisa Rosenbaum, "Reassessing Quality Improvement – The Flawed System for Fixing a Flawed System," *NEJM,* April 28, 2022; 386(17): 1663-1667

[18] Rishi K. Wadhera, Jose P. Figueroa, Karen E. Joynt Maddox, Lisa Rosenbaum, Dhruv S. Kazi, Robert W. Yeh, "Quality Measure Development and Associated Spending by the Centers for Medicare and Medicaid Services," *JAMA*, April 28, 2020; 323(16): 1614

[19] Catherine H. MacLean, Eve A. Kerr, Amir Qaseem, "Time Out – Charting a Path for Improving Performance Measurement," *NEJM*, May 10, 2018; 378(19): 1757

[20] Dhruv Khullar, Amelia M. Bond, Eloise May O'Donnell, Yuting Qian, David N. Gans, Lawrence P. Casalino, "Time and Financial Costs for Phy-

sicians to Participate in the Medicare Merit-based Incentive Payment System: A Qualitative Study," *JAMA Health Forum*, 2021; 2(5): e210527.doi.10.1001/jamahealthforum.2021.0527

[21] Khullar, Time, 1

[22] Jason Hockenberry, "Cost of Compliance with CMS Physician Quality Monitoring-Too High," *JAMA Health* Forum 2021; 2(5): e210684.doi.10.1001/jamahealthforum.2021.0684

[23] Medical Group Management Association, "Annual Regulatory Burden Report," Accessed April 13, 2021.
https://www.mgma.com/resources.government-Programs/mgma-Annual-Regulatory-Burden-Report

[24] Medical Group Management Association, 2019, 6

[25] Medical Group Management Association, 2019, 7

[26] Cart T. Berdahl, Molly C. Easterlin, Gery Rayn, Jack Needleman, Terry K. Nuckols, "Primary Care Physicians in the Meri-based Incentive Payment System (MIPS): A Qualitative Investigation of Participants' Experiences, Self-reported Patient Changes and Suggestions for Program administrators," *JGIM* 2019; 34(10): 2275

[27] Austin B. Frakt, Ashish K. Jha, "Face the Facts: We Need to Change the Way We Do Pay for Performance," *Ann Int Med*, February 20, 2018; 168(4): 291

[28] Eric T. Roberts, Alan M. Zaslavsky, J. Michael McWilliams, "The Value-based Payment Modifier: Program Outcomes and Implications for Disparities," *Ann Int Med*, 2018; 168:261

[29] Rosenbaum, 1666

[30] MacLean, 1757

[31] MacLean, 1758

[32] MacLean, 1760

[33] Wadhera, 1615

[34] Roberts, 261

[35] Carrie H. Colla, Toyin Ajayi, Asaf Bitton, "Potential Adverse Financial Implications of the Merit-based Incentive Payment System for Independent and Safety Net Practices," *JAMA*, September 8, 2020: 324(10): 948

[36] Colla, 949

[37] Jacob Wallace, J. Michael McWilliams, Anthony Lollo, Janet Easton, Chima D. Ndumele, "Residual Confounding in Health Performance Assessment: Evidence from Randomization in Medicaid," *Ann Int Med*, 2022; 175: 314

[38] MacLean, 1760

[39] Sachin D. Shah, Adam S. Cifu, "From Guideline to Order Set to Patient Harm," *JAMA;* March 27, 2018; 319(12): 1208

[40] David J. Nyweide, William B. Weeks, Daniel J. Gottlieb, Lawrence P. Casalino, Eliot S. Fisher, "Relationship of Primary Care Physicians' Patient Caseload with Measurement of Quality and Cost Performance," *JAMA*, December 9, 2009; 302(22): 2444

[41] Nyweide, 2447

[42] Nyweide, 2449

[43] David O. Meltzer, Jeanette W. Chung, "The Population Value of Quality Indicator Reporting: A Framework for Prioritizing Health Care Performance Measures," *Health Affairs*, January 2014; 33(1): 136

[44] Lawrence P. Casalino, "The Unintended Consequences of Measuring Quality on the Quality of Health Care," *NEJM*, October 7, 1999; 341(15): 1148

[45] Rosenbaum, 1664

[46] Rosenbaum, 1664

[47] John M. Eisenberg, "Physician Utilization: The State of Research about Physicians' Practice Patterns," *Medical Care,* 2002;40(11): 1032

[48] Casalino, Unintended consequences, 1147

[49] Casalino, Unintended consequences, 1147

[50] Rosenbaum, 1666

[51] Rosenbaum, 1666

[52] Barken, 37

[53] Cassell, 101

[54] Frakt, 292

[55] Casalino, Unintended Consequences, 1149

"Technologies come into being to serve the purposes of their users, but ultimately these users redefine their own goals in terms of technology."

- Dr. Eric Cassell
  Doctoring: The Nature of Primary Care Medicine

"It's getting worse every year. Data collection is more important than patient care to everyone except the physician actually practicing."

- Anonymous Primary Care Physician

"We may be too busy attending to the popups in the corner of the screen to pay attention to the stories that are being told to us, and to unraveling the meaning."

- Dr. Steve Iliffe
  From General Practice to Primary Care:
  The Industrialization of Family Medicine

CHAPTER 13

The Electronic Medical Record: Unintended Consequences

As health care costs continued to increase during the first decade of the twenty-first century, a new idea was offered to reduce the cost of health care and improve its quality. It was not hard to notice how many businesses and industries in the United States had become computerized, replacing their paper records with electronic records with apparently increased efficiency.

The proposal thus was made to move hospitals and doctors to electronic medical records/electronic health records (EMR/EHR). The poor handwriting of doctors would be replaced by readable text. Communications would be enhanced between doctors and hospitals. The resulting increase in efficiency would cut health care costs. The move started under President George W. Bush, who established the Office of National Coordinator for Health Information Technology (ONCHIT), charged with developing a "health information technology infrastructure" that "reduces health care costs resulting from inefficiency, medical errors, inappropriate care and incomplete information."[1] It was estimated that EHR systems could reduce health care costs by up to 20% annually.[2]

The Bush administration's enthusiasm for EHRs as a magic bullet carried over to the Obama administration, which proposed and persuaded Congress to pass the 2009 Health Information Technology for Economic and Clinical Health Act. This Act, along with its associated Meaningful Use rules, would incentivize doctors and hospitals to undertake the costly and laborious conversion to the electronic medical record. Doctors would be offered carrots first, in the form of increased payments from Medicare, to adopt an EMR. Later, sticks would be used in the form of continually decreasing payments for Medicare patients for doctors who refused to adopt the system.

Proponents anticipated large savings in costs plus improved health care. A Federal government health website in 2008 stated, "Broad use of health IT will improve health care quality, prevent medical errors; reduce health care costs; increase administrative efficiencies; decrease paperwork; and expand access to affordable care."[3]

Over a decade later, billions and billions have been invested in electronic medical records. A whole new industry has been created to supply these records. The majority of doctors, particularly in large practices, are using an EMR.

The cost of the transition was not trivial. One analysis of fourteen practices revealed that the initial costs of going to an electronic health record was $44,000 per full-time equivalent provider with further ongoing costs of $8500 annually per full-time provider.[4]

In 2008 less than 15% of medical practices used an EMR, but by 2012, only four years later, the proportion had increased to 72%.[5] Notably, physicians working in large practices, HMOs and other non-physician-owned practices had much faster adoption of EMRs, which resulted in them receiving meaningful use dollars given for adoption more than the small practices.[6]

What has been the result of the adoption of electronic health records? There are those for which the EMR has been useful. Insurers, both public and private, are collecting vast amounts of data from hospitals and doctors. It is less clear whether this vast electronic warehouse of data has benefited patients or reduced health care costs?

In a study of 4000 hospitals, Himmelstein et al. concluded, "We found no evidence that computerization has lowered cost or streamlined administration."[7]

Nor is this much evidence that electronic medical records improve patient outcomes.[8] An analysis of the performance of seventeen quality indicators over two years of ambulatory visits in the United States showed that visits with an EMR produced improvements in two, worsening in one and no change in the other fourteen.[9]

For the tens of billions of dollars spent, one could argue that almost any other change in medicine could have produced a more significant benefit. Certainly, if the money had simply been given to patients who agreed to quit smoking, the health benefit would have been many times greater.

Are doctors more efficient? Well, no, actually, they are less efficient. One family medicine physician noted, "In the old days writing in a chart was much faster."[10] This may not be a feature of using a computer rather than a paper record specifically. Rather the rapacious appetite of the government, insurers and hospitals for data means that doctors both in the hospital and outside spend a greater amount of time filling out patient charts.

Cassell's prophetic words are descriptive of the EMR problem, for he wrote, "Technologies come into being to serve the purposes of their users, but ultimately their users redefine their own goals in terms of the technology."[11]

I will focus on primary care since this situation is what I know best. I do not know a single primary care physician who sees more patients now than when he used a paper chart. When I asked a family medicine doc at a large group about his patient numbers since the switch to the electronic medical record, he answered, "absolutely less."[12] Studies have shown that primary care doctors spend more total time and more after-hours' time on the electronic medical record compared to specialists. Within primary care, general internists and family physicians spend far more time on the EMR than do pediatricians. Not surprisingly, the adoption of health information technology was faster by large systems than by physician-owned practices.[13]

I have not heard of any doctors who are seeing even the same number of patients as before. Instead, primary care physicians are seeing fewer patients and having to fill out much more extensive charts on each one. Once the government and insurers could easily audit a computerized record, they insisted that each note include more and more things if the physician wanted to be paid for the visit. Responding to a 2019 survey about work, one internist commented, "The EHR (electronic health record) takes so much time. I used to be able to chart on a patient in five to ten minutes for established patients. Now it takes twenty to forty minutes."[14] Another doctor commented, "it's getting worse every year. Data collection is more important than patient care to everyone except the physician actually practicing."[15] Lafferty estimated, "The use of EHRs adds 20-30% more time to a patient's visit with no financial compensation to the doctor."[16] In an AMA survey, 31% of physicians reported being "overwhelmed by the volume of electronic messages received in the office," while 43% said that their EMR made them less efficient.[17]

Studies confirmed that increased time and cost had been imposed by the EMR. One study reported that it increased documentation time among physicians by 17%.[18] A study at Kaiser found that EMR implementation resulted in a 5-9% decrease in office visits.[19]

PCPs receive dozens to hundreds of electronic communications daily. A study found that much was of marginal value, but because the PCP had to read all to figure out how to separate the wheat from the chaff, i.e., to discover what was clinically important, this ate up vast amounts of time.[20] Others note that EMRs eat significantly into the free time of primary care providers.[21]

What about cost savings? There is no one these days who even alleges that the EMRs have cut health care costs by 20% annually. In addition to decreased physician productivity, the

EMRs, by allowing bills to be populated easily with more information, has led to "up coding," where physicians and hospitals bill more for the service by supplying more documentation. This is a clear added cost of having EMRs.

Time spent charting and filling out the increased paperwork as I described in Chapter 10, means there is less time for patients, even if the physician wants to work more hours.

A study of electronic medical records in small practices identified increased physician work as including more time-consuming charting, increased time in ordering and reviewing labs and tasks involved in preventive care and quality management.[22]

From personal experience, I can say that I average about three-quarters of the patients I used to see. Of course, I was younger and more energetic a decade ago, but that really doesn't explain the change. Where a very busy day might have meant seeing twenty-five patients, I now find twenty patients a very busy day, which means that I will have to continue charting at home that evening in order to get the records done.

There has been little written about this consequence of the adoption of the electronic record by primary care. A regression analysis, a sophisticated statistical tool, estimated that having an electronic health record increased primary care time with patients by 1.5 hours a week.[23] While the authors celebrated this as increased time with patients, they did not realize that it meant increased time staring at a screen while in the exam room. I suspect most patients wouldn't value the extra time their doctor spent looking at the computer instead of at them as necessarily a good thing. Nor would most primary care physicians applaud expanding their work week.

There is something else that may be lost. Iliffe eloquently commented, "We may be too busy attending to the popups in the corner of the screen to pay attention to the stories that are being told to us, and to unraveling the meaning."[24] Another doctor noted, "There's a tendency with the computerized record to have things pop out at you, and this also stifles your own thinking, makes you respond to what the EMR is asking you rather than you telling the EMR what you think is relevant to put into the record."[25] The value of getting to know and understand a patient more closely, unfortunately, can't be quantitated. Hence it is disregarded as unimportant. A family physician concluded, "I think people had better relationships before the EMR."[26]

There was another unintended consequence. For large practices, the economies of scale made the changeover financially practicable. For hospital-owned clinics, the hospital could put their doctors on the same computer system as the hospital, which meant that the incentive payments were really a windfall. Studies revealed much greater adoption of information technology for hospital-owned practices than for physician-owned practices, reflecting the resource disparity.[27]

For solo or two to three doctor practices, the meaningful use incentive payments would not cover the cost of the transition. The result was that many of these practitioners opted for early retirement. Others decided to become employees of a large group or hospital-owned practice. Thus, the adoption of the electronic medical record accelerated the consolidation of the health care industry and the drop in the number of physician practices.

Studies have shown that the use of electronic medical records has added to burnout among physicians. Sinsky surveyed a sample of American physicians in 2014, finding that nearly 20% planned to reduce their work hours within a year, with 2% leaving practice altogether. Burnout, dissatisfaction with work-life balance and dissatisfaction with the electronic medical record were all independent predictors of intent to reduce hours or leave practice.[28]

A further analysis of 6375 surveyed physicians found that doctors who used electronic medical records had lower satisfaction, more time on clerical tasks and a higher rate of burnout.[29] The use of computerized physician order entry, where the doctor served as the clerk to put in all the orders, caused particular unhappiness and a sense of burnout. Citing prior research, the study's authors concluded, "Electronic health records have increased the clerical burden on physicians, altered the patient-physician interaction and can distract from the more meaningful aspects of medical practice."[30]

Another study surveyed residents and faculty in nineteen primary care programs. Of the 37% reporting some burnout, three quarters attributed this burnout to the electronic medical record. Those who spent the most time on the electronic medical record were the most likely to report burnout and almost four times as likely to attribute it to the electronic medical record.[31]

Babbott and colleagues studied distinct types of EMRs in different primary care practices. They found that the more functions the EMR included, the more unhappy the physicians were. Those in the group whose EMRs had the most functions complained of the most time pressure, which was associated with burnout and intent to leave the practice.[32] The authors theorized that a fully functional EMR, "may make clinicians aware of the multiplicity of tasks required during each patient visit (health maintenance, quality measures, chronic disease management, social determinants of health and other documentation requirements)."[33] Babbott et al. hypothesized that doctors, "are trying to balance an increase in tasks with no increases in the time allotted."[34] This study showed that overwhelming doctors with too many tasks in too short a time led to increased stress and a sense of time pressure. Perhaps computers would not be overwhelmed by too much to do, but humans can be.

Patients, as well as doctors, are unhappy with the dominant role of the electronic medical record in their visits. A study showed that, "Higher computer use by clinicians in safety-net clinics was associated with lower patient satisfaction and observable communication differences."[35] Ironically, a recent study found that physicians in physician-owned practices were much more satisfied with their EMR than those working for others, which the authors note, "are consistent with previous research reporting that greater physician autonomy and control were associated with greater satisfaction."[36]

Melnick et al. recently argued that increased focus should be on what makes the EMR more usable and easier in actual use. Noting another study that found that doctors spent five hours on the EMR for every eight hours of clinical time, the authors concluded, "Increasingly, evidence indicates that the EHR is imposing an intolerable burden on clinicians and may be degrading, rather than elevating clinical care."[37]

It gets worse. The government declared that electronic medical records had to be "certified," which meant meeting a whole host of exactly defined criteria. Over the years, additional levels of functions needed to be added to meet new levels of certification. Unlike what Melnick and others proposed, these criteria aren't based on what would make a system easier to use in the real world. Indeed, issues of usability and preventing errors in the EMR becomes secondary to what is needed to meet certification.[38]

This ongoing certification requirement had more negative consequences. Whether they were unintended is not for me to say. Since meeting the specific certification requirement was very onerous, many companies that developed EMRs could not meet them and went out of business or at least out of this line of business. The result has been a very rapid consolidation of a new industry into a handful of giant vendors. My economics training tells me that an oligopoly is not the most desirable or efficient model, but this is where we are.

Moreover, akin to teaching for standardized tests, EMRs were developed to meet certification requirements rather than what would be most useful for doctors. For example, current standards mandate the charts include a place where a patient's prior address can be recorded. I don't know why I would want

223

to know this. Another feature is the ability to note over a hundred ethnicities for the patient.

As a primary care doctor, I am interested in the background of my patient, but I don't usually write down their ethnicity. Moreover, many Americans have forebearers who came from different lands. Charts, therefore, should really include multiple ethnicities if one was to be accurate. Yet this has nothing to do with care of the patient. I can only think that there is someone in some agency somewhere who wanted to be able to draw on this data.

Again, for the giant vendors in the EMR field, filling the EMR with options to write down useless garbage may not be a hassle. As a small to medium-sized independent practice, we chose to work with a small independent firm, thinking that they could supply us with something most useful for us. Alas, again and again, their time has been diverted to building in all the things required for certification and recertification rather than the things practicing doctors would find useful. This is a source of frustration for both them and us.

CMS had attempted to increase payments to primary care through a variety of special programs. Several times we have tried to apply for these only to find that we didn't have a certified EMR or, most recently, a certified EMR that included specific functions that the program demanded. Once again, money flows disproportionately to the biggest medical practices and those owned by hospitals at the expense of smaller practices. Robin Hood, or at least CMS, is now robbing the poor to pay the rich.

There is another issue. Different EMRs don't easily communicate. This was a problem the latest certification was supposed to address, but obtaining information from other systems is still challenging.

In some ways, getting information has become difficult. The major hospital where our patients were admitted used to be great about faxing us notes of ER visits, specialty consultations and discharge summaries. When they installed their EMR, they stopped faxing, assuming that everyone was on their EMR.

It has been a year since we asked them to please fax us their notes. Despite now having a huge IT department and multiple discussions with our clinic, they have not figured out how to resume faxing us these notes. I am not an IT person, but I assume that fax technology must be too complex. Yet another part of the same institution, its home health care nurses and physical therapists, continue to fax us their notes for the doctors to sign off and return.

Studies have shown that physician dissatisfaction with the EMR, regardless of which one, is high. By greater than a two-to-one margin, doctors believe that having an EMR has not increased their efficiency.[39]

This brings up another innovation that is being implemented. The Federal government has now passed a new rule stating that all lab and imaging results had to be released instantly to patients. This is in the spirit of the idea that patients should have access to all of their health records. This regulation has been interpreted as meaning that all lab and imaging results should go out whether or not the doctor has even had a chance to see them. The local hospital which runs our send-out labs and pathology is doing that now.

Thus, patients might see results showing that they have cancer first rather than the more traditional and wiser approach of the doctor meeting with the patient to review the results, their implications and treatment options. We have had this happen to our patients.

Internist McHarris commented, "I got an abnormal thyroid ultrasound result saying that the patient needed a biopsy, at the same time, the patient called me about the result, which they had received before I had...This is not helpful to anyone." [40]

Often the patient sees lab results where a bunch of things

are out of the normal range. Previously, I sent out a note with patients' lab results explaining what is significant and what is not, for much of what seems out of the normal range is of no importance whatsoever. I need to explain that the "normal range" is usually a statistical construct usually meant to include 90% of patients who don't have this particular abnormality. By definition, 10% of patients with no disease would fall outside the normal range, yet they are not more ill.

Some tests, such as complete blood counts (CBCs) include a host of measurements of no clinical importance. It is almost as rare as hens' teeth for a RDW just outside the normal range to mean anything. But patients don't know that.

The instant results have generated urgent calls from the upset patients. An enormous amount of patient angst and upset has been generated. The workload for the doctors and their staff having to try to deal with this is greatly increased.

I can only describe the idea that results should reach the patient before the doctor, without any explanation, as, at best, moronic. It would have been so easy to say that results should reach the patient within a few days after the doctor had seen them. This would have allowed time for interpretation and patient education instead of anxiety.

It's just another advance courtesy of the electronic medical record. Or rather, how the powers that be, in their infinite wisdom, have decided it should be used.

---

[1] Jaan Sidorov, "It Ain't Necessarily So: The Electronic Health Record and the Unlikely Prospect of Reducing Health Care Costs," *Health Affairs*, July/August 2006; 25(4): 1079

[2] Sidorov, 1079

[3] David U. Himmelstein Adam Wright, Steffie Woolhandler, "Hospital Computing and Cost and Quality of Care," *American Journal of Medicine*, 1010; 123: 40-41

[4] Robert H. Miller, Christopher West, Tiffany Martin Brown, Ida Sim, Chris Ganchoff, "The Value of Electronic Health Records in Solo or Small Group Practice," *Health Affairs*, September/October 2005; 24(5): 1127

[5] Stewart Babbott and others, "Electronic medical records and physician stress in primary care: Results from the MEMO Study," *J Am Med Inform Assoc*, 2014; 21:e100

[6] Vaishal Patel, Eric Jamoom, Chun-Ju Hsiao, Michael F. Furukawa, Melinda Buntin, "Variation in Electronic Health Recor Adoption and Readiness for Meaningful Use," *JGIM*, 2013; 28(7): 963

[7] Himmelstein, 44

[8] Tait D. Shanafelt and others, "Relationship Between Clerical Burden and Characteristics of the Electronic Environment with Physician Burnout and Professional Satisfaction," *Mayo Clin Proc*, July 2016; 91(7): 844

[9] Jeffrey A. Linder, Jun Ma, David W. Bates, Blackford Middleton, Randall S. Stafford, "Electronic Health Record Use and Quality of Ambulatory Care in the United States," *Arch Int Med*, July 9, 2007; 167(13): 1400

[10] Anonymous, Interview with Gregg Coodley, June 24, 2021

[11] Cassell, 63

[12] Anonymous, Interview with Gregg Coodley, June 24, 2021

[13] Hector P. Rodriguez, Sean P. McClellan, Salma Bibi, Lawrence P. Casalino, Patricia P. Ramsy, Stephen M. Shortell, "Increased Use of Care Management Process and Expanded Health Information Technology Functions by Practice Ownership and Medicaid Revenue," *Medical Care Research and Review*, 2016; 73(3): 308

[14] Kane

[15] Kane

[16] Lafferty, 27

[17] "EHRs Continue to Hinder Physician Job Satisfaction," *Medical Economics*, July 25, 2014; 7

[18] Sidorov, 1080

[19] Sidorov, 1080

[20] Daniel R. Murphy and others, "Electronic Health Record-based Messages to Primary Care Providers: Valuable Information or Just Noise," *Arch Int Med*, February 13, 2012; 172(3): 284

[21] Clement J. McDonald, Michael H. McDonald, "Electronic Medical Records and Preserving Primary Care Physicians' Time," *Arch Int Med*, February 13, 2012; 172(3): 286

[22] Jenna Howard and others, "Electronic Health Record Impact on Work Burden in Small Unaffiliated Community-Based Primary Care," *JGIM*, 2012; 28(1): 110-11

[23] J. Bae, "National estimates of the impact of electronic health records on the workload of primary care physicians," *BMC Health Serv Res*, May 10, 2016; 16:172

[24] Steven Iliffe, *From General Practice to Primary Care: The Industrialization of Family Medicine*, Oxford University Press, Oxford, 2008, 113

[25] Hoff, 61

[26] Anonymous, Interview with Gregg Coodley, June 24, 2021

[27] Rodriguez, 1

[28] Christine A Sinsky, Lotte N Dyrbye, Colin P West, Daniel Satele, Michael Tutty, "Professional Satisfaction and Career Plans of US Physicians," *Mayo Clin Proc*, November, 2017; 92(11): 1625

[29] Shanafelt, Relationship, 836

[30] Shanafelt, Relationship, 837

[31] SL Roberton, DD Robertson, A Reid, "Electronic Health Record Effects on Work-Life Balance and Burnout with the 13 Population Collaborative," *J Grad Med Educ*, August 2017: 9(4): 479

[32] Babbott, e100

[33] Babbott, e105

[34] Babbott, e105

[35] Neda Ratanawongsa and others, "Association Between Clinician Computer Use and Communication with Physicians in Safety-Net Clinics," *JAMA Internal Medicine*, 176(1): 127

[36] Lisa S. Rotenstein, Nate Apathy, Bruce Landon, David M. Bates, "Assessment of Satisfaction with the Electronic Health Record Among Physicians in Physician-Owned vs. Non-Physician-Owned Practices," *JAMA Network Open*, April 21, 2022, 2022:5(4)e228301.doi:10.1001/jamanetworkopen.2022.8301

[37] Edward R. Melnick, Christine A. Sinsky, Harlan M. Krumholz, "Implementing Measurement Science for Electronic Health Record Use," *JAMA*, June 1, 2021; 325(21): 2149

[38] Raj M. Ratwani, Michael Hodgkins, David W. Bates, "Improving Electronic Health Record Usability and Safety Requires Transparency," *JAMA*, December 25, 2018; 320(24): 2533

[39] Shanafelt, Relationship, 844

[40] McHarris

"Consistent with previous research, this study showed more continuity of care in the fee-for-service system than in any other models of care."

- Dr Dana Gelb Safran et al.

"Evidence that pay for performance improves care is scant... practices that care for lower-income or sicker patients received greater penalties, essentially creating a reverse Robin Hood effect."

- Drs. Austin B. Frakt and Ashish K. Jha

"We found no association between physician compensation incentives and the quality of care."

- Dr. David Burstein et al.

"Most CMS value-based payments have failed to meaningfully reduce health care expenditures or improve quality of care."

- Gondi et al (2022)

CHAPTER 14
The Demonization of Fee-for-Service

Arguments about how doctors should be paid may seem peripheral to the plight of the primary care doctor or the concerns of their patients, but it has had important ramifications.

For what is involved are questions of morality and medicine. Cassell wrote, "The basic conflict between what is in the best interest of the doctor versus the best interest of the patient has always existed. It cannot be abolished by regulation. It is part of the moral basis of medicine and can be effectively dealt with only by moral self-regulation by the physician."[1]

Yet arguments over how to pay doctors, in this case primary care doctors, assumes that they are solely economic creatures whose behavior can be most, if not completely, affected by money.

When observers of American health care looked at the situation in the mid-1980s, two facts were clear. Health care costs were rising more than most other costs in the economy. Second, most doctors were paid fee-for-service, meaning that they were paid for the work they did for each patient. This is how almost anyone in the country who is not on a salary is paid, including most other professionals. Dentists, veterinarians, lawyers, architects, farmers, plumbers, electricians, and small business owners are all paid for the services or goods they provide, with more work usually meaning more income, hence creating an incentive to work more.

Prior to 1984, Medicare paid doctors on the basis of "usual, customary or reasonable" fees, which were based on local conditions. This was adopted from the Blue Cross models of the 1960s. However, observers pointed out that this led to very different payments for the same service in different geographic areas.

In 1984 Medicare created a Medicare Economic Index as a first step toward assessing physicians' cost of practice, or overhead, in a bid to reduce payment disparities. This was followed by the adoption of the resource-based relative value scale (RBRVS) in 1989. RBRVS continued to pay primary care doctors on a fee-for-service basis for each discreet service rendered. Gail Wilensky, a health care economist who helped design the system, wrote, "Although the scale was intended to correct for a historical undervaluing of primary care and overvaluing of procedures (which it does not appear to have done very successfully) and for larger differences between urban and rural reimbursements than could be justified by differences in the costs of practice, it retained the use of a largely disaggregated fee schedule."[2]

In the face of rising health care costs, many blamed the concept of fee-for-service, arguing that paying doctors per service done led to excess services being performed and hence increased health care costs. At this time, only a few parts of health care, such as Kaiser-Permanente and the Veterans Administration, as well as public health clinics, gave doctors a salary. Proponents of changing physician payments pointed out that in some other countries where doctors were salaried, health care costs didn't seem to be rising as much.

The conclusion was that fee-for-service was driving unnecessary health care services and spending. The National Commission on Physician Payment Reform looked at factors causing high health care costs in the United States, noting, "Reliance on technology and expensive care, higher payments for medical service performed in hospital-owned facilities than in outpatient facilities, and a high proportion of specialist physicians as compared with generalists were all important cost drivers. But fee-for-service reimbursement stood out as the most important cause of high health care expenditures."[3]

There are major problems with this diagnosis, at least for primary care. First, no one has ever managed to say what the proper amount of care is. For a primary care doctor, what is the correct number of patient visits and what is too little or too much? There was no evidence given that some of the primary care visits were superfluous or proof that PCPs saw patients excessively due to this payment model.

Second, primary care is a tiny portion of the cost of health care, at most 5% of all spending. Having primary care physicians see patients only half as often would only cut the 5% in half. The health care system would have saved 2.5 cents of each dollar spent.

For example, let's suppose a primary care doctor is paid $100 per patient visit. A two-day hospitalization can easily top $50,000 dollars. From a cost-saving perspective, it would be cheaper to pay the primary care doctor for 49 patient visits than pay for the two-day hospitalization. Clearly, "excess" primary care visits due to fee-for-service are not the main driver of health care costs.

The Commission of Physician Payment Reform admitted that primary care wasn't the key culprit, stating, "The sickest 5% of patients consume half of the nations' health care resources...improving their care offers a substantial potential for cost savings."[4] The expensive part of these patients' care mainly occurs in the hospital; very little is due to paying for PCP office visits.

Third, substantial evidence suggests that increased prices rather than increased volume of services is the biggest driver of increased health care costs.[5] Data also suggests that the increase in prices was much greater for hospital prices than for physician services, again suggesting that measures to limit the number of services provided by primary care is almost completely irrelevant to effective cost containment.[6]

Finally, other high-income countries pay physicians in great part on a fee-for-service basis yet have health care costs far lower than in the United States. Gusmano and colleagues noted that, "France, Germany and Japan – appear to achieve economic sustainability in a fee-for-service system."[7] The authors concluded, "Marking fee-for-service as the major cause of high health care spending in the US is problematic, especially as countries with lower prices and expenditures use fee-for-service systems."[8]

The statistics showing the rapid growth of Medicare Part B spending during the 1990s and 2000s lump primary care spending in with payments for specialists and all the other outpatient services. Given the higher number of specialists than PCPs and the much higher incomes, it is clear that the bulk of the increased Medicare spending is not going to PCPs.

Data showed US health care expenditure increased from $810 billion in 2002 to $1617 billion in 2016. The highest category of spending was for inpatient expenses, followed by spending on prescriptions and then for specialty care. These three categories accounted for two-thirds of the increase. In contrast, only 4.2% of the increase was for primary care, which declined as a proportion of all expenditures.[9]

Since much less is spent on primary care in the United States compared to most other industrial nations, blaming the form of primary care payments for the inflated cost of health care is nonsense.

Fee-for-service is, in many ways, a fairer system than some of the alternatives. When I took over as section chief of General Internal Medicine at Oregon Health Sciences University, the section included four tenured full professors and a lot of what they called "worker bees." Income was decided based on political influence, not how much income a doctor brought in. While the four full professors did not like each other much, they agreed that they deserved most of the money that was brought in.

One of the ways we converted the General Medicine Clinic to profitability was by paying everyone a straight percentage of the income they brought in. If you worked more and saw more patients, you earned more.. No one got paid simply because of who they were. As in any system, there were winners and losers. Those who expected a guaranteed income without working for it were, shall we say, less than pleased. Yet the "worker bees" now got paid fairly and worked more, knowing that it meant more income for them. The number of patients seen by the clinic increased dramatically.

Few can make any convincing arguments that too many primary care visits are bad. Indeed, as we have seen earlier, increased primary care is correlated with improved health outcomes, reduced emergency room visits and hospitalizations and increased patient satisfaction.

While the assumption is that primary care doctors paid fee-for-services would generate more health care costs, there is evidence that the opposite might be true. A study looking at the care of hypertension in different practices in Minnesota showed, "Contrary to expectations, physicians paid on a fee-for-service basis use fewer resources to provide these episodes of care than those paid on a salary basis. In these small medical group practices (ten to forty-three physicians), physicians paid on some type of income-generated basis appeared to be more attentive to costs than those paid a salary."[10]

Some have argued that since fee-for-service does not cover everything physicians do, such as electronic and phone consultations, it must be abandoned. A Society of General Internal Medicine (SGIM) task force report in 2004 declared that, "Current traditional fee-for-service financing...will be a barrier to achieving the best possible patient care," arguing that internists should be leading large teams of nurses, pharmacists and other professionals as the care model of the future.[11] Beyond what appeared to be academic hostility to small independent practices, the authors did not provide any data showing why fee-for-service was incompatible with excellent patient care.

Indeed, their argument can be turned around, as happened in the Covid pandemic in 2020–21. Since patients could not always safely come into doctors' offices, doctors turned to telemedicine. Most importantly, the insurers were mandated to pay for it at the same rate as an office visit. Billing was done on a fee-for-service basis. Fee-for-service worked to incentivize primary care doctors to do as many of these visits as possible.

Safran et al. compared PCP performance and patient satisfaction in five different models of care. Contrary to the academic expectations, the model that paid physicians on a fee-for-service basis had their highest scores from patients. Safran et al. also noted, "Consistent with previous research, this study showed more continuity of care in the fee-for-service system than in any other models of care."[12]

The argument against fee-for-service then became that American health care was more expensive because primary care doctors generated a lot more costs by their referrals to specialists and hospitals. Yet the Stark laws clearly prohibit physicians from getting any reimbursement for such referrals or any tests ordered. Thus, removing primary care's fee-for-service payments would have no impact on cutting referrals or any other secondary costs generated by the PCP.

Still, given the health care inflation of the 1970s and 1980s, the powers that be increasingly argued for a different model, suggesting that PCPs be paid on capitation, i.e., a set fee for every patient under their care. This suggestion was implemented in many settings, particularly in health maintenance organizations. Yet if fee-for-service creates an incentive for the doctor to see the patient too much, capitation creates the opposite incentive. Since the doctor is paid whether or not he saw the patient, the incentive is to do too few visits, not too many. Again, this model doesn't give PCPs any incentive to refer less. In fact, referring a patient out for a problem is incentivized, for the PCP gets no added income from seeing the patient themselves. Limits on referrals or other tests in such systems are done on an administrative basis since strict capitation doesn't give financial incentives for this to the PCP. During the two years I worked for an HMO in Boston, referrals and testing sometimes required special authorization, and the administrators worked to discourage these added costs. Patients were angered to find their PCPs acting as "gatekeepers" to limit their specialist referrals. The capitation model gradually fell out of favor.

Paul Starr wrote in 1982, "The more administrative uses the state and other institutions find for professionals, the more they may simultaneously expand and undermine their authority."[13] Patient respect for doctors was decreased when they felt that the doctors were working to help the insurer or HMO more than worrying about the patient.

Interestingly the Covid pandemic, which imposed a large drop in visits and income for many primary care doctors, has brought suggestions for a new capitation model that would protect PCPs financially from similar future disasters. This model suggests incorporating fee-for-service payments for certain limited services, such as patient visits soon after hospitalization. The authors note, "PCPs also want respect for their expertise, autonomy to practice the way they think is best, and flexibility over their time. PCP capitation has to fulfill these goals not just in rhetoric but in action."[14]

The next payment models to be implemented were risk-sharing models. In these models, which paid modest fee-for-service payments for patient visits, there was a set pot of money per patient to cover all that patient's costs. If there was a surplus, a small amount would be shared with the primary care doctor. This created an incentive for the doctor to do as little as possible, whether visits, referrals, tests or hospitalizations. While this creates an incentive to do less, it ignores the underlying problem of what level is really appropriate.

Yet if it is illegal to pay doctors to refer more, etc., under the Stark laws, it is striking, although unnoticed, that these programs pay doctors to do fewer referrals, etc. The surpluses that can be achieved by strictly trying to reduce the services ordered can be a huge percentage of the PCP's annual income. It is argued that PCPs will still do what is needed for their patient even under a risk-based model. Yet it is wholly illogical to assume PCPs under fee-for-service will be wasteful and driven by greed to do too much, but that their moral sense of doing the right thing will overcome a much larger financial gain if they do less.

A variation of the risk-sharing models tries to integrate quality measures along with cost-saving. These measures, dubbed pay-for-performance or value-based care, are being aggressively pushed as providing better care. In 2003 Thomas Scully, head of the federal Centers for Medicare and Medicaid Services, commented, "There's no question that pay-for-performance will work."[15] CMS has, in fact, been rolling out a variety of pay-for-performance models ever since. From 2008 to 2018, CMS spent an estimated $1.3 billion developing quality measures; of the 2200 developed, 800 have been implemented.[16]

CMS put forth a plan a few years ago to, "base 90% of Medicare fee-for-service payments to clinicians on 'value' by the end of 2018 by using performance scores."[17] CMS continues to favor pay-for-performance as the preferred strategy.

Yet most of these pay-for-performance programs showed disappointing results, with relatively small changes induced by the program. Writing in the *New England Journal*, after one study showed less than spectacular results, Dr. Arnold Epstein observed, "CMS may have much to gain from recognizing that pay-for-performance is fundamentally a social experiment likely to have only modest incremental value."[18] A Harvard University review of the literature on paying for quality in health care concluded that there was, "little evidence to support the effectiveness of paying for quality."[19]

Pham et al. pointed out another weakness in pay-for-performance, which is the assumption that, "primary responsibility for care of a beneficiary can be assigned to an individual physician or practice."[20] Instead, their study of 1.79 million Medicare patients showed that many patients saw not only many different specialists but even different PCPs over time. They concluded, "The dispersion of patients' care among multiple physicians will limit the effectiveness of pay-for-performance initiatives."[21]

Meanwhile, implementing these programs has put a major burden on physicians. In a 2019 survey, 84% of physician practices felt that the CMS value-based payment reforms had increased the administrative burden.

The major current tool is CMS Merit-Based Incentive Payment System (MIPS), which evaluates doctors on quality (based on clinical quality measures), improvement activities, costs and use of health information technology to improve care delivery.[22]

The evidence so far casts doubt on whether such an approach will either improve the quality of care or reduce its costs. As Frakt and Jha wrote, "Evidence that pay-for-performance improves care is scant."[23] The authors also concluded that, "practices that care for lower-income or sicker patients received greater penalties, essentially creating a reverse Robin Hood effect."[24]

A 2020 analysis confirmed that safety net practices (where a large percentage of care is provided to vulnerable and poorer populations) did significantly worse in MIPS. Smaller practices, those with a sicker case mix and those in rural areas all did worse overall.[25] This translated into fewer Medicare payments to these practices compared to overall. Is this really a better payment system?

Value-based programs clearly disadvantage doctors who

240

see the sickest patients. Meier noted, "There are few reliable and valid quality measures for patients with the highest need who generate the highest costs...These high-need, high-cost patients are particularly vulnerable under the value-based model of shared savings, whereby care providers share in savings when actual health care costs are lower than expected. Quality measures to guard against underdiagnosis and undertreatment are almost nonexistent."[26]

A recent review found that efforts to do risk adjustment based on the patients' level of illness often failed to accurately assess this.[27] An accompanying editorial concluded, "Spending differences across plans are largely due to patient characteristics that are not accounted for by risk adjustment. Risk adjustment will fail to achieve a central policy goal if its flaws are so severe that insurers can cream skim profitable enrollees."[28]

A review of seventeen pay-for-performance programs gave mixed results. The authors wrote, "Three studies showed that documentation, rather than the actual use of preventive service, improved statistically significantly with a financial incentive."[29] They also concluded, "Adverse selection may have occurred with performance-based contracting in settings where providers can avoid sicker patients."[30]

Moreover, a comparison of different payment models for physicians showed no link to quality of care. The authors concluded, "We found no association between physician compensation incentives and quality of care. Physician compensation incentives have unintended negative consequences."[31]

Moreover, the MIPs program clearly favored large groups at the expense of smaller practices. Almost 20% of the small practices received a negative adjustment in payment compared to 5% of the practices overall.[32] Unless the intention is to wipe out small practices, this pay-for-performance program is severely flawed.

A later analysis using 2019 data again showed that doctors

affiliated with a health system had significantly higher MIPS performance scores. CMS also noted that doctors in large practices scored 71% higher on MIPS than those in small practices.[33] There is no evidence that these differences represented real differences in the quality of care delivered.

Others have noted, "There is no convincing data that payment programs have reduced the inequity that affects marginalized populations...Instead, payment models could worsen disparities for these groups.[34] They argued that equity should be considered along with quality and cost.

The American College of Physicians noted the potential for ethical problems with these types of programs, stating, "Paying physicians incentives could reduce intrinsic reasons or motivations for professionalism, clinical integrity and the sense of medicine as a calling."[35]

There is an excessive cost for physicians to participate in MIPS. Khullar et al. calculated that the mean-per-physician cost to practices participating in MIPS in 2019 was $12,811. Physicians and staff spent an average of two hundred hours per physician on MIPS-related activities during 2019.[36] The survey of 400 practices revealed that, "76% of respondents felt that MIPS is very or extremely burdensome and 87% report that MIPS payment adjustments do not cover the time and resources needed for program participation."[37]

The authors concluded, "that the costs of participating in MIPS may be greater for small practices and primary care practices, which would be consistent with prior work on quality reporting."[38] By contrast, large and hospital-based practices have less costs due to better reporting infrastructure and economies of scale.

Moreover, the MIPS program is based on a fixed budget, i.e., bonuses for good performers cannot exceed cuts for those doing poorly. Thus in 2020, the performers with perfect scores received a positive payment adjustment of 1.68%, an amount for most practices far less than the costs of being in MIPS.[39]

Finally, while paying for better quality, albeit based on flawed measures, or lesser patient costs could be justified as improving medical care, one component used to adjust physician payments is based on the physicians' electronic medical records. Does having a better health information system really merit adjustments in doctor payments? Clearly large institutions and practices are going to have better computer systems than small, rural and safety net practices. Does this really translate into better patient care?

In March 2018, the Medicare Payment Advisory Commission (Med PAC) completed a two-year review of MIPS. It recommended that MIPS be eliminated.[40] They identified multiple problems, including comparison of groups based on different criteria, insufficient patients for each clinician or group to draw accurate statistical analyses, inadequate attention to coordinating care and the massive expense and burden for clinicians to report data. Describing Med PAC's conclusion, Crosson et al. wrote, "MIPS adopts a fragmented approach to quality measurement that is unfair and burdensome to providers, results in unreliable performance scores and does not promote high-quality care...the problems with MIPS are so fundamental that a different approach is required."[41]

Med PAC instead suggested measuring groups of clinicians on a small group of measures, such as hospital readmissions, where the data could be generated from claims data, thus reducing the burden for doctors in supplying information. They noted that it would be better to measure a small set of measures, "that are important to the program and its beneficiaries and can be measured reliably."[42]

In 2012 CMS launched its Comprehensive Primary Care Initiative (CPC), which was tested in seven states. It offered participating practices a monthly "population-based care management fee," i.e., a per-patient capitated fee of a few dollars to help pay for all the tasks the PCP did that were otherwise non-reimbursed. It expanded this in 2017 to the CPC

Plus, which paid the fee to primary care practices with advanced medical homes.[43]

While this concept sounded reasonable, the actual criteria for entry still gave preference to larger groups and health systems. To qualify, primary care doctors had to meet a variety of criteria, one of which was an electronic medical record with certain advanced functions, making the program inaccessible to smaller practices and those in rural or other underserved areas with fewer resources to start with.

The newest payment models are even worse for primary care. Most new "Value-Based Care" programs include more than just a focus on quality. They invariably include a risk-sharing model that creates strong incentives for doctors to do less in order to take home a portion of the surplus thus generated for the insurer.

The latest models propose "down side" risk-sharing for PCPs. What this means is that if too many of the PCP's patients are hospitalized, he or she would have to pay back the extra cost to the insurer. This puts solo or small primary care practices at huge risk if they have patients who happen to get sick. PCPs would have even more incentive not to take care of sick patients.

The risk is less for employed physicians, who would receive less of any surplus and presumably not have reduced salaries if there were losses.

Even as the primary care doctor has less and less control over what happens to her patients, he is asked to take increased risks. The PCP can't control what happens in the hospital since she has been replaced by a hospitalist. Theoretically, all referrals to specialists should come from the PCP. Yet the insurance plans let the hospitalists make referrals, and the specialists make referrals to each other. Recently a hospitalized patient of mine came out with a hospitalist referral for twelve palliative care visits with a palliative care physician. Yet under the risk model the patient was in, the PCP was supposed to control referrals to limit these costs in order to generate savings for the insurer.

The PCP can't control the medicines used in the hospital or by the specialists. The PCP can't control what tests the specialists or hospitalists order. Hence as a practical matter expecting PCPs to be able to control costs when they don't control the decisions that cost money is beyond foolish.

The morality of this should also be questioned. Should the primary care doctor have to choose between hospitalizing a patient who needs it at a huge personal financial cost to the doctor or keeping them out even when this is not good medical care?

Also, of course not everyone shares the risks. The specialists don't take risk. Nor do the insurance company executives, their minions and attorneys agree to get paid less should too many patients need more care. They don't take risk.

Most importantly, patients don't understand the model. It sounds great to focus on "quality" and "value," but how would patients feel to learn that their doctors get paid more the less that is done for the patient. If patients had any power, I don't think they would stomach this.

If the patient did understand this, they might blame their doctor for not doing everything the patient needed in order for the doctor to make more money. Yet primary care doctors didn't design such a system. It is increasingly forced on them in contracts from those more powerful, the insurance companies.

I believe most primary care physicians try to do the number of visits with each patient that they think is appropriate to their care. Having worked with doctors under all these systems, I saw most doctors try to do what they thought was the right amount of care regardless of the payment scheme.

The basic premise of the value-based/pay-for-performance programs is that such physician "professionalism," defines as their intrinsic motivation, is not sufficient to achieve quality. The high administrative costs and meager results of the programs should raise the question whether the marginal benefit in quality over a straight fee-for-system is worth it. Moreover, these programs can further weaken physicians' desire to do the right thing.

Casalino and Khullar point out that value-based programs (VBP) have negative effects on physician motivation. They write, "Professionalism may be decreased when physicians perceive that VBP programs focus on relatively unimportant measures, are unnecessarily complex, increase administrative burden, lack the statistical power to reliably measure performance, rely on checking off boxes (e.g., documenting that a patient was asked about smoking), penalize physicians who care for socioeconomically disadvantaged or complex patients or incentivize inappropriate care...behavioral economics research suggests that providing financial incentives to individuals may undermine intrinsic motivation."[44]

Ironically, even as the flaws in MIPS were revealed, there were those who argued that the real problem was that it still included a fee-for-service component. A group of academics recently wrote in *JAMA*, "if fee-for-service is an inherently misguided approach, a system that preserves its underlying incentives will not fix it."[45]

The basic error is lumping all health care fee-for-service together. While paying huge sums for each additional MRI or PET scan might be folly, paying more for additional PCP visits is not. More visits with a PCP actually results in fewer ER visits and hospitalizations, lowering overall costs. To save overall costs, insurance should increase fee-for-service payments to PCPs to incentivize them to increase patient visits.

Capitation and the risk-based models that followed created perverse incentives. How much a patient needs to be seen really depends on how sick they are. Patients with multiple complex conditions are going to require more visits, at least if they are to get the proper treatment. No doctoring, no matter how brilliant, can make the care of an 80-year-old diabetic patient with heart failure as cheap as a healthy thirty-year-old. Yet flat capitation paid the same fee for each patient. Therefore, there is an incentive to avoid sick and older patients since they will require more care and generate no more income. Risk-sharing models intensify this perverse incentive since these patients will almost certainly use more health care resources and threaten the possibility of there being any surplus to go back to the doctor.

What was the result of these incentives? Whether consciously or subconsciously, some doctors (not to mention insurers) avoided taking on sick complex patients. It also created conflicts between doctors, for those who saw complex patients created higher costs, thus reducing the amount of money available for other doctors with whom they were sharing the risk.

I saw this conflict in the early 1990s when I was Director of the General Medicine Clinic at Oregon Health Sciences University. The clinic generated an overall surplus or profit of some $200,000. We tended to get very complex patients, including many with HIV and advanced diabetes.

However, at the university, General Internal Medicine, which I then headed, was in a risk-sharing model with Family Medicine and Pediatrics for Medicaid patients. Family Medicine pointed out that their patients had lower costs, which they attributed to more efficient management. We answered that Internal Medicine had many more of the very complex patients, such as those with HIV or diabetes, which I believed then and believe now, was the reason they cost more. The bottom line was that the incentive to spend less created conflict among doctors and a strong incentive to avoid seeing complex and therefore costly patients. Risk-sharing turned out to be an effective mechanism for turning PCPs against each other.

When I finished residency in the late 1980s, I became, by

chance, more than design, a doctor with a large practice of HIV patients. I had fewer overall patients than some, but I had a lot of patients I had to see a lot. So maybe I have a built-in bias against capitation. Still the idea that one would do better by avoiding the sickest patients is not why most of us got into medicine.

For insurance companies, they always have made more money if those they covered cost less. For many years, overt "cherry-picking," i.e., trying to just get the healthy patients who would cost less, may have been limited. With the advent of the private Medicare Advantage plans this changed. Of course, no insurer would state right out that they just wanted to cover patients who weren't as sick. Instead, they were sneaky. They included exercise memberships as a bonus for those seniors who signed up on their plan. Those to whom the free gym membership was most appealing tended to be those healthy enough to exercise. I fear any senior who feels pleased that their Med Advantage plan is doing stuff like that for them misunderstands the real motive.

Medicare has tried to correct the problem by adjusting how much they pay Medicare Advantage plans based on how sick a patient is. We will see in the next chapter how Medicare Advantage plans have gamed Medicare to get the maximum money from such adjustments.

What can we conclude about payments to PCPs? First, each payment scheme will create incentives. Doing too little is as bad or worse than doing too much. Certainly, this is true at the level of the individual patient.

Second, how a primary care doctor is paid will not be the biggest determinant of health care costs. Primary care is cheap compared to everything done at a hospital or even a freestanding surgery center. Blaming the primary care doctor for the excessive cost of health care is a distraction from the real drivers of increased health care costs. The aging population is one factor. The inflated cost of new technology and pharmaceuticals that improve our overall health is another. Health care was infinitely cheaper before we could do cardiac bypasses or lung transplants, but no one would want to go back. Insurance company profits is a cost not seen in most other health care systems. Finally, the administrative waste, some of which I have outlined, in the system adds to our costs. Compared to all this, a primary care doctor seeing a patient more often is a trivial cost that has been shown to reduce overall health care costs by reducing hospitalizations and ER visits.

The powers that be view fee-for-service as almost as bad for health care as smoking tobacco. Every article about the subject touts the superiority of "value-based care," where the emphasis is on achieving better quality rather than doing more. Who could be against quality or value? They play a prominent role in advertisements for everything from toilet paper to luxury sedans to now medicine. If insurance plans could figure out how to advertise themselves as having "rich Corinthian leather," they would surely do so. Yet as we have seen in Chapter 12, simply calling something "quality" or "value" doesn't make it so. Nor does anyone propose paying lawyers or plumbers or dentists on the "quality" and "value," for it would be easily apparent that this cannot be done in any way that fairly assesses these for each customer.

At our primary care clinic, we have been forced to do the best we can under all of these models. We try to minimize unnecessary services as long as it doesn't hurt the care of the patient. We check the quality boxes. We have had to play the games with the cards that we were dealt.

Yet what has really allowed us to survive, when so many other practices have not, is paying doctors for their work. Most of the group is part-time. They get to choose how much they want to work, but their pay is based on how much they do, not their seniority or power. I can say from personal experience that the freedom to choose how much you want to work and knowing that you get a fair percentage has been attractive.

I would assert that paying doctors for the work they do, i.e., fee-for-service, is far less corrupt than paying them to do less work. It is much less corrupt than dangling huge bonuses in front of them if they limit how many tests and hospitalizations they permit. It is much, much, much less morally compromising than threatening to claw back even the PCP's basic income should they have too many of their patients who are sick and really need to be treated.

Gondi et al commented in the *NEJM* in July, 2022, "The movement toward value-based payment had been a defining feature of US health care reforms during the past decade. Despite substantial enthusiasm and investment, however, these efforts have been largely disappointing. Most Centers for Medicare and Medicaid Services (CMS) value-based payment models have failed to meaningfully reduce health care expenditures or improve quality of care. Value-based payment models implemented over the past decade have often been regressive, moving dollars away from patients, providers and communities with fewer resources and toward those with more."[46]

The new models of capitation, pay-for-performance and risk-sharing are most concerned with what is best for the insurer. While they theoretically would increase quality and reduce cost, they create immense bureaucracy to try to get there, while the evidence suggests they fall short, even compared to the old model of paying primary care doctors for their services to patients.

---

[1] Cassell, 32-33

[2] Gail R. Wilensky, "Reforming Medicare's Physician Payment System," *NEJM*, 2009; 360:654

[3] Steven A. Schroeder, William Frist for the National Commission on Physician Payment Reform, "Phasing out Fee-For-Service Payment," *NEJM*, May 23, 2013; 368(21):2029

[4] Schroeder, 2031

[5] Laura Tollen, Elizabeth Keating, "Covid-19, Market Consolidation, And Price Growth," *Health* Affairs, August 3, 2020.doi:10.1377/forefront.20200728.592180

[6] Zack Cooper, Stuart Craig, Martin Gaynor, Nir J. Harish, Harlan M. Krumholz, John Van Reenen, "Hospital Prices Grew Substantially Faster than Physician Prices For Hospital-Based Care in 2007-14," *Health Affairs*, February 2019; 38(2): 184

[7] Michael K. Gusmano, Miriam Laugesen, Victor G. Rodwin, Lawrence D. Brown, "Getting the Price Right: How Some Countries Control Spending in a Fee-For-Service System," *Health Affairs*, November 2020; 39(11): 1867-1874

[8] Gusmano, 1872

[9] Martin, 109-1020

[10] John E. Kralewski, Terence D. Wingert, David J. Knutson, Christopher E. Johnson, "The Effects of Medical Group Practice Organizational Factors on Physician Use of Resources," *Journal of Healthcare Management*, May/June 1999; 44(3): 177

[11] Larson, 73

[12] Dana Gelb Safran and others, "Organizational and Financial Characteristics of Health Plans: Are They Related to Primary Care Performance," *Arch Int Med*; January 10, 2000; 16): 73

[13] Starr, 446

[14] Ezekiel J. Emanuel, Farzad Mostashari, Amol S. Navathe, "Designing a Successful Primary Care Capitation Model," *JAMA*, May 21, 2021:E2

[15] *Wall Street Journal*, May 2003; http://online.wsj.com/article/SB10539733189909600.html

[16] Wadhera, 1615

[17] MacLean, 1757

[18] Arnold M. Epstein, "Pay for Performance at the Tipping Point," *NEJM*, 356(6):516

[19] Meredith B. Rosenthal, Richard G. Frank, "What is the Empirical Basis for Paying for Quality in Health Care," Medical *Care Research and Review*, April 2006; 63(2): 135

[20] Hoangmai H. Pham, Deborah Schrag, Ann S. O'Malley, Beny Wu, Peter S. Bach, "Care Patterns in Medicare and Their Implications for Pay for Performance," *NEJM*, March 15, 2007: 356(11):1131

[21] Pham, Care Patterns,1130

[22] Joshua M. Liao, Amol S. Navathe, "Does the Merit-Based Incentive Payment System Disproportionately Affect Safety-Net Practices," *JAMA Health Forum*, 2020:1(5)e200452.doi.10.1001/jamahealthforum.2020.0452

[23] Frakt, 291

[24] Frakt, 291

[25] Liao, Merit Based, 1

[26] Diane Meier, "Private Equity and Healthcare Delivery," *JAMA*, December 28, 2021; 326(24): 2533

[27] Jacob Wallace, J. McMichael Williams, Anthony Loll, Janet Eaton, Chima D. Ndumele, "Residual Confounding in Health Plan Performance Assessments: Evidence from Randomization in Medicaid," *Ann Int Med*, January 4, 2022; 1

[28] Aaron L. Schwartz, Rachel M. Werner, "The Imperfect Science of Evaluating Performance: How Bad and Who Cares?," *Ann Int Med*, January 4, 2022: doi:10.7326/M@!-4665

[29] Laura A. Petersen, LeChauncy D. Woodard, Tracy Urech, Christina Daw, Supicha Sookanan, "Does Pay for Performance Improve the Quality of Health Care," *Ann Int Med*, August 15, 2006; 145(4): 269

[30] Petersen, 269

[31] David S. Burstein, David T. Liss, Jeffrey A. Linder, "Association of Primary Care Physician Compensation Incentives and Quality of Care in the United States," *JGIM*, 2021: 37(2): 364

[32] Amol S. Navathe, Claire T. Dinh, Anders Chen, Joshua M. Liao, "Findings and Implications from MIPS Year One Performance Data," Health *Affairs Blog*, January 18, 2019, 10.1377/HBLOG20190117.305369

[33] Kenton J. Johnston, Timothy L. Wiemken, Jason M. Hockenberry, Jose F. Figueroa, Karen E. Joynt Maddox, "Association of Clinician Health System Affiliation with Outpatient Performance Ratings in the Medicare Merit-Based Incentive Payment System," *JAMA*, 2020; 324(10): 984

[34] Johua M. Liao, Risa J. Lavizzo-Mourey, Amol S. Navathe, "A National Goal to Advance Health Equity Through Value-Based Payment," *JAMA*, June 22/29, 2021; 325(4): 2439

[35] DeCamp, 845

[36] Dhruv Khullar, Amelia M. Bond, Eloise May O'Donnell, Yuting Qian, David N. Gans, Lawrence P. Casalino, "Time and Financial Cost for Physician Practices to Participate in the Medicare Merit-Based incentive Payment System: A Qualitative Study," *JAMA* Health *Forum*, 2021;2(5):e210527.doi.10.1001/jamahealth forum.20210527, 1

[37] Khullar, Time and Cost, 2

[38] Khullar, Time and Cost, 8

[39] Khullar, Time and Cost, 2

[40] Lawrence P. Casalino, Dhruv Khullar," Value Based Purchasing and Physician Professionalism,' *JAMA*, November 2,2019; 322(17): 1648

[41] Francis J. Crosson, Kate Bloniarz, David Glass, James Matthews, "MedPAC's Urgent Recommendation: Eliminate MIPS, Take a Different Direction," *Health Affairs Blog*, March 16, 2018, 10.1377//HBLOG20180309.302220

[42] Crosson, 4

[43] Centers for Medicare and Medicaid Services, "Comprehensive Primary Care Initiative," https://innovation.cms.gov/innovation-models/comprehensive-primary-care-initiative

[44] Casalino, Value-Based Purchasing 1648

[45] Kenton J. Johnston, Jason M. Hockenberry, Karen E. Joynt Maddox, "Building a Better Clinician Value-Based Payment Program," *JAMA*, January 12, 2021; 325(2): 129

[46] Suhas Gondi, Karen Joynt Maddox, Rishi K. Wadhera, "Reaching for Equity-Moving form Regressive to Progressive Value-Based Payment", *NEJM*, July 14, 2022; 387(2): 97, 99

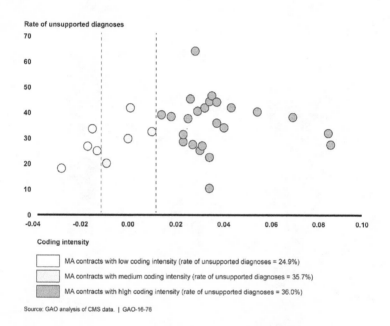

Rate of unsupported diagnoses

Coding intensity

MA contracts with low coding intensity (rate of unsupported diagnoses = 24.9%)
MA contracts with medium coding intensity (rate of unsupported diagnoses = 35.7%)
MA contracts with high coding intensity (rate of unsupported diagnoses = 36.0%)

Source: GAO analysis of CMS data. | GAO-16-76

Medicare Advantage Plans, Rates of Billing without documentation
of the diagnosis.

(Courtesy, Wiki Commons)

CHAPTER 15
Severity Adjustment and the Gaming of Medicare

Medicare is run by the Center for Medicare and Medicaid Services, known as CMS. It is part of the Federal government's Department of Health and Human Services. Although it was originally a publicly managed program, it now is divided into the public program, so-called traditional Medicare, and Medicare Advantage, which are privately owned plans required to offer the benefits of traditional Medicare.

As of the fall of 2021, 42% of Medicare patients were enrolled in Medicare Advantage plans, with some experts predicting that the Medicare Advantage plans will have a majority of patients by 2030.[1]

Payments to Medicare Advantage plans are higher than that of traditional Medicare as, "a reward for higher quality."[2] As we have discussed earlier, measurements of quality are often questionable

Payments from CMS to the Medicare Advantage plans are on a capitated basis, i.e., CMS gives the plans a set amount of dollars for every patient enrolled. Under such a scheme, companies make more money if they have fewer sick and hence costly patients. Plans figured out clever ways to attract healthier older patients, such as by offering free gym memberships to enrollees. Naturally, patients who were too sick to use the gym would be less likely to join that Medicare Advantage Plan.

The folks at CMS did not want doctors or insurers to shun sicker Medicare patients. Therefore, they produced a formula to adjust the risk for patients. Each private Medicare Advantage Plan gets a set amount of money per Medicare beneficiary enrolled in that plan. CMS now put into effect a plan to adjust this money based on the severity of that patient's condition. To do that, they created "highly complex conditions (also called Hierarchical Condition Categories) (HCC)," a group of diagnoses that tended to predict whether a patient would cost more. Each HCC code was given a certain weight in terms of adjusting the money given for that patient. For example, patients with diabetic nephropathy, kidney disease secondary to diabetes mellitus, carried an adjustment factor of over 2. In other words, the Med Advantage Plan would get over double the money if they reported to CMS that the patient had diabetic nephropathy.

It is not hard to understand what happened next. The Medicare Advantage plans had a huge financial incentive to report any HCC diagnosis that their patients carried. Indeed, documenting these codes became as important or more to them than their other quality indicators. Physicians who were diligent in reporting every HCC code were financially rewarded. Since for Medicare, the code didn't carry over from year to year, they needed to be reported in the physician diagnoses every year to keep the waterfall of extra revenue coming.

The insurers didn't want to rely just on the physician diagnosing and reporting these conditions. The extra money paid for the HCC codes was so great that it paid for the Med Advantage insurance companies to hire nurse practitioners (NP) and physician assistants (PA) to make home visits to patients for "checkups." Many patients were puzzled when these NPs and PAs called, saying they wanted to visit. Others were pleased that their insurer cared so much about them. In reality, the insurer cared about having the NP or PA document as many HCC conditions as possible in order to get more money from Medicare.

On March 29, 2021, I received a letter from HouseCalls, an organization hired by one of the Med Advantage plans that, "one of our HouseCalls advance practice clinicians met with T----, who is your patient...in their home on 3/19/21. During their visit, the clinician completed a physical exam...You can see what was done at the visit and what we learned, including any diagnoses made."[3] The reason for the visit is clear in the last seven words, "what we learned, including any diagnoses made."

What do primary care physicians think about this? Speaking for myself, I am irritated that the insurer is paying someone else for a house call on my patient rather than trying to promote primary care or continuity. I think it is duplicitous to claim that any of this is for the patient's benefit. It is to make sure that all HCC codes are reported to maximize the amount Medicare would pay that Med Advantage plan.

Yet we knew we had to play the game too to stay in business. Our doctors would not make up HCC conditions that patients didn't have, but they did make an effort to report true HCC diagnoses. At our monthly staff meetings, doctors complain that none of this does anything to actually help patients. No one rebuts them for there is no rebuttal.

Yet the insurers have gone further. After the patient has had one of these home visits, we have had patients be told by their insurer that they don't need to see their regular physician for a checkup. Fortunately, most patients ignore this advice.

Primary care physicians (or other doctors for that matter) did not go to medical school to become coding experts. For this coding is a specifically American process. As far as I know, the list of codes (called DRGs, or diagnosis-related groups) and HCC (the highly complex conditions) are not used outside of the United States. Blood and muscles are integral to medicine; DRGs and HCCs are not. This is yet another burden that fills the primary care doctor with dismay.

I should mention that while insurers are gratified if

specialists list HCCs, they do not depend on them to do so. This is a task for the PCP.

Many Med Advantage plans rate physicians on what percentage of last year's HCC codes they put in their visit notes and pay more if PCPs capture all of the prior HCC codes. For capturing more codes means more money paid for this patient's care from Medicare to the patient's Med Advantage plan.

None of what is being done is illegal. The insurers hopefully are not trying to get codes reported that do not exist. The question is how the system makes coding the most essential element in a patient's care.

Naturally, the HCC system is much more complex than I just described. Different HCCs interact differently with each other, some adding to the weight of the other while others do not. Thus, if two HCCs in the same hierarchical category are noted, only the highest weighted HCC in that category is counted.[4]

It is worth considering how much effort, personnel and spending goes into these calculations each year by CMS, as well as all the effort, personnel and cost put out both by physician offices and insurance companies to create the risk scores for each Medicare patient each year. None of this is caring for the patient. It all just has to do with all the money being divided up.

I also want to mention that none of this existed when Medicare was started and before private Med Advantage plans were created. Physicians were paid fee-for-service when they saw a patient. They would list the diagnoses dealt with at the visit, but they were not expected to game the system to generate more money. If there was more cost from patient visits, at least it was in actual patient care, rather than the administrative complexity and costs of the current system.

Of course, not trying to adjust for severity creates a major issue when the idea is that doctors and or clinics are paid depending on the costs their patients generate. Under a capitated system, doctors receive a set fee per patient based on the average costs of patients overall. However, having sicker patients mean that the doctor will be providing more services, thus reducing the average fee per patient. For example, a patient with diabetes is likely to need multiple visits in a year, while a healthy patient might have one. The doctor is paid the same fixed cost in either case.

The situation is worse for the pay-for-performance plans where the doctor is judged both on "quality" and "cost" for her patients. Sicker patients mean more quality measures that have to be met. Sicker patients are also the most costly. Pay-for-performance turns out to disadvantage the safety net clinics and anyone else who cares more for the poor and the sick.

For the last two to three decades, these alternative payment schemes have led to cherry-picking by both insurers and sometimes, sad to say, by doctors. This can take the form of not taking certain types of patients. Other times doctors act such that the more complex patients vote with their feet to move to better arrangements. I have had multiple patients who changed to establish care with me because their prior doctor was not interested in their mental health issues or sympathetic to their chronic pain or decided to discharge them when they wouldn't or couldn't follow his advice to stop smoking or lose weight.

For all the cries that fee-for-service led to doctor corruption by overuse, as was seen in prior chapters, primary care visits then and now made up a tiny fraction of the overall cost of healthcare. Is it really worse for the PCP to have more visits when the patient is sick or with mental health or substance abuse issues? How does this compare to a system that either encourages doctors and insurers to shun sick patients or to focus more on the documentation of their serious illness than their management? Which system is really more corrupt?

---

[1] Gail Wilensky, "The Future of Medicare Advantage," *JAMA Health Forum*, May 5, 2022; 2022:3(5): e221684.doi.10.1001/jamahealthforum.2022.1684

[2] Wilensky, Future

[3] Gottlieb, March 29, 2021, 1

[4] Janet Franklin, "The ABCs of HHS-HCCs: Taking a Closer Look at the Commercial Risk Adjustment," *Journal AHIMA*, October, 2014; 86(10): 76

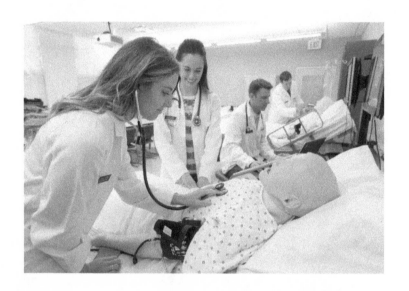

Physician Assistant Program at ODU.

(Courtesy, Wiki Commons)

CHAPTER 16
The Advent of the Physician Substitutes

Shortage of primary care physicians is not new. Nurse practitioner (NP) and physician assistant (PA) programs began in the 1960s, driven by PCP shortages in underserved areas as well as the increased funding from the formation of Medicare and Medicaid.[1] Another factor in the start of the physician assistant program was, "the desire to make good use of experienced hospital corpsman and combat medics returning from Vietnam."[2]

Physician assistants work under physician supervision, with the physician ultimately having some liability for their actions. Physician assistants go through specific training programs and are traditionally regulated by states' medical practice acts. The scope of what PAs could do varied tremendously between different states.[3] Recently there has been a push to rename them "physician associates."

Nurse practitioners start by being trained as registered nurses (RN), for which there were different training programs ranging from two to four years. Nurse practitioners are one of several categories of advanced practice nurses. They have an estimated average of 500 hours of clinical training and are certified in a specialty area of practice, such as primary care or mental health. They can practice independently with their scope of practice being governed under the nurse practice acts of each state.[4]

The expansion of nurse practitioners really began in the

1990s. In 1992 there were an estimated 48,000 nurse practitioners nationally.[5] Sandy and Schroeder commented, "Managed care promoted the growth of nurse practitioner and physician assistant programs, both to enhance the productivity of physician practices and to offer a more cost-effective form of primary care itself."[6] The number of NPs/PAs doubled from 1992 to 1997.[7]

By 2006 there were over 200,000 NPs/PAs in the United States. They spread out from doing primary care to specialization. The growth of both NPs and PAs was significantly faster than the growth in the number of physicians over the two decades before 2006.[8]

By 2006 some 11.5% of practices and 16.5% of physicians were working with nurse practitioners and physician assistants, known as mid-levels, in the practice.[9] There are differences between physician assistants and nurse practitioners, although in the real world they are often used interchangeably.

Our practice has long had nurse practitioners working as part of our group. Our mental health nurse practitioner both offered therapy and prescribed meds. Our women's health nurse practitioner did everything from routine PAPs to management of different gynecologic issues. For many years we had an adult nurse practitioner who both covered in the office for doctors for acute issues such as urinary tract infections or bronchitis, and had her own practice of patients. All three were excellent clinicians. However, they did not feel that they were the equal, in terms of clinical knowledge, of our psychiatrists, or a gynecologist or an internal medicine physician. For more complex issues, they would refer patients to the appropriate physician.

The issue is not whether nurse practitioners or physician assistants can offer good clinical care, for they clearly can in many situations. The problem is when health care systems view them as interchangeable with physicians, except for being less expensive. From feedback from those who have worked in our local county health department, nurse practitioners and physician assistants are often viewed in this way. Hospitals that hire nurse practitioners as hospitalists to take care of complex, very ill patients certainly are implying that they are comparable enough to hospitalist physicians to substitute a number of them for the higher-priced physicians.

The last two decades have seen the increasing use of nurse practitioners and physician assistants taking the place of doctors. A patient referred to one of the surgical specialties usually will have initial or follow-up visits with a physician assistant (PA). Since surgeons make their income largely through procedures, they can maximize income by doing more procedures while having physician assistants or nurse practitioners do, in many cases, the office consult and, even more often, post-surgical visits. The same rationale applies to procedure-heavy medicine specialties such as Cardiology. This morning I received a discharge summary on my patient who had received a hip replacement. It was by the PA of course.

Very often, patients assume that the nurse practitioner or physician assistant they have seen are physicians. Many patients have reported that some have actually introduced themselves as doctors. Other times patients report that the cardiologist or endocrinologist suggested so and so treatment, never realizing that the advice was coming from a nurse practitioner or physician assistant. Recently a patient told me of several visits with an orthopedist, including two cortisol injections in her shoulder that proved ineffective, followed by a referral to physical therapy. All of these were done by a physician assistant. She never saw the orthopedist. When they learn the truth, patients are often very upset.

For primary care physicians, the situation is often frustrating and frankly insulting. I manage heart disease of many types in large numbers of patients. When I finally get to the point when I think the patient needs more of a specialist given the complexity of their disease, I want them seen by the cardiologist, not a physician assistant. While there may be cases when the physician assistant knows more about a narrow specialty, this is not always the case.

For example, I have managed perhaps ten thousand patients with congestive heart failure (CHF) over my years in practice. This level of experience is not matched by a Cardiology PA a year or two out of school.

These situations, which happen increasingly as specialists add mid-levels to maximize their income, is discouraging to primary care physicians. I am sure that many PCPs ask why they spent years in training only to be presumed less able to manage patients than the physician assistants in the specialist offices.

The irony is that the void is at least in part the fault of organized medicine. As described in Chapter 4, graduating 3000 American doctors a year who are unable to practice because they cannot find a residency position is the first part of this.

The scorning of general practitioners by residency programs who feel they are inadequately trained is the second component of this problem. For a general practitioner would have over twice the clinical experience of a physician assistant and three to four times that of a nurse practitioner when each started to practice.

Finally, the closure of so many medical schools following the Flexner report created a shortage of doctors willing to practice in many locations.

The absence of general practitioners who would deliver primary care, besides contributing to the physician shortage in small towns and poorer neighborhoods of the cities, meant that care would devolve on non-physicians.

In replacing PCPs with NPs and PAs, the assumption made is that primary care is simple basic care. Instead, primary care may be the most complex of any part of medicine, for the doctor cannot just limit themselves to one system, one disease, but must look at and understand the whole patient.

At the primary care level, nurse practitioners and physician assistants are often suggested as alternatives due to the shortage of primary care physicians. This is all well and good and may fill gaps admirably in the short run. The powers that be, all the same, need to stop and ask why there are not enough primary care doctors.

---

[1] Hoff, 13

[2] Donaldson, 162

[3] Donaldson, 163

[4] Donaldson,159

[5] Donaldson, 159

[6] Sandy, 263

[7] Sandy, 263

[8] Dill, 65

[9] United States Department of Health and Human Services, "Characteristics of Office Based Physicians and Their Practices: United States 2005-2006," Vital and Health Statistics, Series 13, Number 166, April 2008, 13

Free standing "Doc in the Box" Urgent Care.

(Courtesy, Wiki Commons)

CHAPTER 17

Skimming the Fat: Urgent Care and Pharmacy Clinics

Of course, not everyone has a primary care physician. Many patients wait until they are sick and then go to the Emergency Room (ER). Historically, this has been especially true for uninsured patients or for patients on Medicaid who may not have been able to find a doctor who was willing to take them on, given the lower reimbursement.

Emergency room care involves long wait times and high expense for both patient and their insurer. To address this, many hospitals created "urgent care" as a part of their emergency rooms. Patients who were less sick would be seen in the urgent care side of the ER, often by a so-called mid-level, a nurse practitioner or physician assistant who were cheaper for the hospital than the emergency room physicians.

Another approach to reducing ER usage and cost was the promotion of the "medical home" model. Under this, primary care doctors would assume increased responsibility for managing their patients, including providing extended hours beyond what was customary. This often included weekend, early morning or evening hours.

For insurances having primary doctors see the patient was cheaper than having them go to the emergency room. Insurances now began requiring primary care physicians to be part of a "medical home" in order to get contracts with that insurer. Of course, any new innovations in health care require extensive legal paperwork. Medical homes now have to be certified either by a state or national medical home credentialing entity and recertified on a regular basis.

The paperwork required to become a "medical home" was substantial, thus adding to the administrative burdens of the primary care doctor. It was particularly onerous as yet another administrative hurdle for solo or small practices, and may have been another factor in the closure of so many.

Nevertheless, while the medical home approach tried to address keeping a doctor's existing patients out of the emergency room, it did nothing for patients who lacked a regular doctor. A reasonable percentage of these were young, healthy adults. Many of them lacked health insurance or opted for a high deductible plan that meant seeing a doctor was very expensive.

Cassell pointed out that the view that first-contact care can be done well by anyone is simplistic, writing, "It requires clinical skill to diagnose at an early stage, and the correct diagnosis often makes an important difference in the outcome of illness."[1] We have seen that patients who have primary care doctors do better.

Nevertheless, at this point, many entrepreneurs and companies saw an opportunity to make money, so they took a different approach. They created free-standing urgent care/retail clinics with limited staff, where the care was usually provided by a mid-level. In many of them, patients had to pay cash. In exchange, patients received quick, convenient service for minor illnesses.

These urgent care clinics expanded rapidly over the last forty years. From only fifty nationwide in 1987, the number quadrupled in just three years.[2] They are aptly summed up as, "fast food concept applied to medicine."[3]

Hoff explained, "Convenience, speed and price are the main reasons retail clinics gained popularity over the past few years...they seek to carve out a market niche for common acute illnesses, health promotion activities such as physicals and screening, basic laboratory testing and immunizations...they provide flexible hours of operation including evenings and weekends, do not require appointments and are intended to move the patient through the visit in a short time period."[4]

Analysis showed that these clinics were most appealing to young adult patients, patients without a regular source of care and patients without insurance, but with an ability to pay cash for care.

The urgent care and retail clinics are only interested in those able to pay. There is no great rush, indeed no desire at all, to provide after-hours or more convenient care to the indigent, or at least those without insurance.

Subsequent years saw everyone from hospitals to venture capital to physicians to pharmacies starting these urgent care clinics, which usually generated large profits for their owners. Retail clinic visits increased fourfold from 2007 to 2009, reaching six million annual visits.[5] The number of retail clinics was almost 2000 in 2016.[6] By 2018 there were over 10,000 clinics representing a $15 billion dollar industry.

A decade ago, Barken predicted this, writing, "How will the other half receive health care? Again, in the absence of a public policy that encourages physicians to take up primary care, entrepreneurship in retail and the economics of creative destruction will find a new way...the niche product...is the immediate and affordable treatment of an array of acute, self-limited illnesses...this is a consumer-driven model of care for acute illness, more like putting out the occasional small fire than sustaining a conventional, comprehensive and continuous relationship between a patient and a provider of health care."[7]

Primary care doctor offices, like emergency rooms, have a lot of fixed costs that add to the cost of care. These include everything from billers to referral specialists to nurses. This allows primary care doctors to be able to care for complex, ill patients.

These new retail clinics, which included some operated by

hospitals, did not have all these costs. By asking for cash and, in many cases, not asking if patients have insurance, these clinics could offer cheaper care to the least complicated, best-paying patients. The result has been to undercut the financial position and ability to practice of the primary care physicians.

Even as these urgent care clinics expanded to take patients with Medicare and even Medicaid, their operating costs were still less than that of PCPs.

In a doctor's schedule, the hope is that there will be some uncomplicated patients who will take up less than the time scheduled for the appointment. This allows doctors to take care of ill patients who take more time than they are listed for. For example, seeing a patient for a urinary tract infection might take only ten of the allotted twenty minutes. In contrast, a diabetic patient with heart failure and kidney disease will certainly take more than the twenty minutes for which they are booked. A *New England Journal of Medicine* commentary explained, "The current reimbursement system renders simple acute health problems high margin work that can offset losses from treating more complex problems."[8]

By taking away all the simple care, the retail clinic makes it that much harder for primary care practices to survive financially. McHarris observed, "If they skim off the simplest patient problems and we care for all the complex patients who have twenty things wrong, it makes it that much harder to stay afloat."[9]

For health care as a whole, having the first point of contact of a patient for a new condition be an urgent care will result in increased costs. Substantial evidence demonstrates that, "first contact with a primary care physician is associated with more appropriate, more effective and less costly care."[10] A study using insurance company data refuted the conventional wisdom that retail clinics offered a cheaper alternative that would lower the costs of health care. Rather than replacing more expensive visits in ERs or with PCPs, 58% of retail clinic visits for low acuity conditions, such as colds or back pain, were added utilization of the health care system; the overall annual costs were higher for patients who used retail clinics.[11] Spending on low acuity problems increased by 21% overall when patients used retail clinics. When care for minor problems is cheaper, it makes sense that people would use such care more; hence overall health care costs would increase.

In addition, many patients are transferred from urgent care clinics to emergency rooms. One analysis showed that 35.9% of these transfers were unnecessary, while 64.2% were discharged from the emergency room.[12] These unnecessary transfers add to total health care costs. Moreover, studies of retail clinics show that they do not reduce low acuity emergency room visits.[13]

Recent evidence confirmed that urgent care centers raise overall health care costs. Wang et al. found that thirty-seven additional urgent care center visits were associated with a reduction of a single low acuity emergency room visit. Therefore even though the single emergency room visit cost about ten times as much as the urgent care visits, the combined annual cost of emergency room and urgent care visits for patients on average rose 45% from 2010 to 2019.[14] Clearly urgent care clinics raise, rather than reduce, overall health care costs.

The retail clinics also aim to satisfy the client. Thus, it is not surprising that a 2014 study showed overuse of antibiotics for viral upper respiratory infections is greatest at retail and urgent care clinics. Antibiotics were prescribed at 39% of urgent care visits, 36.4% of retail clinic visits, 1.8 % of ER visits and 7.1% of traditional physician office visits.[15] Further analysis suggested that inappropriate prescriptions for colds occurred in 17% of retail clinic visits and 16% of urgent care visits compared to 6% of medical office visits. While the 450,000 retail and urgent care visits that year were dwarfed by over nine million medical office visits, the retail and urgent care visits accounted for 40% of the outpatient antibiotics prescribed.[16]

Indeed, another analysis showed that 54% of visits to retail and urgent care clinics were for respiratory infections. In a commentary titled "The Fast and the Spurious," the authors commented, "Lowering barriers for an office visit to such a degree may prompt visits for mild self-resolving illnesses that would be better treated with rest and symptom management at home."[17]They concluded, "We all pay – in increased insurance premiums and increased antibiotic resistance – from the overprescribing of antibiotics for upper respiratory infections."[18]

A study reported the top ten reasons patients are seen in retail/urgent care. Of these, six of the top seven, such as sinusitis or bronchitis, are most often viral, where patients are better off not receiving antibiotics or other treatment.[19]

The antibiotic overprescribing seen in retail clinics supports concerns, "that nurses who staff clinics in drug stores will be encouraged to prescribe antibiotics and other medications. Drug stores may be willing to subsidize the operation of these clinics to capture the income from the sale of pharmaceuticals."[20] Perhaps the pharmacy chains are innocent of such machinations, and the increased prescribing of antibiotics is coincidental. Nevertheless, the evidence suggests otherwise.

Visits to retail clinics decrease continuity of care. A study of over 127,000 patients from 2007 to 2009 showed that each retail clinic visit resulted in decreased subsequent visits with their PCP and significantly reduced continuity of care. The authors observed, "Each retail clinic visit could represent one fewer visit to a PCP, one fewer opportunity to build a primary care relationship."[21]

Another study in Minnesota similarly concluded that, "Continuity of care was lower for patients who used retail clinics than for patients who did not use retail clinics,"[22] A 2015 analysis from Houston among Medicare patients showed that patients who had retail clinic visits had a lower likelihood of seeing their PCP and lower continuity of care.[23]

Decreased continuity is associated with worse outcomes; conversely, having more visits along with a health maintenance visit with a PCP is associated with increased preventive care.[24] Continuity of care among the elderly is associated with fewer hospital/ER visits and lower overall health care costs.[25]

On the other end of the age spectrum, pediatricians are also unhappy with the retail clinics. Most believed that they disrupted continuity of care, while only 15% reported being notified by the retail clinic within twenty-four hours of the visits. A large number of the pediatricians concluded that the retail clinics provided suboptimal care.[26]

Such concerns were outweighed by the profits generated by operating urgent care and retail care. The biggest entities opening new retail clinics are the large pharmacy chains, particularly CVS and Walgreens. A 2013 study reported that two-thirds of these clinics were owned by pharmacy chains, 18% by hospitals and 12% by private investors.[27] For the giant pharmacy corporations, any clinic losses would be offset by the benefits of, "New prescription customers, active store foot traffic and brand differentiations."[28] However, while such in-store clinics may boost profits for CVS or Walgreens, they decrease continuity of care as patients are not seeing their PCP for care.

It is ludicrous to imagine that these pharmacy chains had anything in mind other than making more money. The issue came up during the ongoing effort to have pharmacies administer the Covid vaccine. Politico reported, "CVS Chief Officer Jon Roberts discussed the company's 'opportunity with vaccines,' to convert newcomers into long-term customers, starting with the 15-minute period patients are supposed to wait in the store after receiving a Covid shot. During the observation period, he said, store employees could try to sell patients on the company Minute Clinics for regular health care visits."[29]

Few of the free-standing or pharmacy clinics waste time or money informing the primary care doctor about their patient's visit. It is left to the PCP to contact these entities to try to find out what happened. The situation is better in closed systems such as Kaiser or other large health entities, but communications to the PCPs were still poor. A Kaiser doctor observed, "We didn't know patients were in urgent care unless we were looking in the chart."[30]

Hoff argued that the growth of these clinics may, "contribute to the shifting perception of generalist medicine within our society from a relationship-oriented brand of total care to a transaction-oriented series of compartmentalized visits."[31]

While urgent care clinics operated by hospitals are usually willing to see Medicare or Medicaid patients, this is not true for many of the free-standing urgent cares. The hospitals try to benefit by getting the patient to affiliate with them for further care, even if they have an existing doctor. We often have patients come in saying how the urgent care suggested that they change PCPs to someone within that hospital's employ.

A new aspect is the push by some retail clinics into limited management of chronic conditions. In 2013 Walgreens announced that their stores would begin "chronic care management, assessment and treatment" for conditions such as high blood pressure, elevated cholesterol and diabetes.[32]

In 2014 Walmart opened its own nurse practitioner staffed clinics, "to offer services expected from a primary care provider with referrals to specialists as needed. Services include wellness and preventive care such as check-ups and physicals and treatment of common conditions like high blood pressure and high cholesterol, along with basic acute care."[33] Walmart employees would only have to pay a $4 co-pay, with other customers paying a $40 co-pay. Here the corporation is again trying to carve away the healthier patients, leaving those with multiple chronic conditions or mental health issues for PCPs.

It is these patients with multiple issues, disproportionately the poor and the elderly, who will suffer the most when their PCP is forced out of business.

Insurers have added to the growth of retail clinics by adding them to their provider networks. Some even waived co-pays for these services while others marketed them to their members.[34] The studies noted earlier suggest that this will raise rather than lower overall health care costs.

Observers saw this expansion as further damaging to primary care. Jeffrey Cain, vice president of the American Academy of Family Physicians, commented, "Our healthcare system is already fragmented, and our concern is that the expansion of retail clinics into chronic care will lower quality, increase costs and pose a risk to patients' long-term health outcomes."[35]

For even if a chain of retail clinics proposed to treat a few chronic conditions, with physician substitutes following clinical guidelines, they were not offering comprehensive coverage for all of the patients' chronic diseases. This is different from primary care, which focuses on all of the problems a patient might bring in, thus requiring a broader level of expertise than that being proposed by the retail clinics. Nevertheless, these additional offered services increase the damage to primary care. Dr. Ateev Mehrotra, a professor at the University of Pittsburgh School of Medicine, noted, "Primary care providers risk a slow but steady decline in their scope of care if they do not offer a viable alternative to these new convenient care options."[36]

The issue of after-hours care is a real one. Yet destroying continuity and skimming off the easiest patients will harm primary care.

The implications for primary care practices and the overall health care system are not a concern for the entrepreneurs or pharmacy chains who create Urgent Care or mini-clinics. These entities are happy to leave the PCP with a disproportionate number of elderly, sick or dysfunctional patients whose Medicare or Medicaid insurance pays the least of any insurance. The retail mini-clinics are not interested in these patients. As Barken wrote, "The fast-food model of service meets its nemesis when it greets its first customer who is eighty-nine, has a litany of medical complaints, lacks adequate social support and had more than a touch of forgetfulness."[37] The CVS of the world are not interested in attracting these patients to their in-store clinics. The consequence that many primary care physicians cannot survive just caring for these sick elderly patients is not the urgent cares' problem.

Of course, for the wealthiest patients, there is another alternative. Recent years have seen a burgeoning of concierge practices. There the doctor sees only a small population comprised of those willing to pay premium monthly retainers in order to have the attention and availability of their PCP. The wealthy will always have options.

Is this just another nail in the coffin of primary care for the ordinary person? It may or may not be. It is worth consideration for those who wrestle with how to improve health care in the United States. There is nothing that says that primary care doctors will always be there.

Cassell, 38

[2] Starr, 439

[3] Eleanor Siegel, "Emergence of Emergicenters," *Boston Globe,* June 8, 1981

[4] Hoff, 14

[5] "AAFP Fires Back at the 'Convenience Care Revolution' Begun by Retailers," *Medical Economics,* June 25, 2013, 14

[6] J. Scott Ashwood, Martin Gaynor, Claude M. Setodji, Rachel O. Reid, Ellerie Weber, Ateev Mehrotra, "Retail Clinic Visits for Low-Acuity Conditions Increase Utilization and Spending," *Health Affairs,* 2016; 35(3):449

[7] Barken, 201

[8] John K. Iglehart, "The Expansion of Retail Clinics – Corporate Titans vs. Organized Medicine," *NEJM*, July 23, 2015; 373(4): 302

[9] McHarris

[10] Starfield, Contribution of Primary Care, 483

[11] Ashwood, 449

[12] Tony Zitek, Ignasia Tanone, Alexzza Ramos, Karina Frama, Ahmed S. Ali, "Most Transfers from Urgent Care Centers to Emergency Departments are Discharged and Many are Unnecessary," *Journal Emergency Medicine*, 54(6): 882

[13] Zitek, 886

[14] Bill Wang, Ateev Mehrotra, Ari B. Friedman, "Urgent Care Centers Deter some Emergency Department Visits But, on Net, Increase Spending," *Health Affairs*, April 2021; 40(4): 592

[15] Danielle L. Palms and others, "Comparison of Antibiotic Prescribing in Retail Clinics, Urgent Care Centers, Emergency Departments and Traditional Ambulatory Care Settings in the United States," *JAMA Internal Medicine*, September 2018; 178(9): 1267

[16] Palms, 1267

[17] Michael A. Incze, Rita F. Redberg, Mitchell H. Katz, "Over prescription in Urgent Care Clinics – The Fast and the Spurious," *JAMA Internal Medicine*, September 2018; 178(9): 1269

[18] Incze, 1270

[19] Amer Kaissi, Tom Charland, "The Evolution of Retail Clinics in the United States 2006-2012," *Health Care Manager*, 2013;32(4):337

[20] Berman, 1124

[21] Rachel O. Reid, J. Scott Ashwood, Mark W. Friedberg, Ellerie S. Weber, Claude M. Setodji, Ateev Mehrotra, "Retail Clinic Visits and Receipt of Primary Care," *JGIM*, 2012;28(4): 504

[22] James E. Rohrer, Kurt B. Angstman, Gregory M. Garrison, Julie A. Maxson, Joseph W. Furst, "Family Medicine Patients Who Use Retail Clinics Have Lower Continuity of Care," *Journal Primary Care and Community Health*, 2013:4(2): 150

---

[23] N. Ogechi Abara, Nicole Huang, Mukaila A. Raji, Yong-Fang Kuo, "Effect of Retail Clinic Use on Continuity of Care among Medicare Beneficiaries," *J Am Board Fam Med*, 2019; 32: 531

[24] Rohrer, 152

[25] Abara, 532

[26] Jane M. Garbutt and others, "Pediatric Providers' Attitudes Toward Retail Clinics," J Pediatr, 2013; 163: 1384

[27] Kaissi, 340

[28] Kaissi, 340

[29] Mohana Ravindranath, Susannah Luthi, "Pharmacies Score Customer Data in Vaccine effort. Some are Crying Foul," *Politico*, April 3, 2021

[30] Anonymous, Interview with Gregg Coodley, June 21, 2021

[31] Hoff, 16

[32] "AAFP Fires Back," 14

[33] Inglehart, 301

[34] Ashwood, 454

[35] "AAFP Fires Back," 14

[36] "AAFP Fires Back," 14

[37] Barken, 202

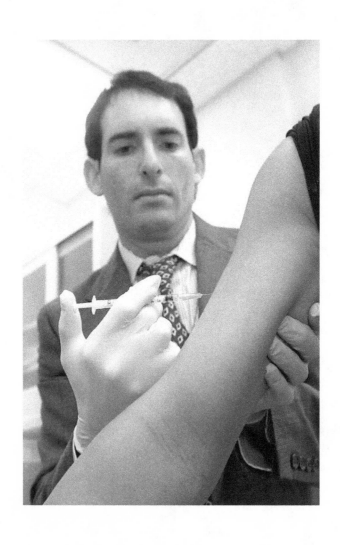

American Physician Giving Vaccination.

(Courtesy, Wiki Commons)

CHAPTER 18
Losing Vaccines

The second half of the twentieth century saw the advent of a host of new, extremely effective vaccines, such as for measles, mumps, Hepatitis A and B and others. Vaccinations became an important part of what doctors did, especially pediatricians. Children would receive a series of vaccinations from their pediatrician or family physician. For adults, there were fewer, but still an important series of vaccinations, such as booster shots against tetanus or against the pneumococcus.

Then, under President George W. Bush, Congress passed a law to pay for drug coverage for Medicare patients, what was known as Medicare Part D. The law had a little-noticed effect on vaccinations for Medicare patients. Suddenly there were certain vaccinations, such as tetanus/diphtheria/pertussis (Tdap) vaccine, which would not be paid for if given in the doctor's office.

Instead, patients had to have these vaccines administered by a pharmacy as they were considered "medicines" that fell under Part D coverage. Physicians could still give other vaccinations, such as influenza. What was different between the vaccines that one could still be given by doctors and others that couldn't is not explainable. To complicate things further, commercial plans might still pay for the doctor administering these vaccines. Thus, I can give my patient Tdap if he is sixty-four, but if he is sixty-five, he has to go to the pharmacy.

Patients are amazed and startled by this. Let's say I review preventive care with my seventy-year-old patient. I tell her she is due for a mammogram, tetanus booster and flu shot. I have to explain that I could give her the flu shot but that she would have to go to a pharmacy for the tetanus booster. I can't give her any rational explanation why this is so.

What is clear is that vaccinations have been increasingly removed from physicians. For the big pharmacy chains that increasingly dominate the industry, vaccinations have become a big source of revenue. Even for shots that physicians give, payment policies drive patients to get the shots at the pharmacies. If insurance payments mean that shots at pharmacies are free while they will have a cost at physicians' offices, many patients will opt to get the shot where it costs them less.

Primary care doctors, when they think about this, are infuriated by yet another part of their job being taken away. Even when primary care doctors are able to give vaccinations, payments for such services may be made untenable. Pediatrician Stephen Berman commented that health plans, "often reimburse pediatricians less money than it costs to purchase and administer vaccines."[1]

In our practice, we looked at giving Shingrix, the new shingles vaccine. Each vaccination costs hundreds of dollars. Insurance payments were such that we might make $10 from giving the shot. In the interim, we would have to spend thousands of dollars to purchase the vaccine, then wait two to three months after giving the vaccine to receive insurance company payment. We simply couldn't afford to essentially borrow money to give the vaccines when the reimbursement would be so low and so much later after we spent the money to buy them. And even the tiny profit per dose assumes that no doses would be spoiled or wasted or otherwise not be eligible for payment. For, in that case, we would lose money giving the vaccines.

Nevertheless, primary care doctors still provide a huge percentage of vaccinations. A study of Medicare patients in fee-for-service programs in 2017 found that primary care physicians provided 46% of all vaccinations, with 45% being provided by mass immunizers such as pharmacies.[2]

Thus, the decreased role of physicians in the new Covid vaccinations was striking. The initial plan was to give available vaccines to states. In Oregon, as in many states, early vaccine shipments were given to the big hospital systems. Independent primary care doctors could not get any vaccine despite their pleas. Health care workers were given first priority to be vaccinated. Yet our doctors and staff had to go to the vaccination sites of the big hospital chains to get vaccinated.

We had signed up to be a site for vaccinations in December. Then we heard nothing from the state. A letter to a local political leader brought the declaration that a certain percentage of the available vaccines would be reserved for independents, doctors and clinics not owned by the hospitals. I e-mailed Patrick Allen, the chief of the Oregon Health Authority, who was in charge of the vaccinations in Oregon. He quickly replied on December 22, "Commissioner Meiran is correct. Vaccination will be provided to entities and providers not tied to major health systems...it may be a while, based on the pace at which vaccine ships."[3]

The next entity to receive vaccines to give to patients was not doctors. Instead, pharmacies were given vaccines from a Federal government program to give to patients.

Our phones were ringing off the hook as we would field hundreds of calls a week asking if and when the clinic would be giving vaccinations. We had to keep saying that we were told that we would be a vaccination site but had been given no information about when this would start. To say patients were upset is a gross understatement. In place of being able to come to their regular doctor, patients had to navigate a very frustrating online enrollment that baffled many of the patients, particularly the elderly. Then they had to find their way to the convention center or the airport to be vaccinated. I had a delightful eighty-four-year-old patient of several years come into my office crying uncontrollably because she couldn't get the vaccine. She begged for my help to get vaccinated. I won't forget my complete inability to help her.

I would e-mail the Health authority again on February 8 and March 1, saying on the latter occasion, "It would be very helpful for our patients and our staff to get an idea as to the timetable we might be able to start vaccinating patients here."[4]

Even as the vaccination programs progressed across the nation, the possible role of primary care physicians was rarely mentioned. Multiple opinion articles were written about how to persuade vaccine-hesitant patients to take the vaccine when available. Ideas were bruited about of having political leaders, celebrities and clergy help convince patients to get vaccinated. Do the powers that be think primary care doctors are so insignificant that patients might not ask their doctor's opinion about vaccination?

The media was full of articles begging for additional people to serve as vaccinators, claiming this was a limiting factor in the campaign. And yet, we had a clinic of twenty doctors and multiple nurses experienced in giving vaccinations, with a population of sick patients who wanted it, and we could not get the time of day from anyone. And people wonder why primary care doctors feel disrespected and discouraged.

Again and again, primary care doctors were ignored. On March 29, Politico reported how pharmacies seem to be giving many more shots than the mass vaccination sites. The article quoted an unknown Biden administration official saying, "It is clear that Americans feel comfortable relying on their local pharmacies for the vaccine. The retail pharmacy program will keep growing...."[5] Nowhere in the article is there any mention of enlisting primary care doctors in the vaccination program.

On March 15, I e-mailed the Oregon Health Authority and the Multnomah County Health Department, saying that we were ready and willing to give vaccinations but that, "maybe the idea of primary care doctors being involved in vaccination is too radical to consider."[6] This e-mail generated a response, although it told me that I had to contact someone else who, in turn, passed me on. Eventually, I was directed to a fourth person, this time at the Multnomah County Health Department. After a slew of e-mails where I restated our willingness and ability to give two hundred shots a week to patients, I received an e-mail from Kim Toevs at the County Health Department on March 18, stating, "I'll confirm by mid-week this week that you can expect to receive a direct delivery of 200 doses per week starting the week of March 29, if vaccine comes in as expected."[7]

With at last a ray of hope, the clinic held a series of planning sessions to nail down every aspect of how we would do the vaccinations. Still, we did not get a confirmation as the county stated that they were waiting for the state for information on how many vaccines would be available. The March 29 start date came and went. We were told that not enough vaccine had arrived for any to be available for us to administer.

Finally, on April 5, the Clinic received the first Covid vaccine, the Johnson and Johnson vaccine. We administered this vaccine on a Thursday and Friday after receiving it. On the following Monday, the CDC/FDA recommended not giving further doses of the vaccine until a series of seven blood clots in women receiving the vaccine could be investigated.

Fortunately, the Multnomah County Health Department came through magnificently. By Tuesday, we were able to get a supply of the Moderna vaccine to give to patients.

We have been giving the Moderna, and when given the green light, the Johnson and Johnson vaccine ever since. Most of our patients over sixty-five have already been immunized. The Multnomah County Health Department has come through to make sure we had enough supply time after time. I cannot thank them enough.

Particularly among those under sixty-five, there is a fair amount of vaccine hesitancy. However, the mere fact that we have the vaccine on site meant that we were able to persuade those of our staff members and many of our patients who were hesitant to get immunized.

We have also had multiple conversations with our patients encouraging them to be vaccinated and answering their questions about it. We have not succeeded in persuading everyone. Yet I have not had any patients who have refused to listen to the conversation. Our patients respect our opinions and knowledge even if they don't always agree.

There is evidence supporting the crucial role of primary care in vaccination against Covid-19. Lo and colleagues found the number of primary providers correlated with the rate of Covid-19 vaccination, with each additional ten PCPs per 100,000 population associated with a 0.3% higher vaccination rate. Similar correlations occurred even in areas of the most vaccine resistance, such as rural areas or the ten states with the highest Republican vote share.[8]

Thus, vaccinations should remain an integral component of primary care. The policy that doesn't permit certain vaccines to be paid for in the doctors' office is an absurdity created by Medicare regulations. It benefits only the pharmacy chains that can make more money by being the only ones approved to give certain vaccines for which they will then be paid.

Nor is it a role that most pharmacists seek. Leaving aside the Covid pandemic, most pharmacists do not particularly want to give shots. It is not something that is a key part of pharmacy education. Instead, the impetus comes from the chief executives of the pharmacy chains, who see it as additional revenue.

Moreover, primary care doctors are the ones who know vaccines best and are the people who should be seeing the patient if there is a side effect. Almost all PCPs have patients who present for a visit with some reaction from a vaccine, such as pain or swelling at the injection site or an allergic reaction with hives. It is not the chief executives of the pharmacy chains or their minions who will be taking care of these problems.

Nor is it the best role for pharmacists, for they don't go into the field to be doctors. When a patient has a complication or symptoms from a vaccination, they will almost certainly be advised to see their doctor, not come back to the pharmacy. It is the pediatrician who can best explain to parents the risk of measles and how deadly a disease this can be. It is the pediatrician (or family physician) who should be giving the measles vaccine. Similarly, it should be the role of any of the primary care providers to explain to patients the rationale for immunization against diphtheria or tetanus. They should be the ones who can give the vaccines. Medicare or other insurers should pay for these vaccines even if, and especially if, given by the patients' doctor.

---

[1] Berman, 1123

[2] Elizabeth Wilkinson, Anuradha Jetty, Stephen Peterson, Yalda Jabbarpour, John M. Westfall, "Primary Care's Historic Role in Vaccination and Potential Role in Covid-19 Immunization Programs," *Ann Fam Med*, 2021;19.online. https//doi.org/10.1370/afm.2679

[3] Patrick Allen, Communication to Gregg Coodley, December 22, 2020

[4] Gregg Coodley, Communication to Kristen Dillon, March 1, 2021

[5] Erin Banco, "Biden Administration Remakes Vaccination Strategies after Mass Vaccination Sites Fizzle," *Politico*, March 29, 2021

[6] Gregg Coodley, Communication to Kristen Dillon and others, March 15, 2021

[7] Kim Toevs, Communication to Gregg Coodley, March 18, 2021

[8] Chun-Han Lo and Others, "Association of Primary Care Physicians Per Capita with Covid-19 Vaccination Rates Among US Counties," *JAMA Network Open*, February 10, 2022:592):e2147920.doi:10.1001/jamanetworkopen.2021.47920

Marriage A-la Mode: The Lady's Death by William Hogarth,
Circa 1743.

(Courtesy, Wiki Commons)

Percentage of American Physicians Employed by Hospitals and
other Institutions

1940 12.8%

1957 26.5%

2022 75%

"Our results suggest that the common assumption that bigger
is better should not be accepted without question."

- Dr. Lawrence P. Casalino et al.

CHAPTER 19
The Shrinking of the Independents

Most American physicians succeeded in remaining independent for most of American history. Nevertheless, even a hundred years ago, doctors complained about the difficulty this required. An Ohio physician wrote to *JAMA* in 1902, "The members of the profession are constantly humiliated and insulted by wealthy corporations, state, county and city officials."[1] He noted that a steel manufacturer wanted to pay less for his services, noting, "If I do not accept the fees the company offers, the work will go to another physician, and the company knows it can get plenty of doctors to do their work for whatever they are willing to pay."[2]

Yet there were only limited doctors working for larger entities for most of the twentieth century, mainly centered in certain industries, such as coal, mining and timber, where the companies saw value in purchasing medical care for their employees. Cynics wondered if the doctor working for the coal company really had the interests of patients as the top priority.

The American Medical Association fought against corporate employment of physicians for years, commenting in 1935, "Where physicians become employees and permit their services to be peddled as commodities, the medical services usually deteriorate, and the public which purchases such services is injured."[3] Indeed up until the last few years, doctors were successful in keeping their autonomy. Paul Starr observed, "A key consideration here is that the costs of going into individual practice were not inordinately high."[4] Another factor in preventing corporate control was the relationship the physician had with the patient, a situation unique to physicians among the self-employed artisans fighting against being swallowed up by industry.

This was to change post World War II, with further acceleration in the 1960s and onward. Paul Starr explained, "Prior to the rise of third parties, doctors stood in direct relation to their patients as healers...it meant that doctors did not face any larger and more powerful organization that could dictate their income and conditions of practice."[5]

Employee health programs existed before World War II but expanded rapidly during the War. Worker pay was frozen in many industries, and companies could not raise it to attract workers. Then in 1942, the War Labor Board allowed companies to offer new fringe benefits, such as health coverage, to attract workers.

This helped attract both insurance companies and the relatively new Blue Cross/Blue Shield to offer health coverage. Coverage grew rapidly post-war, often with unions negotiating it for their members. In the 1960s Medicare, health insurance for the elderly, and Medicaid, health insurance for the poor, were started.

The more these third parties covered health care costs, the more control they sought. The rise of health maintenance organizations was an effort to control costs. Large health maintenance organizations had their own salaried physicians. Patients covered under this insurance coverage could no longer be seen by independent doctors. In 1940 only 12.8% of physicians were employed by institutions. By 1957 that proportion had risen to 26.5%.[6]

Competition from HMOs and others led to an increasing number of doctors joining groups rather than starting individual practices. Where only 1.2% of physicians were part of groups in 1940, this had increased to 12.8% by 1969. Groups gave the physicians the numbers to offer ancillary services such as x-rays and labs. Consultant Jeff Goldsmith commented, "Ancillary profits are a significant incentive for the formation of groups, one which is likely to become more powerful as market pressures reduce the profitability of the physicians' services component of what a practice produces."[7]

Yet this would be of limited benefit compared to the other changes occurring. As far back as 1982, Starr wrote, "Corporations have begun to integrate a hitherto decentralized hospital system, enter a wide variety of other health care businesses and consolidate ownership and control in what may eventually become an industry dominated by huge health care conglomerates."[8]

For-profits replaced non-profits, especially hospitals. Local institutions lost autonomy, being replaced by huge chains of hospitals, pharmacies and chains of clinics. For example, by 1981, the Hospital Corporation of America owned or managed over 300 hospitals with 43,000 beds.[9]

In some areas, companies began to offer vertically organized care, where they owned the insurance company, the hospital and the physicians. In Portland, Oregon, for example, the Sisters of Providence owns Providence Insurance, Providence St. Vincents and Providence Portland Hospitals and employs thousands of physicians in the Providence Medical Group. It also owns Providence Physical Therapy, Providence Home Health and a variety of other ancillary services.

Health care expert David Feinwachs summarized the situation, writing in February, 2022, "Vertical integration now dominates our health system. Physician practices are acquired by hospitals, hospitals are acquired by health systems, health systems 'align' themselves with one of an ever-decreasing number of insurance companies, and now the insurers are being acquired by national drugstore chains."[10]

The last thirty-five-plus years has seen a huge drop in the number of independent physician practices. The trend has been toward consolidation. Contributing factors have been the rise of health maintenance organizations, hospital purchases of practices, the regulatory environment making solo and small group practice increasingly difficult and most recently, the purchase and consolidation of practices by private equity firms.

Data showed that the percentage of PCPs who were employed increased from 23% in 1983 to 48% in 1995.[11] From 1983 to 2014, the number of doctors in solo practice dropped from 44% to 19%.[12]

The changes in the 1990s paralleled the growth of HMOs. In 1991 515 HMOs covered 35 million patients. By 1996 HMOs covered 66.8 million patients.[13]

The worst carnage has been recent. Even fifteen years ago, more than 75% of primary care practices employed five or fewer physicians.[14] Over one-third of doctors were in solo practice.[15] Only 9% of doctors were in practices with eleven or more physicians.[16] In 2006 65.2% of PCPs were still owners or part owners of their practices."[17]

Multiple factors have contributed to driving small and independent practices into extinction. Such small practices often did not have the resources to meet the increasing expectations of them. First, insurers demanded more and more "quality" data, a daunting task for solo or small practices.

The second blow was the move to shift physicians to electronic health care systems. Even with large financial subsidies, adopting such an EMR was far easier for large groups and hospital-employed physicians who could rely on the services of a whole information technology department and spread the costs of adoption over a much larger group of physicians. After the initial "carrots" of extra Medicare payments for adopting an EMR, those who had not done so faced the "sticks" of reduced Medicare payments, worsening each year without an EMR. The consequence of the push to electronic records was the closing of many smaller practices as doctors either retired early or joined larger groups.

A third factor was the new model of the medical home, with the concept of a larger primary care team being responsible for managing patient care. Dr. David Meyers wrote. "A substantial hurdle facing these projects is the costs of transforming the typical small primary care practice into a medical home...Small primary care practices are unable to support full-time quality improvement officers, chief information officers, social workers, health educators, mental health professionals and care coordinators."[18] Ironically, the concept of the medical home was developed to try and strengthen the role of primary care.

A fourth factor was decreasing reimbursement by Medicare, followed to a degree by private insurers, for primary care physicians.[19] Casalino and colleagues noted, "physicians in small practices have no negotiating leverage with health insurers, so insurers typically pay them much lower rates for their services than they pay to physicians who practice in large groups or are employed by hospitals."[20]

Medicare also pays more for the same service when offered in a hospital than in an outpatient setting. A facility fee law, enacted in 2003 after lobbying by hospitals, allows hospitals to be paid for an additional facility fee in addition to the charge for the service.[21] Thus, independent practitioners and their practices would receive less reimbursement for the same service, whether labs, imaging or minor procedures, than those providing the same outpatient services on the grounds of the hospital. The differences can be staggering. Where a chest x-ray and lab panel done by an independent doctor might be reimbursed $87 and $23, respectively, a hospital would be paid $375 and $277, respectively.[22]

The ability of hospitals to receive more for the same service certainly contributes to rising health care costs, but it is also one more factor that contributes to the inability of independent practices to compete. The hospital can afford to offer higher salaries to doctors, nurses and other staff, given the higher reimbursement.

Finally, the Affordable Care Act (ACA) offered doctors incentive payments that required them to be part of larger networks.[23] The theory was that such networks would help improve quality and reduce costs. Again, the working assumption is that paying primary doctors fee-for-service in a decentralized manner would be the most expensive program for the least quality.

The changes in health care organizations were little noticed or understood in most discussions of the Affordable Care Act. However, this "Dark Side of the Force" aspect of the ACA had a profound and disastrous effect on primary care in America.

A second negative consequence of the ACA was to inadvertently cause an increase in high deductible health plans. A *NEJM* article in 2013 explained, "Mandating coverage while requiring affordable premiums without enacting other cost-control mechanisms gives rise to increased cost-sharing as the simplest mechanism for reducing premiums."[24] So the good goals of not allowing insurance companies to deny patients with pre-existing conditions affordable insurance and expanding coverage for the uninsured at an affordable rate led insurers to try to make more money by increasing the amount patients had to pay out of pocket for services. The high deductible plans, considered 'blunt instruments' that indiscriminately reduce utilization of both appropriate and discretionary care, led many patients to reduce visits to their PCP, except for the worse issues.

The ACA was part of new demands from government and insurers for quality improvement, electronic records and medical homes, which dramatically contributed to the closing of some practices and the merger of others into large entities. The more this consolidation occurs, the more the remaining independent practices must compete against larger health care systems with more resources.[25] An increasing percentage of primary care doctors are employed by hospitals, who see them as a captive source for referrals, testing and hospitalizations. By February 2014, an estimated 60% of family physicians and pediatricians were employees.[26]

Muhlestein and Smith chronicled the changes from June 2013 to December 2015. In this thirty-month period, the percentage of doctors in groups of nine or fewer dropped from 40.1 to 35.3, while those in groups of 100 or more increased from 29.6 to 35.1.[27] By 2015 over a third of physicians were in practices of 100 or more.[28]

The biggest change was for primary care. The number of primary care doctors practicing in the smallest groups (one to two physicians) dropped 24% in that thirty-month period, while the percentage in groups of 500 or more increased by 28%.[29] Thus, a quarter of solo or two-person primary care practices closed over that two-and-a-half-year period, while the greatest growth was in huge networks of employed physicians.

From 2010 to 2018, the number of primary care physicians employed by hospitals or health care systems doubled, from 28% to 50%.[30] This is an astonishing and yet unnoticed change in such a fleeting period.

The trend toward consolidation is continuing. In an eighteen-month period from July 2016 to January 2018, hospitals and health systems bought up over 8000 practices. As a result, fourteen thousand previously independent physicians became hospital employees.[31]

The Covid pandemic made things far worse. A 2022 analysis reported that three of four American doctors were now employed by hospitals or other corporate entities. Some 108,000 physicians left independent practice in the three years ending in 2021, with 76% of this occurring after the onset of the Covid pandemic in March 2020. Kelly Kenney, chief executive of the Physician Advocacy Institute, commented, "Covid-19 drove physicians to leave private practice for employment at an even more rapid pace...The pressure of the pandemic forced many independent physicians to make difficult decisions to sell their practices."[32]

Rebecca Etz, a director of a health care nonprofit, commented, "For primary care doctors, the coronavirus is 'an extinction-level event.'"[33] An August 2020 survey found that 8% of the doctors who shut their practices due to coronavirus were primary care physicians. Greg Griggs, executive vice president for the North Carolina Academy of Family Practitioners, stated, "Covid, I think, has exposed everything that is wrong with the health care system. You have these financial challenges; you have higher costs, and you have logistical challenges. All combined are pretty much a nightmare for primary care practices."[34] Naturally, it is the small independent practices that may not have the deep pockets to weather this, not the hospital or corporate-owned practices. McHarris noted, "I think there is an analogy between medicine and retail, with small independent practices being forced out by large corporations."[35]

Paradoxically one study showed that the larger the size of a practice, the less chance that they have remained independent. By 2019 only one-third of family medicine physicians remained in independent practice. While 80.6% of solo practitioners remained independent, only about a fifth of those in groups of six or more doctors were still independent.[36]

Traditionally hospitals were believed to lose money by employing a primary care doctor. Hospitals didn't need to employ PCPs because they could count on referrals to their specialists and hospitalizations from independent PCPs continuing on a usual basis. Kocher and Sahni wrote in 2011, noting, "Today, aggressive hiring of PCPs is returning, in part because hospitals fear physicians becoming competitors by aggregating into large integrated groups that direct referrals and utilization to their own advantage."[37]

Hospitals now envision increased benefits from having

larger doctor networks of employed doctors. First, this gives the hospital greater power in negotiating contracts with insurers. Second, as there are increased risk-based contracts, this vertical integration gives the hospital much more control over the process at every stage, potentially capturing more shared savings.

Sometimes this vertical integration extends one step further as the hospital/physician companies link with insurance companies, leaving independent doctors outside looking in.

Many studies have looked at the effect of such vertical integration. Post et al., in a review of the available data, concluded, "There is evidence that prices and spending increase with greater levels of vertical integration between physicians and hospitals, while the relationship between integration and quality is not yet established."[38]

As discussed earlier, MIPS, the Medicare program that seeks to incentivize doctors for improved quality and lower costs, favors large hospital linked practices over those which are either independent, rural, small or serving large numbers of poorer patients.

The Federal government has not been a neutral player in terms of whether doctors stay independent. Instead, its policies, even if inadvertent, in the last two decades have aggressively hurt independent doctors and led to them choosing to become employed by hospitals and corporations. Government in recent years, whether led by conservatives or liberals, has favored the rich, the powerful and large in healthcare at the expense of the poor and the small.

Paul Starr speculated in 1982 that, "compared with individual practice, corporate work will necessarily entail a profound loss of autonomy...there will be more regulation of the pace and routines of work. And the corporation is likely to require some standard of performance, whether measured in revenues generated or patients treated per hour."[39] Ironically, there is evidence to suggest that such tighter monitoring can be counterproductive, causing those supervised to reduce their work effort.[40]

Earlier studies of primary care doctors' experience in managed care systems suggest that consolidation and the changes it encompasses will further decrease happiness among PCPs.

All of this has come to pass. Perhaps some corporate employed physicians do not feel like they have made a Faustian bargain, trading independence for security.

Trying to remain independent of the big health care systems, private practices have sometimes chosen a different risky alternative, that of private equity. Private equity firms have made money historically by buying up money-losing companies and theoretically restoring them to profitability. In reality, such purchases have frequently resulted in slashing of payrolls and production, consolidation of different companies and then a quick sale of the whole for a generous profit by the private equity firms.

Private equity firms are now involved in a major way in health care, with purchases comprising 18% of all private equity deals in 2017, while the value of private equity deals in health care was $42.6 billion globally, an increase of 17% from the prior year.[41] Physician practices have been a key component of this.

For physician practices that are hard-pressed, private equity offers a source of funding. Physician sales of practices are taxed at the lower capital gains rate. Gondi and Song from Harvard Medical School wrote in *JAMA*, "New requirements and mounting uncertainty as the health care system moves toward value-based purchasing may have also made physicians more interested in selling their practices. Some physicians may sell because of concerns that they can no longer compete for insurance contracts as an independent practice in an increasingly consolidated market."[42]

Conceivably the private equity firms could increase administrative efficiencies. However, the private equity firms' focus is on short to medium-term profits. Boston University business school professor Joseph Restuccia noted, "Venture capital firms are looking to make money for their investors. That means the doctor's agency on behalf of their patient is drastically reduced because (they) have a harder time being the patient's advocate."[43]

At best, physicians will lose some autonomy and decision-making. At worst, there may be tremendous pressure to do more profit-making procedures and focus on seeing commercial patients for which the reimbursement is much higher than Medicare and Medicaid.[44] As Zhu and Polsky wrote in a recent *NEJM* article, "As more investors enter health care and drive value creation, it's worth considering for whom value is being created."[45] Since the loss of physician autonomy and decision-making is an important component of disenchantment among primary care doctors, this development, whether or not beneficial for the larger health care system, is not good for the doctors. There is also concern that the private equity firm, having consolidated a fragmented market, would be in a position to drive the remaining independent practices out of business.[46]

Those who are most likely to lose when these primary care practices close are those patients who are less desirable to those who see medicine mainly as a business. They will be disproportionately the poor, minorities and those with mental health or substance abuse issues.

Noting that private equity firms typically try to sell the practices they purchased within a few years, DeCamp and Sulmasy wrote, "The desire to sell the practice soon after acquisition can create the incentive to sell off parts of the practice or undertake drastic short-term cost-cutting measures, including staff layoffs, to make a potential sale more attractive."[47]

One of the most shocking examples of this recently, albeit at a larger scale, was the purchase of the venerable Hahnemann University Hospital by a for-profit firm and its abrupt closure one year later, giving staff and patients only four weeks' notice.[48]

Ironically, theoretically, most states prohibit the, "corporate practice of medicine," yet with enough exceptions that, "the legal doctrine and practice reality may not align. In 2018 employed physicians outnumbered those owning their own practices."[49]

The size of these companies is astonishing. Premise Health claims that its doctors treated eleven million employer-sponsored members from 1600 companies and municipal governments in 850 health centers, generating a profit in 2020 of over $1 billion.[50] One Medical started by offering care for a membership fee of $199 plus billing for services. It claimed 600,000 members by the end of March 2000, mainly from contracts with employers. One Medical CEO, Amir Rubin, claimed, "without changing how the system pays, we can still reduce the cost of care."[51] If One Medical's stock rose enough, Rubin was in line for an annual salary of $199 million a year.

If the operations of these private companies must generate enough money to pay such salaries and make profits for the investors, the extra money needed to do so must come from somewhere. It is not hard to imagine that it will come from the pockets of the primary care doctors, or such doctors will be driven to work more, as directed by the managers, to create the surplus. I suspect that neither would increase the morale of the PCPs.

Other companies have adopted the concierge model. Forward Health asks members to pay $149 a month as a subscription.[52] Ironically, even the model where the rich pay more for special "personalized" care has now become a target for corporate ownership and profit generation.

Even Amazon decided to get in the game in the last year, offering telehealth and home visit service initially for employees. Amazon has now rolled out Amazon Care for the general population, described as, "a hybrid virtual and in-person experience, in which providers who might need a little bit more information can dispatch a nurse to the home."[53] Kristen Helton, director of Amazon Care, explained that it, "could cover a significant percentage of care with a virtual provider coupled with an in-person nurse."[54] Amazon Care medical director Sunita Mishra explained, "In time, we believe it will replace other types of care."[55] Amazon has supplemented this foray into care with an online pharmacy starting in November 2020. Based on their recent history, it is possible that they may be able to out-compete everyone else. Dr. Elizabeth Rourke commented in the *NEJM*, "Its primary care offering necessarily lacks comprehensiveness...It can thus either provide care exclusively to healthy people with only minor problems, or it can exacerbate the fragmentation of sicker patients' care...I worry about the financial viability of already stressed primary care practices if substantial numbers of young, healthy patients get their care from Amazon, leaving only the sickest and most difficult-to-treat patients behind."[56]

Amazon's plans are part of a wave of new "virtual-first" primary care, where care is accessed first by telehealth. Some models offer both a virtual and regular PCP, while others only have a virtual PCP.[57] If patients need further testing or a physical exam, they are referred to a local lab or urgent care. Besides the hope of profits that lure big companies into offering this service, Whitehead and Mehrotra note, "The shift to virtual-first models is motivated by the fact that for some patients, access to in-person PCP visits may be limited."[58] Thus the existing shortage of PCPs is used as a rationale for corporate programs that will siphon off the younger, healthier and more tech-savvy patients, leading to the further decline of existing primary care practices. Whitehead and Mehrotra note, "The advantages of virtual-first primary care are largely theoretical...By preferentially enrolling healthier people...the plan can be profitable regardless of whether the plan leads to improved care." [59]

Amazon is proving to be the biggest shark in the ocean. On July 22, 2022 Amazon announced the purchase of One Medical. Senator Elizabeth Warren (D-MA) commented," Amazon already has too much economic power, a terrible track record with workers, and alarmingly little clinical experience, which raises major questions about how the deal could impact consumer prices and health care choices."[60]

There is no clear evidence that consolidation reduces cost or improves quality. There is considerable evidence that it could increase costs. Baker and colleagues showed that areas with less competition showed higher price increases.[61] In their analysis from 2003 to 2010, they concluded, "We saw substantial amounts of concentration in the markets we studied, which raises concerns about potentially harmful implications for consumers."[62] Austin et al. reported, "Counties with the highest average physician concentration (i.e., fewest competing groups of physicians) had prices 8-26% higher than the prices in the lowest counties."[63]

Analysis of data in Massachusetts and Virginia separately showed that prices were higher the greater the market share of the medical entity.[64] Hospital ownership of physician practices has also been associated with higher prices and spending.[65]

Each private corporation adds both its own costs and a profit margin to the overall cost. McHarris argued, "Corporatization of medicine is one of the primary reasons for the excessive cost of health care in this country."[66]

Benefits to patients from consolidation are the most illusory, with evidence suggesting that hospital acquisition by another hospital or system results in worse patient experiences.[67] Hospitalized patients have been shown to have better outcomes in more competitive compared to less competitive hospital markets.[68]

Private equity ownership also may lead to more instability.

In the 1990s, many physician practices were bought by physician practice management companies. Economist Uwe Reinhardt described the results in 2000, "The business model originally promoted by the industry...as a vehicle for endowing physicians with the financial capital they would need...the advertised idea was to create genuine value that could be shared at least by physicians and their capitalist allies in the financial markets, but also perhaps by patients, in the form of lower prices or higher quality. On paper, it is an attractive business strategy...Be that as it may, much of the PPM (physician practice management) industry now lies in shambles."[69] For the PPMs ended up adding another layer of costs rather than value.[70] Many large physician groups closed in the aftermath. Whether the current private equity ownership wave will have similar consequences remains to be seen.

Corporate ownership has also been shown to result in higher use of health resources, i.e., testing, etc. A recent study looked at factors affecting the overuse of health care in 676 US health care systems. The study found that, "higher amounts of overuse among health care systems was associated with investor ownership and fewer primary care physicians."[71]

What is hard to understand is why so many brilliant people who helped design and implement these so called 'reforms' of the last two decades in the name of increased efficiency and coordination did not see that converting from a world of multiple independent doctors and hospitals to a few behemoths would lead to increased pricing power and higher costs. Perhaps we needed more economists who understand oligopolies and fewer lawyers and information technology experts involved in the process. Or perhaps some independent primary care physicians who could have explained the implications.

Unlike independent physicians, hospital-employed physicians are expected to use the hospital and its employees for any medical tests or procedures. Since Medicare pays more for some tests when done in the hospital, this alone guarantees increased costs. Health care economist Robert Mechanic noted, "In many places, the trend will almost certainly lead to more expensive care in the short run."[72] Writing in the *New York Times*, Elizabeth Rosenthal commented, "Hospitals also know that doctors they employ can better direct patients to hospitals owned labs and services."[73]

The American College of Physicians, which represents internal medicine physicians, noted the possible ethical issues, writing, "Physicians employed in large organizations experience challenges to the exercise of clinical judgment, professional integrity or the ability to put patients first...there is the potential for dual loyalty when physicians try to be accountable to both their patients and their employers."[74] Others have argued that the contracts doctors sign with employers, "may be part of a growing class of subtle but protean and pernicious restrictions on employed physicians' professionalism and autonomy. These provisions may financially benefit employers and their management."[75] One example was financial incentives for hospital-employed physicians to refer within their system, regardless of patient needs.[76]

Dr. Arnold Relman, long-time editor of the prestigious *New England Journal of Medicine*, worried about how the commercialization of health care affected medicine, writing, "When physicians think of themselves as being primarily in business, professional values recede and the practice of medicine changes...the current focus on money-making and the seductions of financial rewards have changed the climate of US medical practice at the expense of professional altruism and the moral commitment to patients."[77]

Ironically, even as the number of independent practices diminished, there was increasing evidence that they might be more effective and less costly than the larger groups. Casalino et al. surveyed 1045 primary care practices from 2007 to 2009, at a time when almost two-thirds of American office-based physicians worked in practices of less than seven doctors.

Casalino et al. reported that compared to practices of ten to nineteen physicians, practices with one to two physicians had 33% fewer preventable hospitalizations, while practices with three to nine physicians had 27% fewer.[78] Preventable or ambulatory care-sensitive admissions were those where good primary care could potentially abort such hospitalizations.

The study also showed that groups owned by physicians also significantly lower ambulatory case-sensitive admission rates than those owned by hospitals (4.3 per 100 patients per year compared to 6.4 per 100 patients per year).[79]

On the other hand, neither the presence of a medical home nor pay-for-performance incentives, nor risk-sharing for hospital costs, significantly affected the rate of these hospitalizations.[80] Thus, all the special measures that are thought to improve care and reduce costs did not matter. Casalino and others concluded, "These findings were unexpected since small practices presumably have fewer resources to hire staff to help implement systematic processes to improve the care they provide."[81] The authors speculated, "It is possible that small practices have characteristics that are not easily measured but result in important outcomes, such as fewer ambulatory care-sensitive admissions...it is possible that physicians, patients and staff know each other better in small practices and that these close connections result in fewer avoidable admissions."[82] McHarris, an independent internist, suggested another possible explanation, observing, "we all spend more time with patients than corporate providers...is that sustainable?"[83]

Multiple other studies found results supporting these conclusions. J. Michael McWilliams and colleagues reported that small practices, averaging seven doctors, had lower readmission rates than medium (average forty-three doctors) and large practices (averaging 217 doctors). Overall, Medicare costs did not differ significantly between the different sized physician-owned groups, but hospital-based groups had higher costs.[84] The authors concluded that, "spending was lower for those with strong primary care orientation."[85]

In contrast, multiple studies found that hospital acquisitions of physician practices resulted in increased prices of healthcare services.

Koch found that spending and costs for Medicare patients increased after hospitals acquired the practices of the physicians caring for these patients.[86] Capps et al. showed that prices for services provided by hospital-acquired physicians increased an average of 14% post-acquisition.[87] Baker et al. reported that an increase in the market share of hospitals with the most ownership of physician practices was linked to higher hospital prices and spending.[88]

Robinson and Miller looked at costs for commercial HMO patients in California. After adjustment for patient severity, they found the highest costs in physician groups owned by multihospital systems, almost 20% more than physician-owned groups. Physician groups owned by local hospitals had the next higher costs, still 10% more than physician-owned groups. Among physician-owned groups, the largest groups had expenditures 9.2% more than the smaller physician groups. The authors concluded, "These findings are in contrast to the hope and expectation that organizational consolidation of physicians would result in greater coordination and hence lower expenditures."[89]

Young et al. looked at the effect of independent doctors becoming hospital employees on the ordering of magnetic resonance imaging (MRI). They reported that the odds of a patient receiving an inappropriate referral for an MRI increased by over 20% after a physician transitioned to hospital employment, with most patients referred to the hospital employing the physician.[90]

Kralewski and colleagues, in a study of over 133,000 Medicare patients with diabetes in 234 group practices, found that smaller practices had fewer ambulatory-care sensitive admissions and lower overall cost of care.[91] The study also showed that having an electronic medical record did not reduce costs while, "a higher ratio of nurse practitioners and physician assistants in practice increased costs."[92]

Some have argued that greater consolidation would improve quality of care. The evidence does not prove this fanciful claim. Scott et al., studying US acute care hospitals from 2003 to 2012, found that hospitals that increased the employment of physicians did not show any improvement in any of four primary composite quality measures.[93]

Safran et al. found greater patient satisfaction among those seeing mainly independent doctors being paid fee-for-service than those seeing physicians employed by HMOs and others. The authors noted that this might reflect consistent differences in attitudes between independent and employed doctors, stating that the independent physicians were much more concerned with their patient relationships. They concluded that, "physicians in open-model systems knowingly assume responsibility for building and maintaining their patient panel as part of their professional life, while physicians in closed-model systems (such as staff model HMOs and hospital-employed doctors) were said to largely rely on their plan to provide them with patients."[94]

Restuccia commented, "When (a physician) is practicing on their own, they have much more discretion about how much time they spend with a patient. They can forego some of their income...to provide the patient the best care."[95]

Another study looked at the management of hypertension in multiple practice settings in Minnesota. The study revealed that, "Patients treated in practices that emphasize entrepreneurism, group solidarity and decentralized decision making have lower costs for episodes of care for hypertension. However, physicians in practices with cultures that favor organizational formality and those with cultures that stress cost-effective practice styles appear to use more resources to care for patients. Practice cultures oriented towards rules and regulations appear to diminish the physicians' ability (or motivation) to control resource use."[96]

As Casalino et al. concluded," "Our results suggest that the common assumption that bigger is better should not be accepted without question."[97]

Policymakers do not consider such heresy, instead operating on the assumption, as stated earlier, that decentralized uncontrolled fee-for-service payments for the doctors was the root of the rapidly rising health care costs.

Ironically, the Stark laws effectively remove any financial incentive for independent doctors to overuse imaging, labs or hospitalizations. However, when a physician is employed by a large institution, the same prohibitions may apply on the surface, but incentives for any kind of behavior can be buried within the salaried arrangement. Even if not explicitly present, the referrals of the hospital-employed doctors to their own institutions are more likely for the physicians are most likely to prosper when their employer is doing well. Indeed, the data shows that hospital-owned practices had more potentially preventable admissions than those owned independently by physicians.[98] A review of hospital employment of doctors concluded that, "vertical integration generates higher prices, higher spending and ambiguous changes in quality."[99] In another analysis, Baker et al. concluded that, "vertical integration appears to lead to statistically and economically significant increases in hospital prices and spending."[100]

The situation is most problematic in small cities and towns, which may be left with a single hospital and their employed physicians in place of the multiple small practices they previously enjoyed. There is no evidence in any other sector of the economy where a monopoly resulted in lower costs or prices.

The trend accelerated even more recently as the number of physician practices owned by hospitals or non-hospital corporations increased 25% in 2019–2020, with much growth in practices owned by insurers or private equity.[101] Some 48,000 physicians left independent practice during that time to become employees of these corporations.[102] By July 2021, 69% of doctors were employed by hospitals or corporate entities, an increase of 12% from 2019 to 2021.[103]

The fewer independent practices, the harder it is for the remaining ones to survive, as the big systems have less and less motivation to work with them. McHarris remarked, "The more primary care clinics close, the harder it is for the rest of us to survive...It affects everyone. Everybody has a body... people should care."[104]

The shrinking of independent practices threatens more than a loss of a competitive market, giving patients a variety of choices of physicians and settings. To the extent that the loss of autonomy is another factor discouraging doctors from choosing to go into primary care, the consolidation may lead to fewer and fewer personal physicians being available for patients.

---

[1] F. H. Todd, "Organization," *JAMA*, October 25, 1902; 39:1061

[2] Todd, 1061

[3] American Medical Association, Bureau of Medical Economics, *Economics and the Ethics of Medicine*, Chicago, 1935, 49-50

[4] Starr, 218

[5] Starr, 236

[6] Starr, 359

[7] Jeff Charles Goldsmith, *Can Hospitals Survive? The New Competitive Health Care Market*, Dow Jones-Irwin, Homewood, IL, 1981, 35-36

[8] Starr, 428

[9] Starr, 430

[10] David Feinwachs, It's time to bring competition back to health care," *Medical Economics,* February 2022;7

[11] Buchbinder, 701

[12] Dhruv Khullar, Gregory C. Burke, Lawrence P. Casalino, "Can Small Physician Practices Survive? Sharing Services as a Path to Viability," *JAMA,* April 3, 2018; 319(3): 1321

[13] Buchbinder, 702

[14] Meyers, 272

[15] United States Department of Health and Human Services, Characteristics of Office Based Physicians and their Practices, United States 2005-6, Vital and Health Statistics, April 2008; 13(166)

[16] United States Department of Health and Human Services, Characteristics

[17] United States Department of Health and Human Services, Characteristics, 9

[18] Meyers,

[19] Elizabeth Rosenthal, "Apprehensive, Many Doctors Shift to Jobs with Salaries," *New York Times,* February 13, 2014

[20] Lawrence P. Casalino and others, "Small Primary Care Practices Have Low rates of Preventable Hospital Admissions," *Health Affairs,* September 2014:33(9): 1687

[21] Lafferty, 21

[22] Lafferty, 22

[23] Rosenthal

[24] J. Frank Wharam, Dennis Ross-Degnan, Meredith B. Rosenthal, "The ACA and High Deductible Insurance – Strategies for Sharpening a Blunt Instrument," *NEJM,* October 17, 2013; 386(16): 1481

[25] Jane M. Zhu, Daniel Polsky, "Private Equity and Physician Medical Practices – Navigating a Changing Ecosystem," *NEJM,* March 18, 2021; 384(11): 981

[26] Rosenthal

[27] David B. Muhlestein, Nathan J. Smith, "Physician Consolidation: Rapid Movement from Small to Large Group Practices, 2013-15," *Health Affairs*, September 2016; 35(9): 1638

[28] Khullar, Can Small Practices, 1321

[29] Muhlestein, 1640

[30] Colla, 948

[31] Physicians Advocacy Institute, "Updated practice acquisition study: national and regional in physician employment, 2012-2018," February 2019, http://www.physiciansadvocacyinstitue.org.portals/0/assets/docs/01191 9-Avalere-PAI-Physician-Employment-Trends-Study-2018-Update.pdf?ver=2019-02-19-162735-117

[32] Aine Cryts, "3 in 4 Doctors Are Employed by Hospitals, Corporate Entities: Report," *Medscape;* April 2022; https://www.medscape.com/viewarticle/972604_print

[33] Christopher Rowland, "Diagnosis for Small Family Doctors: Less Money, Greater Hardship and Patients on Video," *Washington Post*, September 8, 2020

[34] Rowland

[35] McHarris

[36] Diane R. Rittenhouse, Andrew W. Bazemore, Zachary J. Morgan, Lars E. Peterson, "One-Third of Family Physicians Remain in Independently Owned Practice, 2017-2019," *J Am Board Fam Med,* 2021; 34: 1033

[37] Robert Kocher, Nikhil R. Sahni, "Hospitals race to Employ Physicians – The Logic behind a Money-Losing Proposition," *NEJM*, May 12, 2011; 364(19): 1791

[38] Brady Post, Tom Buchmueller, Andrew M. Ryan, "Vertical Integration of hospitals and physicians," *Med Care Res Rev*, 2018; 75(4):422

[39] Starr, 446

[40] Bruno S. Frey, "Does Monitoring Increase Work Effort? The Rivalry with Trust and Loyalty," *Economic Inquiry*, October 1993, volume XXXI: 663

[41] Suhas Gondi, Zirui Song, "Potential Implications of Private Equity Investments in Health Care Delivery," *JAMA*, March 19, 2019; 321(11): 1047

[42] Gondi, 1047

[43] Aine Cryts, "Nearly 70% of Physicians working for Hospitals or Corporate Entities New Survey Reveals," *Medscape Medical News,* July 1, 2021

[44] Zhu, 981

[45] Zhu, 983

[46] Gondi, 1048

[47] Matthew DeCamp, Lois Snyder Sulmasy, for the American College of Physicians Ethics, Professionalism and Human Rights Committee, "Ethical and Professional Implications of Physician Employment and Health Care Business Practices: A Policy Paper from the American College of Physicians," *Ann Int Med, 2021;* 174: 847

[48] DeCamp, 847

[49] DeCamp, 844

[50] Bernard J. Wolfson, "Can a Subscription Model Fix Primary Care in the United States," *Washington Post,* June 3, 2021

[51] Wolfson

[52] Wolfson

[53] Elizabeth Rourke, "In Clinical Care, Will Amazon Deliver?" *NEJM,* December 23, 2021; 385(26): 2402

[54] Rourke, 2402

[55] Rourke, 2402

[56] Rourke, 2403

[57] David C. Whitehead, Ateev Mehrotra, "The Growing Phenomenon of 'Virtual-First' Primary Care," *JAMA,* December 21, 2021; 326(23): 2365

[58] Whitehead, 2365

[59] Whitehead, 2366

[60] Cristiano Lima, Aaron Schaffer, "Amazon Foes Fear Company's Health Care Acquisition will Cement its Power," *Washington Post,* July 22, 2022

[61] Lawrence C. Baker, Kate Bundorf, Anne B. Royalty, "Physician Practice Competition and Prices Paid by Private Insurers for Office Visits," *JAMA,* 2014; 312(16): 1653

[62] Baker, 1659

[63] Daniel R. Austin, Lawrence C. Baker, "Less Physician Practice Competition is Associated with Higher Prices Paid for Common Procedures," *Health Affairs*, October 2015; 34(10): 1753

[64] Kocher, 1792

[65] Gondi, 1048

[66] McHarris

[67] Beaulieu, 51

[68] Nancy D. Beaulieu, Leemore S. Dafny, Bruce E. Landon, Jesse B. Dalton, Hedayo Kuye, J. Michael McWilliams, "Changes in Quality of Care after Hospital Mergers and Acquisitions," *NEJM*, January 2, 2020; 382(1): 52

[69] Uwe E. Reinhardt, "The Rise and Fall of the Physician Practice Management Industry," *Health Affairs*, January-February, 2000; 19(1): 50-51

[70] Reinhardt, 52

[71] Jodi B. Segal, Aditi P. Sen, Eliana Glanzberg-Krainin, "Factors Associated with Overuse of Health Care Within US Health Systems: A Cross Sectional Analysis of Medicare Beneficiaries from 2016-2018," *JAMA Health Forum* 2022; 3(1)e214543.doi.10.1001/jamahealthforum. 2021.4543

[72] Rosenthal

[73] Rosenthal

[74] DeCamp, 845

[75] Roy M. Poses, Wally R. Smith, "How Employed Physicians' Contracts May Threaten Their Patients and Professionalism," *Ann Int Med*, July 5, 2016; 165(1): 55

[76] Poses, 55

[77] Arnold Relman, "Medical Professionalism in a Commercialized Health Care Market," *JAMA*, December 12, 2007: 298(22): 2668

[78] Casalino, Small Primary Care and Admissions, 1680

[79] Casalino, Small Primary Care and Admissions, 1684

[80] Casalino, Small Primary Care and Admissions, 1684

[81] Casalino, Small Primary Care and Admissions, 1685

[82] Casalino, Small Primary Care and Admissions, 1685-6

316

[83] McHarris

[84] McWilliams, 1447

[85] McWilliams, 1453

[86] TG Koch, BW Wending, NE Wilson, "How Vertical Integration Affects the Quantity and Cost of Care for Medicare Beneficiaries," *Journal of Health Economics*, 2016; 52: 19

[87] Cory Capps, Daniel Dranove, Christopher Ody, "The effect of hospital acquisitions of physician practices on prices and spending," *Journal of Health Economics*, 2018; 59: 139

[88] Laurence C. Baker, M. Kate Bundorf, Daniel P. Kessler, "Vertical Integration: Hospital Ownership of Physician Practices is Associated with Higher Prices and Spending," *Health Affairs*, May 2014; 33(5): 756

[89] James C. Robinson, Kelly Miller, "Total expenditures per Patient in Hospital-Owned and Physician-Owned Physician Organizations in California," *JAMA*, October 22/29, 2014; 312(16): 1668

[90] Gary J. Young, E. David Zepeda, Stephen Flaherty, Ngoc Thai, "Hospital Employment of Physicians in Massachusetts is Associated with Inappropriate Diagnostic Imaging," *Health Affairs*, May 2021; 40(5): 710

[91] John E. Kralewski, Bryan E. Dowd, Yi Xu, "Medical Groups Can Reduce Costs by Investing In Improved Quality of Care for Patients with Diabetes," *Health Affairs*, August 2012; 31(8): 1832

[92] Kralewski, Medical Groups Can reduce Costs, 1833

[93] Kirstin W. Scott, E. John Orav, David M. Cutler, Ashish K. Jha, "Changes in Hospital-Physician Affiliations in US Hospitals and Their Effect on Quality of Care," *Ann Int Med*; January 3, 2017; 166(1): 1

[94] Safran, 74

[95] Cryts

[96] John E. Kralewski, Terence D. Wingert, David J. Knutson, Christopher E. Johnson, "The Effects of Medical Group Practice Organizational Factors on Physicians' Use of Resources," *Journal Healthcare Management*, May/June 1999; 44(3): 176-177

[97] Casalino, Small Primary Care, 1686

[98] Casalino, Small Primary Care, 1680

[99] Post, 418

[100] Baker, Vertical integration, 762

[101] Paige Winfield Cunningham, Alexandra Ellerbeck, "The Health 202: One Hundred Million Eligible Americans still Haven't Gotten Vaccinated," *Washington Post,* July 1, 2021

[102] Cunningham

[103] Aine Cryts, "Nearly 70% of Physicians Working for Hospitals or Corporate Entities New Survey Reveals," *Medscape Medical News*, July 1, 2021

[104] McHarris

St. Patrick Day Parade, Pittsburgh, 2008.

(Courtesy, Wiki Commons)

CHAPTER 20

Between Scylla and Charybdis: Private versus Public Insurance

It would seem like a major omission to say nothing about the choice between public and private insurance. This is really a question of a single public payor versus the current mix of private plans and public coverage. Before moving to discuss this, it is worth trying to understand and learn from the models used in other advanced nations.

In Germany, care is funded by public Sickness Funds that pay on a fee-for-service basis, with some resistance to proposals for capitation. Primary care is provided by general practitioners who provide initial diagnosis and treatment.[1] In the Netherlands, health care is funded by a combination of private and public health insurance, with providers being largely private rather than public employees. The Dutch system gives general practitioners the role of first contact physician for all patients. GPs are paid based on a combination of capitation and fee-for-service.[2] In Great Britain, most care is provided by the National Health Service with physicians employed by the Health Service. Finally, Canada offers universal public health insurance coverage. Half of doctors are family practitioners who provide most ambulatory care. While patients can see specialists without referrals, specialists receive lower reimbursement under these circumstances.[3]

It is not that primary care doctors in other countries don't have complaints. Doctors complain that "General practice in the United Kingdom is being industrialized."[4] Fewer doctors than needed are choosing primary care in Canada and Sweden.[5]

However, analysis comparing the experience of adults in Australia, Canada, Germany, the Netherlands, New Zealand, the United Kingdom and the United States is not too flattering. Schoen et al. wrote, "The United States spends by far the highest share of national income on health care, yet it is the only country that leaves a high percentage of the population uninsured or poorly protected in the event of illness."[6] The survey showed that vis-à-vis their health system, "US adults held the most negative views and were the most likely to report affordability concerns."[7]

The grim comparison continued. "One-fifth of US adults reported serious problems paying medical bills in the past year – more than double the rates in the next highest countries."[8] Americans were the most likely to perceive administrative waste. Americans were less likely to have a regular primary care doctor than any other country.[9]

Schoen et al. continued, "Canadian and US adults were the least likely to report same-day access and the most likely to report long waits.... (they) were most likely to have gone to a hospital ER in the past two years, to have multiple visits and to say that they went to the ER for the care their doctor could have provided if available."[10] I don't think we should be relieved that on this one measure, someone else scored as badly as us.

The authors noted, "Affordability was of particular concern in the United States, where 42% of chronically ill adults said they had skipped medications, not seen a doctor or forgone recommended care because of costs – a rate two to eight times higher than rates in other countries."[11]

The current American system has much to dislike. There is a huge amount of administrative waste that contributes to costing Americans more for health care than anywhere else in the world.

In terms of the problems discussed earlier, what would be the benefits of moving to a single payor system? A single payor would mean a single entity to receive credentialing for doctors rather than having to duplicate a process for each insurer. It would not eliminate the need to get hospital privileges and state licensure.

Second, a single payor theoretically would mean that there would be only one system for referrals with the elimination of worrying whether the doctor was referring in-network or not.

For prior authorizations, there would be one list of drugs needing authorization, rather than different, changing ones for each insurer. This would be a huge time saver.

There would be one list of quality measures to meet rather than different lists for each insurer, again introducing a degree of increased rationality and simplicity to the system.

There would likely be less micromanagement of practice, as CMS sends far fewer messages about how to manage patients than do private insurers.

The change might improve continuity of care as patients would not have to shift doctors due to changes in their insurance.

Elimination of private Medicare Advantage plans would eliminate the emphasis on finding "high complexity codes" in order to increase the money the plans get from Medicare.

Eliminating private insurers would reduce the administrative costs of the health care system, potentially freeing up money for better patient care or less costs to patients.

Eliminating private insurers might eliminate high deductible plans, which keep patients from seeing their PCP until illnesses become dire.

Eliminating the private insurers would mean eliminating the health care dollars that go to their profits. I do not know what the head of CMS is paid, but it is almost certainly less than the millions to tens of millions that the CEO of each large health insurer takes home annually.

It would eliminate the billions going to the private companies now employing doctors to generate substantial profits for their managers and investors. None of that actually improves health care.

The current system consumes a higher percentage of the gross domestic product than most or perhaps all other countries. A 2018 *JAMA* article by Papanicolas et al. compared the United States to ten of the highest-income countries. While the United States spent 17.8% of its gross domestic product on health care, the spending in other countries ranged from 9.6 to 12.4%.[12] The United States had the highest proportion of private health insurance (55% versus 10% in the next highest, Germany). Life expectancy was the lowest, and infant mortality highest in the United States. Administrative costs accounted for 8% of the total in the United States versus 1–3% in the other nations. Cost of medications was far greater in the United States than in any of the other countries.[13] These statistics do not make a very effective argument for keeping our current system, where we are spending more to achieve less health than in other nations.

As was discussed earlier, the fee- for-service system has been blamed for the higher US health care spending. Papani-colas and colleagues argued that it was not a major driver of this cost, for American health care utilization did not vary much from other countries. The authors instead concluded, "The data suggest that the main driving forces were likely related to prices, including prices of physician and hospital services, pharmaceuticals and diagnostic tests, which also likely affected access to care. In addition, administrative costs appeared much higher in the United States."[14] The inability of the mixed private-public system to control prices via market mechanisms, plus the grossly higher amount of money spent on administration, is a powerful argument for switching to a public single payor system.

Arnold Relman, for many years the editor of the *New England Journal of Medicine*, wrote in 2007, "Health care has become a $2 trillion industry, largely shaped by the entry and growth of innumerable private investor-owned businesses that sell health insurance and deliver medical care with a primary concern for the maximization of their income...in no other health care system do investor and business considerations play such an important role. In no other country are the organizations that provide medical care so driven by income and profit-generating considerations. This uniquely US development is an important cause of the health care crisis that is destabilizing the entire economy."[15]

In 2011 Berwick and Hackbarth estimated that waste accounts for 20-30% or more of health expenditures in the United States.[16] It is conceivable that this might be reduced significantly by a change to a single payor, if only by reducing the complexity of doing the same process in multiple ways depending on the insurer.

In 2019 Shrank et al. looked at the waste in the health care system again. They estimated that the cost of waste in the US health care system ranged from $760 to 935 billion annually, or about 25% of health care spending. They broke this down to failure of care delivery $102 to 165 billion, failure of care coordination $27 to 78 billion, overtreatment or low value care $75 to 101 billion, pricing failure $230 to 240 billion, fraud and abuse $58 to 83 billion and administrative complexity $256 billion.[17]

There are components of this waste that wouldn't necessarily be improved by switching to a single payor model. Problems in care coordination, like the inadequate communications by hospitalists and emergency rooms with PCPs, is one such example. However, the two categories of pricing and administrative complexity equal half a trillion dollars and potentially could be, to a great extent, eliminated by a change to a single payor.

Traditionally private coverage was seen as providing better coverage than Medicare. Evidence increasingly suggests that this is no longer the case.

An analysis by Catlin et al. showed that out-of-pocket spending from 2007 to 2010 increased rapidly for patients with employee-sponsored commercial insurance. Over the same time, out-of-pocket costs declined for patients on Medicare.[18] This may have reflected more high deductible commercial plans along with more comprehensive coverage by Medicare.

More data was provided by a 2010 survey that found that patients with employer-sponsored commercial coverage, "were more likely than Medicare beneficiaries to forego needed care, experience access problems due to cost, experience medical bill problems, and be less satisfied with their coverage."[19] The study also compared patients on traditional Medicare to those on private Medicare Advantage Plans. Patients on the Medicare Advantage plans reported lower out-of-pocket costs but also were more likely to rate their insurance poorly and report difficulty accessing care.[20] Those with Medicare Advantage noted difficulties with bills and accessing care at a level equal to younger adults with commercial insurance. Medicare patients were also more likely to have a primary care doctor to provide broad care. The authors concluded that, "Medicare is doing a better job than employer-sponsored plans at fulfilling the two main purposes of health insurance: ensuring access to care and providing financial protection."[21]

Recent data also shows that patients covered by public insurance were more satisfied with their care. In a study of 149,290 people from 2016 to 2018, those with private insurance were less likely to have a personal physician, more likely to report unstable insurance coverage, more likely to have difficulty seeing a doctor due to cost, less likely to take medications due to costs and more likely to have medical debt compared to those on Medicare. Compared to Medicare, those with employer-sponsored insurance were less satisfied with their care.[22]

Medicaid, which provides coverage to the poor, had traditionally been viewed as inferior to commercial insurance. Yet, in this study, compared to patients on Medicaid, those with commercial employee-sponsored insurance were more likely to have medical debt, while the satisfaction with care was the same for the patients on Medicaid and those on commercial insurance. Medicaid patients did have a harder time finding a physician.

Recent prior studies suggested that patients with Medicare or with military/veterans coverage were the most satisfied with their health insurance.[23]

This large survey is a powerful statement of patients' unhappiness with private insurance.

And yet, and yet, there is reason to hesitate. For there is much that government has done to worsen the plight of the PCP and the care of the patient.

It is CMS that has set the payment policies that result in so much more being paid to specialists and for procedures than to primary care doctors for talking to patients. Eliminating private insurers won't change this pay differential that has contributed to the shrinking of primary care and the disillusionment among its practitioners.

Moving to a single payor would not of itself help the job-education mismatch for primary care nor improve communications between hospitalists and primary care physicians.

Moreover, much of the insanity and absurdity in medicine results from the insurers following the lead of CMS. The coverage for screening for cancer with expensive procedures such as mammograms and colonoscopies while screening for disease with inexpensive blood tests such as sugar, cholesterol and prostate antigens is denied, is based on CMS guidelines.

It is CMS that has taken the lead in demonizing fee-for-service and pushing value-based/pay-for-performance plans over the last two decades. As we have seen, the benefits in quality have been small; the administrative cost has been high, and the policies have favored hospital-employed physicians and large groups at the expense of smaller and independent practices and those in rural areas or caring for the poor.

It is CMS that has spent billions developing such a large array of quality measures that to achieve them would exceed all the hours the PCP practices each day.

It is the Federal government that pushed for the adoption of electronic medical records by physicians. The cost and complexity of this has been a factor in the shrinking of smaller practices in favor of large groups and hospitals.

The CMS initiatives to improve care and quality by pushing doctors to become part of large networks or to create medical homes are other innovations that have contributed to the massive conversion from a large mass of independent doctors to near-monopoly vertically integrated networks in some areas. The economics of creating oligopolies or monopolies results in higher health care costs, while the evidence that consolidation has improved quality is scant.

It is Medicare rules that mean that certain vaccines will not be paid for if given in doctors' offices. It is the Federal and state governments that set the rules for distribution of the Covid vaccine that gave low priority to primary care doctors.

In my state, it was the state health authority that ignored any thought of benefit from continuity of care in allowing the reassignment of Medicaid patients away from their long-term doctors. While the powerful in the private sector do not care much about the interests and well-being of primary care doctors or patients, the public sector seems equally not to care compared to the political considerations of who has the most power. This is much more likely to be the huge health care entities than the small doctor offices.

As a primary care doctor, I find myself in the position of Treebeard in *The Two Towers* when he says, "I am not altogether on anybody's side, because nobody is altogether on my side."[24] Still, in a different age of the world, he might have been thinking of certain insurers when he concluded, "And there are some things, of course, whose side I am altogether not on; I am against them altogether: these-burarum (he again made a deep rumble of disgust) – these orcs and their masters."[25]

---

[1] Fitzhugh Mullan, "The 'Mone Lisa' of Health Policy: Primary Care at Home and Abroad," *Health Affairs*, 17(2): 122

[2] Mullan, 123

[3] Mullan, 123

[4] Iliffe, 7

[5] Iliffe, 189

[6] Cathy Schoen, Robin Osborn, Michelle M. Doty, Meghan Bishop, Jordon Peugh, Nandita Murukutla, "Towards Higher-Performance Health Systems: Adults' Health Care Experience in Seven Countries, 2007," *Health Affairs*, 2007; 26(6): w718

[7] Schoen, w720

[8] Schoen, w722

[9] Schoen, w722

[10] Schoen, w724

[11] Schoen, w728

[12] Irene Papanicolas, Liana R. Woskie, Ashish K. Jha, "Health Care Spending in the United States and Other High Income Countries," *JAMA*, March 13, 2018; 319(10): 1024

[13] Papanicolas, 1024

[14] Papanicolas, 1025

[15] Relman, 2668

[16] Berwick, 1513

[17] William H. Shrank, Teresa L. Rogstad, Natasha Parekh, "Waste in the US Health Care System: Estimated Costs and Potential for Savings," *JAMA*, October 15, 2019; 322(15): 1501

[18] Mary K. Catlin, John A. Poisal, Cathy A. Cowan, "Out of Pocket Health Expenditures by Insurance Status, 2007-2010," *Health Affairs*, January 2015; 34(10): 111

[19] Karen Davis, Kristof Stremikis, Michelle M. Doty, Mark A. Zezza, "Medicare Beneficiaries Less Likely to Experience Cost and Access Related Problems Than Adults with Private Coverage," *Health Affairs*, August 2012; 31(8): 1866

[20] Davis, 1871

[21] Davis, 1873

[22] Charles M. Wray, Meena Khare, Salomeh Keyhani, "Access to Care, Cost of Care and Satisfaction with Care Among Adults with Private and Public Health Insurance in the US," *JAMA Network Open*, 2021;4(6)e2110275.doi:10.1001/jamanetworkopen.2021.10275

[23] Wray, 8

[24] J.R.R. Tolkien, *The Two Towers*, Ballantine Books, New York, 1965, 95

[25] Tolkien, *The Two Towers*, 95

The Garden of Eden by Jan Brueghel and Peter Paul Rubens,
circa 1615.

(Courtesy, Wiki Commons)

CHAPTER 21

Restoring Rhyme and Reason: Some Solutions to an Impossible Task

It is, of course, impossible to simply rewind the clock to a state when many of the problems I have discussed did not exist for primary care. As Frodo said, "I wish it had not happened in my time."[1] Yet, as Gandalf answered, "So do I and so do all who live in such times. But that is not for them to decide. All we have to decide is what to do with the time that is given us."[2]

So let us look forward and discuss the necessary and positive steps that would improve the field of primary care, stem the continuing loss of primary care doctors and improve the care of patients in America.

First, we must affirm that primary care physicians add value. Most patients accept this notion automatically, for most choose to establish care with their "regular" doctor. Even most patients who don't have a regular doctor wish they did.

Beyond the intrinsic value that patients place on primary care, the evidence is overwhelming that primary care reduces other health care costs, from cutting the use of an emergency room and unnecessary hospitalizations to promoting preventive care. Phillips and Bazemore asserted, "that doubling primary care financing to 10–12% of overall health care spending would be likely to pay for itself, via resulting reductions in overall health spending."[3] McHarris asked, "Why aren't we paying for primary care up front instead of paying later for dialysis or ventilators or other catastrophic care?"[4]

Should they realize the potential benefits, there are many who would benefit from the health of primary care. UCSF professor Thomas Bodenheimer summed it up well fifteen years ago, writing, "Who might support a national policy to rescue primary care? Employers and insurers, public and private, may get a return on investment by fostering a more effective primary care sector that would reduce health care costs. The public would benefit from micro-system improvement, with fewer appointment delays, higher quality and more meaningful interpersonal relationships. Even specialists might recognize that they would suffer if primary care deteriorates."[5]

Dr. Ada Stewart, president of the American Academy of Family Physicians, suggested, "investing in primary care as a public good. The current cost-based model only emphasizes the cost of delivering care without accounting for the value of care patients should receive."[6]

If we accept that primary care doctors are of value, we must look at how the field can be improved so more new graduates would go into it and fewer drop out. The morale of existing primary care docs is not a negligible factor for new graduates. If the new graduates see those practicing primary care as beaten down, overwhelmed by the paperwork and made servants of the insurance companies, you will not easily convince them to join the field. Instead, as Cassell penned, "If new systems treat physicians as the solution rather than the problem, rising morale will help spread new ideas."[7]

Most of the lay commentary on shortages of primary care blame it on the lower incomes relative to specialists. No doubt this plays a role. Yet doctors are not simply driven by money. People who go to all the trouble and work to become doctors want to enjoy their work and feel that what they do is making a positive difference. More health care spending won't fix that. Instead, I will discuss solutions that would reduce the overall cost of health care.

First, we need to look at medical education. Many have

argued that medical schools' choice of students should focus more on those likely to go into primary care, with strong evidence that certain characteristics predict those most likely to go into primary care.[8] Students from rural areas are those who are most likely to want to practice there; the same applies to students coming from underserved communities in the cities. While this is not a hard and fast rule, it is worth taking into account if we want to get more primary care doctors to practice in these areas.

Second, we need to look at the length of medical training. Does it need to take so long and, as a corollary, cost so much? For science training that is not really used by most clinicians, we certainly should question repeating it in both college and medical school. Biochemistry is of major importance to researchers. Its utility to clinicians is much less. Particularly, we must question the value of memorizing bits of knowledge that will be forgotten since they are never used. For example, in medical school, we had to memorize the structures of each of the amino acids. I doubted its relevance at the time but hoped that my further career would show how necessary it was. That has not happened.

Much of the medical education program is designed for those going into medical research. I am not against research, having participated in almost two hundred such projects during my career. The design of some medical education to promote research should certainly be maintained. However, before almost all American medical schools adopted the John Hopkins model of a four-year curriculum heavy on basic sciences to help graduate physician-researchers/teachers, many schools had shorter training schedules and focused more on graduating practitioners for the local area. The reform, while increasing the overall professionalism of the field, has resulted in shortages of physicians, particularly in rural areas. These shortages persist today.

There have been proposals to shorten medical school for

those going into family medicine as a way to make the specialty more attractive since reduced years of medical school also mean reduced costs for medical training and hence less debt.[9] This idea should be considered more widely. Reducing the time needed to start practicing would certainly give primary care one advantage in competing with specialties for medical school graduates.

Another suggestion is to replace the four-year medical school curriculum with a three-year curriculum plus a one-year primary care residency. This would replace the fourth year of medical school, where students have elective time to get exposure to other specialties, with the first year of residency. Again, this would create a financial benefit from going into primary care of a shorter time in training.

In fact, several American medical schools in the 1970s and 1980s, as well as some Canadian medical schools, offered three-year programs. Raymond and colleagues reported, "The broad array of published data...suggests that students in three-year programs perform as well as their four-year counterparts at all stages of their careers."[10] Reducing medical school to three years for primary care doctors could save them tens of thousands of dollars in reduced tuition, offering a powerful incentive to choose primary care careers.

Another idea to encourage more medical school graduates to go into primary care would be to partially rebate their medical school tuition if they went into primary care. The National Health Service Corps essentially attempted to do this. In exchange for practicing for a set period of time in a medically underserved area, physicians would have their medical school tuition paid for. This concept could be expanded to reduce the medical school costs for anyone going into primary care while giving additional bonuses to those committing to practicing in medically underserved areas.

The United States needs to be able to utilize the 3000 doctors who graduate from medical school each year but are unable to practice since they cannot obtain a residency position. The number of residency spots could be increased to guarantee these graduates at least a one-year position. If these positions were in primary care, the system would have just added 3000 more PCPs, in the form of general practitioners, a year for negligible cost since residents usually pay for themselves at the hospitals where they are trained.

In increasing the number of residency positions, the Federal government should lift the cap on the amount of direct graduate medical education (GME) funding that helps pay for it. New residency slots should be in primary care, with an emphasis on increased positions in areas of the nation with the worst shortages of primary care doctors. In exchange, there could be a reduction in the amount of indirect GME, which is given to hospitals to compensate them for the supposed increased cost of having residents work there. The Medicare Payment Advisory Commission found that less than half of these indirect payments, based on complex formulas from the 1980s, were justified by the evidence.[11] This money, which makes inpatient care more lucrative, could be redistributed more to support outpatient and community health care.

If primary care doctors are never going to manage inpatients once they finish residency, we need to shift the training from being so hospital-focused. Most internal medicine residents currently might have an outpatient clinic one half-day a week. My primary care internal medicine residency increased this to two half days a week. Still, 80% of the training was with inpatients. This was useful when I got to manage my patients in the hospital, but now I would suggest it is of decreasing utility as most inpatient care, save in some rural or low-income areas, is managed by hospitalists.

If primary care doctors really are going to be shut out of hospital care, as is so often the case today, the time spent in the hospital could be cut to the first year of residency, which is called internship. The primary care doctor should spend all of the second year in an outpatient setting, while the third year could be eliminated. Prospective PCPs would get far more practical training for what they will be doing than the current model of spending a half-day a week for three years. Primary care residencies could be cut to two years yet still offer far more outpatient training than is currently the case.

One of the factors revealed in surveys of students and residents is that many opt not to go into primary care in part because of limited exposure to it during their training. Kassler wrote, "A curriculum that increased students' exposure to primary care could help them appreciate how caring directly for patients, providing continuity of care and being involved in the psychosocial aspects of care can be gratifying aspects of medical practice."[12]

To prioritize primary care, the Federal government, particularly Medicare, has to change the way it finances residency training. Money needs to be redirected from hospitals and hospital-based training to paying for training in an ambulatory, primary care setting. Instead of just hospital-employed specialists receiving financial support for their role in training, primary care doctors could receive money to cover the cost of having residents learn in their offices. Moreover, it is not that the Federal government nor the medical schools are passive bystanders in terms of how many medical students choose primary care residencies. This number could be increased by fiat either by the Feds or the medical schools. Moreover, the number of specialty fellowships could equally be reduced by an administrative decision. This change in the number of residencies and fellowships won't solve the problem by itself, for residency slots in primary care will be insufficient if not enough students choose to fill them. Petersdorf suggested raising the salaries of primary care residents relative to that of specialty residents and fellows to help encourage more students to choose the primary care option.[13]

Again, Canada offers a model for the Canadian medical

education system that has made sure a balanced, appropriate number of PCPs and specialists are produced.[14]

Next, the disparity in income between primary care doctors and specialists has long been pointed out yet not fixed. Part of this disparity rests on how much doctors are paid for procedures compared to talking to and examining patients. There are ongoing attempts, particularly by Medicare, to reduce the disparity by reducing how much is paid for procedures and paying more for the things primary care doctors do. Cuts in their income has met fierce resistance at times from different specialties.

In the ideal markets theorized by Adam Smith, scarcity, such as of primary care doctors, would lead to an increase in their price or, in this case, income. A glut of specialists would similarly result in a declining price or income. Yet, CMS, and the insurers who followed its lead, have fixed prices for both. The fact that the AMA advisory committee that advises CMS on how to adjust the value of different services is dominated by specialists has contributed to the market distortion.

As a result, CMS has looked for other mechanisms to try to steer more money to primary care, from the medical home to the MIPS program. As we have seen, these are complicated schemes that don't really make up the primary care-specialty income gap while disadvantaging solo and small practices and those taking care of the indigent.

The simpler solution would be for CMS to radically adjust the relative value units on which physician payments are based. Since specialty incomes are approximately double that of primary care, a 25% increase in payments to primary care and a 25% decrease in payments to specialists would go a long way to reducing the disparity while still maintaining a substantial differential. CMS, in fact, has the data to make the changes to most impact those specialties in surplus while sparing those where there is not an excess.

The impact of increasing primary care and decreasing the

amount of specialty care would not be immediate, for the existing workforce would not radically change overnight. However, over time the lessened financial disadvantage of primary care should lead to more medical students choosing it as a career.

Moreover, this need not be a one-time intervention. If the amount of the change does not result in a sufficient increase in the number of new PCPs, CMS could make further adjustments until the numbers are what are needed nationally. Since this is simply a redistribution to fit market conditions, there would be no additional cost to the health care system.

If primary care doctors appear besieged and often discouraged, it is hard to lure new graduates to the field and hard to keep existing practitioners going. Thus, the rest of this chapter will focus on concrete steps to improve the life of primary care docs.

Let's start with the concept of continuity of care. If it is important to have and maintain a long-term relationship with a doctor, patients should not have to give this up if their insurance changes. We accept this now, but this is a recent phenomenon. The Federal government could mandate that insurers could not force patients to change primary care doctors but instead must pay the same for any PCP, whether "in-network" or not. Some, but not all, states have mechanisms in place to allow this to happen. It should be made universal.

The reality and the great irony are that this change, despite insurance companies' certain opposition, would save insurers money. Doctors who have known a patient for years are not going to have to recreate the wheel by ordering a variety of new tests. Moreover, when you know a patient, the doctor can better sense when someone is sick or not, thus meaning that some ER visits or specialty referrals might not happen.

Indeed, there is abundant evidence that continuity of care by a primary care doctor for a patient does indeed lower other health care costs.

What about insurers maintaining their networks? The expensive part of health care for the insurer takes place in the hospital and, to a lesser extent, in outpatient imaging, surgery and specialty consultations. The insurer could still insist that the PCP refer this to "in-network" when needed.

What would be lost by this change to allow a patient to keep his PCP, no matter the insurance? Only a tiny modicum of control by the insurer. In exchange, their costs would be less and the patient and physician satisfaction greater.

One of the other barriers to continuity is the high deductibles and co-pays that many insurers now offer as a standard part of their plans to hold down overall costs. Insurers usually cover one physical or preventive care visit a year by primary care without it falling under the deductible or requiring a co-pay. Insurers could allow all other primary care visits to be excluded from the deductible and/or require a lower or no co-pay so that the high deductible plans don't prevent many patients from getting routine care due to cost. Increased primary care visits would be cheaper for the insurer than having the patient end up in the emergency room or hospital as a result of the problem not being treated.

Again, since good primary care has been shown to lower overall medical costs, it would be in the insurers' interest to make the cost of such visits to patients minimal so patients utilize primary care services. Since data also show the stronger the bond between the patient and the primary care provider, the lower the average cost, it again would be financially prudent for insurers to encourage more visits to the PCP to strengthen this relationship.

Today, while most insurers may have a slightly lower co-pay for primary care than seeing a specialist, the primary care services under high deductible plans are paid for by patients out of pocket, creating a strong financial disincentive for this care. Indeed, most insurance plans focus more on the differential charge to patients for in-network versus out-of-network visits than on encouraging more primary care.

Moreover, insurers need to stop weakening continuity of care by paying for home visits by other practitioners, both nurse practitioners and doctors, than the PCP. There is no data that having more cooks making the broth will make either a better or cheaper product. Instead, as shown in Chapter 5, increased continuity of care will result in both better and less expensive care for patients.

The challenge of how to encourage patients to see their PCP instead of a specialist as the first contact for a problem has been dealt with in America either by making the PCP the gatekeeper from whom the patients need a referral for specialty care, or by giving patients complete freedom to see whoever they wish. An alternate solution is offered by Canada, where patients can see specialists without a referral, but where the specialist then receives lower fees in such cases. Adoption of such a system in the United States would use a market-based solution to encourage specialists to have patients see their PCPs first while removing PCPs from the role of the gatekeeper. As we have seen, denied referrals often result in increased patient dissatisfaction with their PCP.

What about care in the hospital? I don't think it is possible to put the genie back in the bottle, to have PCPs again take over the management of their hospitalized patients. For better or worse, hospitalists are here to say.

What can be changed is communication between the ER, the hospitalists and PCPs. The ER should be mandated to talk to the PCP before deciding to admit a patient. It should be mandatory for hospitalists, at a minimum, to contact the PCP every time their patient is admitted and when they are discharged. This would not only improve continuity but improve hospital care. Even if the hospitalist has the patient chart, there are nuances that only the PCP would know. For example, I frequently see hospitalists start patients on a medication that

341

the patient has already tried and rejected. Patients may have had a prior evaluation of a medical problem. Knowing this would save the hospitalist from having to evaluate it all over again.

My patients tell me afterward that they asked if the hospitalist had been talking to me during the hospitalization. Many times they are assured that this is the case, when it never is. Wouldn't it be better if the hospitalist actually had to talk to the PCP?

When I have suggested this to the hospital administrators, the answer often is that the primary care doctors don't want to be interrupted to hear about their patients in the hospital. I don't necessarily believe this is true. Regardless, there needs to be communication between the hospitalists and PCPs, even if inconvenient for either.

This would also help with the issue of management by nurse practitioner hospitalists. I think they would be able to do a better job if they talked to the PCP at the start of the hospitalization. This would help them know when the problem was something they could manage versus when the patient should receive additional physician management and consultation.

One of the most problematic aspects of hospitalist care is their desire to refer everyone to palliative care or hospice. There are times when this is appropriate, but the discussion would be better if it occurred between the patient and their own doctor. As it stands, patients are too often referred for hospice when the hospitalist concludes on the basis of a brief meeting that they are elderly and ill and, therefore, must not have enough quality of life to want to keep living.

I can be confident in making the assertion that there are few primary care doctors who like insurance companies. At best, as when Gandalf answered Frodo's assertion that Gollum was evil, they can answer about whether insurers are evil, "perhaps not wholly so."[15] How can this relationship be improved? I will go into more detail, but it comes down to insurance companies being willing to give up some control with the possible reward of increased profits

Let's start with the issue of credentialing, by which each insurer requires each physician to fill out new paperwork each year in order to be able to see patients with that insurance. This certainly creates a cost for both the insurer and physician. I would argue that medical licensure should be enough for insurers. However, if they insist on additional certifications, there are multiple ways in which it can be made less burdensome and costly. There could be one common form for all insurers. Certification could be for five years rather than one year. Perhaps doctors who had never had a malpractice judgment against them could have to recertify less often. After all, even if doctors have to swallow the cost of all this paperwork, the staff the insurer employs to read and keep track of it surely adds to their costs.

A second source of physician and patient aggravation is prior authorizations for drugs. This, again, is a recent phenomenon. My wife, who is a pharmacist, noted that a few years ago, patients would be outraged to learn that they couldn't get the medicine their doctor prescribed.[16] Now, like the frog getting used to the ever-increasing temperature of water set to boil, patients are more resigned to it, but still incredibly aggravated.

There are many ways in which this process could be reformed to reduce aggravation to physicians without costing insurers. First, there should not be prior authorizations required for inexpensive or generic drugs. Requiring prior authorization for a drug that is $4 a month is more costly for the insurer in terms of its employee's time than anything saved by denying this. Second, there is a more efficient way to reduce drug costs, one that the insurers are already using. Insurers put medicines on different tiers, with the higher tiers for the more expensive drug having much higher out-of-pocket costs for patients. One could call this a market-based solution rather than the regulatory one of the prior authorizations. The most expensive drugs, particularly those for which there is an equally efficacious, less expensive alternative, could be priced high enough that patients would opt for the cheaper substitute. This already happens every day. Patients call saying that the prescribed antibiotic was too expensive and request a cheaper alternative.

Eliminating or drastically reducing the prior authorization process would be a great relief to doctors. By reducing the costs of staff for the insurers to handle drugs of trivial cost, it would actually save insurance companies money. They would just have to practice a little less medicine.

Another step that would reduce time and trouble for everyone is if there was a single list of drugs that required prior authorizations rather than varying radically from one insurer to another. Another useful reform would be if the cost of each drug could be known by doctors and patients in advance rather than being secret and differing between insurances. Doctors and patients could talk in advance about whether the patient could afford the medication.

Here is another idea. Imagine what might happen if insurers had to pay physicians for their time to do prior authorizations. This would make sure insurers only asked for it for the limited numbers of drugs that were so expensive to make it worth it.

This illustrates another point. If insurers had to pay for physician time for everything they asked them to do currently without pay, they would stop requiring lots of useless information that currently costs them nothing and the physician a lot, what is called in other contexts unfunded mandates.

What about patient referrals? Since PCP referrals to specialists on an insurance company panel have an approval rate of 100%, the entire process is a costly waste of time for both physician and insurer. At a minimum, such referrals by the PCP to these specialists could be automatically authorized. The insurance company could dispense with all their employees who review these and always say yes.

Referrals could still be required for doctors, testing or hospitals not on the insurance company panel. This is a small part of all those that are done.

What about referrals for imaging, where the PCP has to jump through a bunch of hoops to get a test authorized for their patient? Perhaps this does occasionally cut the insurer costs, but a system designed to cut costs by making the process so aggravating that the physicians give up in dismay hardly seems to be the best design for health care. By eliminating this requirement, insurers could dispense with hiring the outside consultants and companies they use to evaluate their value, saving enormous amounts of money.

Since insurers know which doctor orders what, they could require this extra step of begging for authorization of an MRI or CT scan only for doctors who consistently order far more than the average. As it stands, all PCPs are aggravated so that the insurers could deter the actions of a few.

Moreover, insurers might save money by eliminating limits on PCPs when such limits don't exist for specialists. For example, when the PCP can't get authorization for a knee MRI, he will refer the patient to the orthopedist who will order it. Thus, the insurance has to pay for both the MRI and the specialty consultation, while authorizing the MRI in the first place might have eliminated the need for the referral.

Few things are more aggravating to the PCP than the daily barrage of suggestions from the insurance companies as to how they should practice. Doctors really don't like receiving these directives as to what they should prescribe and what tests they should do. The process is not free for the insurers; they are either having their staff send all these suggestions or hiring outside companies to do it. I have not seen any studies that showed that it either improved patient care or saved money for insurance companies. In the absence of that, I would urge that the insurance companies stop practicing medicine. At a minimum, they could keep the blizzard of suggestions for the 10% of doctors who do the least preventive care. There is a cost to aggravating all primary care doctors, for when the insurers are done, they may find that there are a lot fewer PCPs.

For all physicians, the burden of paperwork is worse than fifty years ago. For none is it worse than for the primary care doctor. I would go out on a limb to say that no PCP chose to go into the profession for the opportunity of spending hours a week on all the things that are dumped on them.

Much of the paperwork seems to exist to transfer liability from others onto the PCP should anything happen. Thus, a nursing home may send a message every time the patient didn't get one of two dozen pills or banged their elbow without any injury. Is this really protecting the patients or covering one's butt? I have to sign off on every plan by a physical therapist. Yet the reality is that they know what to do in their own field far more than I do.

We are asked by oral surgeons to clear patients for tooth removal. Sometimes there is a legitimate concern, but it feels that more often, it is so I can be responsible instead of them if anything goes wrong.

I am not sure what the answer is. I think a good place to start would be to have someone, whether Medicare or some other entity, review all the things PCPs have to do in terms of paperwork to see what is really necessary for good care and what is just protecting someone else, in theory, from an overzealous, hungry attorney.

Noting how much of PCPs' days are wasted in clerical work, Shipman and Sinsky argue that improved efficiency would be another way to increase primary care provider capacity, suggesting a variety of system improvements in physician offices.[17] Process improvements are always good, but the real problem lies upstream in terms of the clerical tasks placed on doctors. Eliminating this excessive clerical work gets at the cause of the problem rather than just trying to ameliorate it.

Insurers and the government push the idea of increasing quality. This is defined as making sure that patients get their mammograms or colonoscopies, or diabetic feet exams as per quality guidelines. The problem is not that much of this isn't a worthy goal. It is instead that the PCP cannot possibly do all of the ever-increasing number of quality measures. Nor do the insurers take circumstances into account when seeing doctors meet their quality guidelines. A few years ago, an insurer complained that certain patients had not had their mammograms. When we explained that these were women with prior bilateral mastectomies, we were told that they still counted in our totals since the quality program had already taken that into account.

I said earlier that it feels akin to teaching for a standardized test rather than teaching to maximize knowledge. A PCP often is discouraged to find that all the other care they lavish on their patient doesn't count, that only the things on the insurer's lists matter.

For Med Advantage patients, much of this originates from Medicare. It is ironic that no one measures if I order mammograms for my patients on straight Medicare. It only matters if they are on the Med Advantage plans where meeting the quality goals will give that insurer a higher rating, i.e., more stars. The Med Advantage plans all dream of having five stars, which allows patients to transfer to them anytime in the year. I thought we were practicing medicine, not doing reviews of restaurants for the Michelin Guide.

Health care expert Dr. Donald Berwick wrote how the current era, "has brought with it excessive measurement, much of which is useless, but nonetheless mandated. Intemperate measurement is as unwise and irresponsible as is intemperate health care."[18] Berwick suggested that the CMS, insurers and regulators should commit to reducing by 75% the volume and cost of measurements currently used in health care.[19]

Bolstering this case is the evidence that focusing on fewer measures would produce most of the potential health gain.[20] Drastically reducing the number of measures to focus only on those with the proverbial "biggest bang for the buck" would be a very wise and helpful step. This would allow more room for clinical judgment and individual patient preferences.[21]

Beyond greatly reducing the quality measures asked for, another useful step would be to create a single list of required measures that would be the same for all insurers rather than the current situation where every insurer has its own list of different guidelines and quality measures.

Casalino offered another idea. Addressing the problems of value-based programs, he suggested that physicians could be offered innovative motivators. He suggested that practices that performed well could, "be rewarded with an exemption from prior authorization or other reporting requirements."[22] I can think of little that would be more motivating to my partners than to be freed from the curse of prior authorizations, not to mention any other reductions in paperwork.

Few innovations in medicine in recent years have been more oversold than electronic medical record systems. They were touted as something that would increase efficiency and reduce cost.

At a cost of tens of billions of dollars, doctors were pushed to adopt them. They were promoted as so useful that it would pay the Federal government to subsidize doctors to adopt them.

Yet the cost of health care has not fallen. Instead, almost every primary care physician sees fewer patients than they did when using old-fashioned paper charts. It is not that typing things into a computer is inherently less efficient than writing them down with a pen. Instead, the problem is that computerized records empowered both the government and insurers to demand more information. In the old days, a doctor might see a patient for congestive heart failure and high blood pressure, jot down the relevant details from the history, exam and treatment plan, submit a bill for a moderately complex visit and be done. In recent years billing for the same visit, the doctor had to make sure that both the history and the assessment had enough detail to support this claim. The visit note had to include a certain number of components from a review of system and a certain number from the physical exam, etc. Thus, the doctor's note became longer, not because the patient had changed but because Medicare and the insurers required much more information to be present in order to be willing to pay the bill. The electronic medical record also facilitated the way for insurers to ask for more information to assure "patient quality."

Government regulation helped drive the industry created to produce electronic medical records. The Federal government has required certification every few years, with each time requesting that the EMRs meet very narrow specifications. This certification requirement helped drive many companies that made EMRs out of the business.

First, the government needs to abandon this wasteful demand for certification. The government doesn't regulate the computer systems of the auto industry or the banks, or major league baseball. This would potentially allow more competitors to enter the industry, which, overall, is more likely to reduce costs than an oligopoly arrangement where a few companies can control prices.

Second, both Medicare/Medicaid and private insurers need to demand less information. Electronic medical records shouldn't be designed to record patients' prior addresses or their ethnicity in a detail that puts the census to shame. Hartzband and Groopman said this well when they wrote, "The (EHR)...has become a tyrannical, time-consuming billing tool; it must be reconfigured to work for physicians rather than forcing physicians to work for it."[23]

CMS has taken an initial step toward demanding less information by allowing notes where complexity is based on time spent rather than by checking off a certain number of items in each of multiple categories.

This promises to be a major step forward. Since whatever CMS does is usually aped by private insurers, this could allow a significant reduction in the checking of boxes previously required for each bill. It will depend on the implementation. I am cynical enough to question whether the insurance industry will be satisfied with this approach or will instead demand additional information to be able to reduce or delay visit payments to physicians.

If the powers that be stop demanding as much information, primary care doctors will be able to see more patients. Again, I would suspect that most PCPs would opt for more patient visits rather than more complex visit notes; they would rather spend more time talking to the patient than more time writing the note of the visit. I think it likely that patients would prefer if their doctor spent more time talking and listening to them rather than staring at the computer screen. Perhaps that is an old-fashioned viewpoint, but I think it is correct.

One of the biggest causes of burnout for physicians is loss of autonomy. Allowing doctors flexibility in their schedules is one of the few things that reduce burnout, so it would be a wise intervention for those organizations employing physicians.[24]

One of the more recent frustrations for PCPs has been the need to focus on recording high complexity codes for the Med Advantage plans so that these plans can receive more money from Medicare, with some trickling down to the PCPs. Of course, the first reason this occurred is the mere presence of private companies managing Medicare patients. When there were no private Med Advantage companies, Medicare paid directly to the physician for their services without any need to figure out much an intermediary needed. The easiest practical solution, although the most difficult politically, would be to abolish private intermediary companies managing Medicare (and, in my state, Medicaid) patients.

Medicare formerly paid fee for service directly to physicians. It is the creation of value-based plans under Medicare Advantage that requires risk adjustment to avoid penalizing those caring for the sickest patients. Primary care, which again is a negligible part of health care costs, should be paid for directly from Medicare to doctors. Adjustment in payments to insurers based on severity would be derived automatically from hospital records, eliminating the need for and the time spent gaming the system.

Instead of offering new primary care initiatives that require huge administrative efforts to join and participate in, CMS could simply reward PCPs more directly by paying them more for seeing Medicare patients. This would be simpler and cheaper and eliminate the current bias toward these special programs rewarding the hospital and large group practices disproportionately.

There is a virtue in a simple, easily understood system of payments for physicians that treats all equally. It certainly would reduce the complexities of payments for both private and public entities, reducing administrative costs. Like democracy, fee-for-service may be the worst system except for all the others.

The increasing use of nurse practitioners and physician assistants would be a positive good if they were not seen as substitutes for primary care physicians. Policymakers should not assume either that there is no other way to fill the gap in the number of needed primary care doctors or that these physician substitutes are exactly equivalent. NPs and PAs are different from primary care doctors and shouldn't be seen as a cheap solution that would allow continued inaction toward the decreasing numbers and morale of primary care doctors. I have discussed how the proliferation of privately owned urgent care clinics will have a negative long-term effect on primary care. The first step might be to prevent them from cherry-picking, i.e., only seeing healthy well-paying patients. When I was licensed In Massachusetts, a condition of licensure was that I needed to see Medicaid patients. The free-standing urgent care clinics should not be allowed to shun the poor and the old if they want to deliver care.

Second, the growth of urgent care clinics in pharmacies has come with the increasing replacement of local pharmacies by huge chains. One driver has been the insurance companies who force patients to get their drugs from where it is cheapest for the insurer. If patients were allowed to get their medications wherever they chose, this might slow the closure of the local pharmacies. Second, oligopoly, control of an industry by a few large entities, is no more desirable for pharmacies than any other industry. The anti-trust laws should be used to stop the increasing consolidation of the industry as pharmacies and pharmacy chains are swallowed up by larger and larger conglomerates. Finally, there are strict regulations on doctors dispensing medications. It is thought to be a conflict of interest for doctors to write prescriptions for drugs they would then dispense. If doctors are prohibited from dispensing drugs, pharmacies should be prohibited from practicing medicine.

Insurers should also incentivize patients to see their primary care doctor over going to urgent care by increasing co-pays for urgent care visits and lowering them for the PCP visit. Evidence is clear that this would lower health care costs and costs to the insurer.

Few things are as absurd as primary care doctors being prevented from giving needed vaccinations. If I know at his physical that a sixty-five-year-old man needs a tetanus booster, it is crazy that I can't give it right then and there. Instead, I have to tell him that Medicare requires that he get it at a pharmacy.

Medicare and private insurers should be mandated to pay for any licensed vaccine, whether given by a doctor or a pharmacy.

The Covid vaccination campaign has largely ignored doctors. Yet after those willing are vaccinated, those in doubt are going to be most influenced by their doctors. In the future, primary care doctors should be the spearhead of vaccination campaigns rather than an afterthought or not thought of at all.

The private versus public insurance debate ignores another option, which is that of most utilities, such as water and electricity. These are often private companies whose rates and profit are closely regulated. There is no reason the administrative overhead for private insurers can't be set at a more reasonable amount – if not the 3% of Medicare, perhaps 5% rather than the current double-digit levels. There could be reasonable limits on their profits and restrictions on the income of their chief executives. Relman argued, "Physicians should not accept the industrialization of medicine, but should work instead toward major reforms that would restore the health care system to its proper role as a social service that society provides to all."[25] Limiting all the opportunities for everyone, from private equity to huge pharmacy chains to make large profits, regardless of secondary consequences, might help limit costs and focus the system more on this service aspect. The danger, of course, is that too often, the regulated, especially if large and powerful, take over the regulators.

There are many factors driving the loss of physician practices and the increasing number of physicians who are employees of large entities. These include the large debt burdens that many physicians graduate with and hence the need for an assured income to be able to pay this back. Another large factor is the ever-increasing requirements that are asked of primary care doctors, whether this be switching to an electronic medical record that meets rigid guidelines, having to do the paperwork to create a medical home, or the need to report more and more data to the insurers and government.

The number of new practices that are started these days is far, far fewer than fifty years ago. One factor is that elevated levels of debt make the lure of a job with an assured salary far more appealing and less risky. In addition, medical training teaches nothing about the non-medical side of having a medical practice.

Our group, the Fanno Creek Clinic, is one of the few new primary care practices in Portland in the last twenty-five years. I was fortunate to have had management experience running the General Medicine Clinic at the University before taking on the challenge of independent practice, with no one to bail me out if I failed. To start the practice, we had to get a Small Business Administration loan, for which the bank required personal guarantees where failure would have meant that they would have taken everything but my firstborn.

Even twenty-four years ago, the idea of opening a new primary care practice was viewed as wildly "risk-seeking," with hospital administrators predicting we would close in six months.[26] Of course, such predictions spurred the doctors involved to make sure we succeeded.

Opening or even joining an independent practice is far riskier today, where the deck is stacked in favor of the big players.

As we have explored, these driving factors are not inexorable. We should reduce what is asked of independent primary care doctors before we drive them all to extinction. The tax incentives given to hospitals as "non-profits" should be considered for primary care doctors opening a practice. No one has considered that because no one really values independent primary care, yet there is much evidence that such care has been shown to be both cheaper and better than that from large entities.

It may be inevitable that the future will see each American

city dominated by one or very few huge vertically integrated entities, including insurance, hospital and employed physicians. From an economic standpoint, situations of monopoly, where one company, and oligopoly, where a few companies dominate a market, are distortions, leading to higher prices, less efficiency and less freedom. Why those administrators pushing coordination and consolidation as the answer to achieve higher quality and lower cost think medicine will be different from any other economic endeavor in terms of the effects of bigness and oligopoly is baffling. Of course, the same thing is happening to pharmacies, where independents are being forced out in favor of a few huge pharmacy chains.

Insurance companies and governments need to be forced to give up their bias toward the biggest and most powerful entities in healthcare. They need to stop thinking of primary care doctors as widgets; mindless commodities that can be easily manipulated and forced to do what they are told. For bigness fosters such thinking, patients become "covered lives," and doctors become "providers."

Let us imagine what a future with the implementation of these reforms might look like. Their cost and length of education reduced, their relative incomes increased, large numbers of medical students flocked to practice primary care. Existing PCPs, their burden of "busy work" slashed dramatically, would wax poetic to the students about the fulfillment of having long-term relationships with patients and their families.

With the time that must be spent on filling out the electronic medical records drastically less, each primary care doctor can see more patients. There would be enough primary care doctors for every person in the nation. Patients would know that going to the primary care doctor, in the absence of copays and deductibles, would be less expensive than going to urgent care. Increasing numbers of PCPs would mean fewer emergency room visits and fewer hospitalizations, resulting in lower overall health care costs. Patients would not be forced to change doctors due to switching insurance, allowing more long-term relationships. Going to a doctor who knows them would result in better quality and lower-cost care.

With hospitalists mandated to talk to the PCP about each hospitalized patient, wasteful repletion of tests and drugs that have already failed could be avoided. There would be far fewer major problems in the transition of care, fewer errors, and less patient confusion. Patients could trust that the hospitalists were actually talking to and working with their doctors.

By giving up micromanaging PCPs, insurers would allow them to be more efficient. The cost savings from this and from the changes above would lead to higher insurance company profits and/or less increase in health care premiums.

Without the burden of massive debts, more physicians would opt for the autonomy offered by private practices rather than feeling financially compelled to work for large entities. Tax incentives for opening a new primary care practice would help dramatically. A reduction in the information requested by both public and private health care entities would allow doctors to focus on patient care rather than documentation. Having more, smaller individual practices, would lead to more choices for patients, more personal care and perhaps reduced overall costs.

Electronic medical records could be designed for simplicity and ease of use, as is the case in most other industries, rather than focused on meeting government specifications. Doctors and insurers would no longer have to focus on coding high complexity conditions to garner more Medicare dollars. The doctors could once more focus on patient care.

Preventing a few large behemoths from dominating the business of pharmacy and medicine will reduce the increased costs that oligopoly and monopoly situations always result in.

Complicated payment schemes that require massive administration would be replaced by simple, easily understood incentives. Physicians, as well as nurse practitioners and physician assistants, could focus on a limited number of those quality objectives that add the most value rather than trying to chase an impossible number.

Patients could get most referrals and prescriptions without needing insurance company approval, reducing everyone's time and cost, including that of the insurers. The insurers would focus on trying to reduce the few most expensive drugs and procedures only.

Every aspect of such a future is still possible, but it won't happen without changes to our current way of doing business.

It is a worthy goal that each American have the means, i.e., insurance, to have their own regular doctor. It won't do much good if there simply aren't enough primary care doctors around. We must encourage the growth and flourishing of such doctors, both for their sake and that of their once and future patients.

---

[1] J.R.R. Tolkien, *The Fellowship of the Ring,* Ballantine Books, New York, 1965, 82

[2] Tolkien, *Fellowship, 82*

[3] Phillips, Robert, Primary Care, 808

[4] McHarris

[5] Thomas Bodenheimer, "Primary Care – Will It Survive?" *NEJM,* August 31, 2006; 355(9): 863

[6] Ada D. Stewart, "Prioritizing Primary Care Can Save the U.S. Health Care System," *American Family Physician,* July 2021; 104(1): 15

[7] Cassell, 16

[8] Colwell, 392

[9] Shi

[10] John R. Raymond, Joseph E. Kerschner, William J. Hueston, Cheryl A. Maurana, "The Merits and Challenges of Three-Year Medical School

Curricula: Time for an Evidence-Based Discussion," *Acad* Medicine, October 2015; 90: 1318-9

[11] Ahmed, 4

[12] Kassler, 43

[13] Petersdorf, 408

[14] Mullen, 123

[15] Tolkien, *Fellowship,*

[16] Karen L. Coodley, Conversation with Gregg Coodley, March 31, 2021

[17] Scott A. Shipman, Christine A. Sinsky, "Expanding Primary Care Capacity by Reducing waste and Improving the Efficiency of Care," *Health Affairs,* November 2013; 32(11): 1990

[18] Donald M. Berwick, "Era 3 for Medicine and Health Care," *JAMA*, April 5, 2016; 315(13): 1329

[19] Berwick, Era 3, 1329

[20] Meltzer, Population,

[21] Hartzband, 2487

[22] Casalino, Value Based, 1648

[23] Hartzband, 2487

[24] Hartzband, 2487

[25] Relman, 2688

[26] Tom Heckler, Communication to Gregg Coodley, 1997

APPENDIX
List of Proposed Reforms

Education and Training

1) Reduce the length of medical school from four to three years; optional 4th year for those specializing or going into research.

2) Guaranteed first-year residency position in primary care to all medical school graduates; encourage option of doctors becoming general practitioners after one year of residency.

3) Reduce primary care residencies (Internal Medicine, Family Medicine and Pediatrics) to two years; 2nd year is all outpatient training.

4) Change number of residency positions to increase number in primary care and reduce number in specialty care.

5) Reduce subsidy to hospitals for training specialists; redirect money to PCPs for mentoring and training new PCPs.

6) Reduce medical school costs for those going into primary care.

Income Adjustment

7) CMS to adjust relative value units on which physician payments are based; increase payments to primary care by 25% and reduce those to specialists by 25%.

8) Equalize payments for services, whether done in hospital or outpatient, to reduce incentive to consolidate services within hospitals and increase fairness.

Encouraging Continuity

9) Patients can keep PCPs no matter their insurance to increase continuity.

10) Eliminate or reduce co-pays/deductibles for any PCP visits to encourage patient to see PCP rather than more expensive alternatives.

Reducing Administrative/Clerical Burden

11) Eliminate necessity of referrals within networks; eliminate referrals for imaging/other tests except for 10% of doctors ordering most studies.

12) Specialists are paid more if the patient has a referral.

13) Insurers credential doctors for five years rather than annually; consider eliminating recertification for doctors with no malpractice claims.

14) Insurers to stop practice suggestions for doctors except for 10% of doctors doing least preventative care.

15) Government and insurance to reduce amount of information demanded via the electronic medical record to allow more time to focus on patients rather than charting.

16) Government to stop certification of EMRs, allowing companies to focus on the most usable product rather than building to government specifications that are irrelevant to practice.

Prior Authorizations

17) Eliminate prior authorizations for generic or inexpensive drugs.

18) Use different tiers of insurance payments to encourage patients to use cheaper alternatives when available.

19) CMS to create a single list annually of very expensive drugs where insurers could ask for PAs.

20) Insurers have to pay doctors for each PA, encouraging them to use PAs only for most expensive agents.

21) Prices of each medication to be publicly available to doctors and patients.

Hospital Care

22) Emergency room doctors and hospitalists must talk to PCP before each hospital admission and before patient discharge.

Quality of Care

23) Limit quality measures to a small number of the most important interventions.

Medicare

24) Eliminate Medicare Advantage plans or limit them to inpatient care; severity adjustment in the latter case based on hospital records only. This would eliminate the focus on generating more high complexity codes.

25) Medicare to pay PCPs directly, mainly fee-for-service with limited bonuses based on a brief list of quality measures.

Preventing Other Bad Things

26) Allow PCPs flexibility in scheduling to reduce burnout.

27) CMS and insurers must pay for all vaccinations given at a doctor's office (if the vaccine is covered elsewhere).

28) Retail and urgent care clinics mandated to communicate

about visits to PCPs; insurers to have higher co-pay/ deductible for these entities to encourage patients to see their regular doctor instead.

Preventing Oligopolies and Monopolies

29) Regulate private corporations employing physicians to limit overhead/profits and to avoid focus on short-term gains.

30) Give tax incentives to PCPs opening new practices to encourage expansion of primary care with reduced oligopoly and monopoly situations.

31) Use anti-trust laws to prevent excessive or reverse excessive consolidation in both medical care and pharmacies; preventing monopoly or oligopoly will reduce costs via competition.

BIBLIOGRAPHY

Aaronson, Alexandra L. Katherine Backes, Gaurava Agarwal, Joshua L. Goldstein, Joan Anzia, "Mental Health during residency training: assessing the barriers to seeking care, *Acad Psychiatry* 2018; 42(4): 469-472

Abara, N. Ogechi. Nicole Huang, Mukaila A. Raji, Yong-Fang Kuo, "Effect of Retail Clinic Use on Continuity of Care among Medicare Beneficiaries" *J Am Board Fam Med*, 2019; 32: 531-8

Aetna Active Health Management, Communication to Gregg Coodley, March 22, 2021

Agency for Healthcare Research and Quality, The Number of Practicing Primary Care Physicians in the United States, last revised July 2018, Rockville, MD, https://www.ahrq.gov/research/findings/factsheets/primary/pcwork1/index.html

Agency for Healthcare Research and Quality, Medical Expenditure Panel Survey (MEPS), 2008-2018, Rockville, MD, ClinCalc Drug Stats Database version 21.1, ClinCalc.com

Ahmed, Harris. J. Bryan Carmody, "On the Looming Physician Shortage and Strategic Expansion of Graduate Medical Education," *Cureus*, July 15, 2020; 12(7): 1-7

Allen, Patrick. Communication to Gregg Coodley, December 22, 2020

American Medical Association, Bureau of Medical Economics, *Economics and the Ethics of Medicine,* American Medical Association, Chicago, 1935, 49-50

364

American Medical Association, Physician Characteristics and
Distribution in the United States 1995/1996 Edition, Chicago,
1996

American Medical Association, 2016 AMA Prior Authorization
Physician Survey, American Medical Association, 2017

"American versus European Medical Science," *Medical Record 4*,
May 15, 1869, 133

Anonymous, to Gregg Coodley M.D., June 21, 2021

Anonymous, to Gregg Coodley, June 24, 2021

Arch Int Med, July 9, 2007; 167(13): 1400-1405

Ashwood, J. Scott. Martin Gaynor, Claude M. Setodji, Rachel O.
Reid, Elleri Weber, Ateev Mehrotra, "Retail Clinic Visits for
Low-Acuity Conditions Increase Utilization and Spending,"
Health Affairs, 2016; 35(3): 449-455

Atlas, Steven J. Richard W. Grant, Timothy G. Ferris, Yuchiao
Chang, Michael J. Barry, "Patient-Physician Connectedness and
Quality of Primary Care," *Ann Int Med*, March 3, 2009; 150(5):
325-335

Austin, Daniel R. Laurence C. Baker, "Less Physician Practice
Competition is Associated with Higher Prices Paid for Common
Procedures," *Health Affairs*, October 2015; 34(10): 1753-1760

Babbott, Stewart. and others, "Electronic medical records and
physician stress in primary care: Results from the MEMO
Study," *J Am Med Inform Assoc*, 2014; 21:e 100-106

Bae, J. "National estimates of the impact of electronic health
records on the workload of primary care physicians," *BMC
Health Serv Res*, May 10, 2016; 16:172

Baicker, Katherine. Amitabh Chandra, "Medicare Spending, The Physician Workforce and Beneficiaries' Quality of Care," *Health Affairs*, April 7, 2004; W184-W196

Baker, Laurence C. Kate Bundorf, Anne B. Royalty, "Physician Practice Competition and Prices Paid by Private Insurers for Office Visits," *JAMA* 2014; 312(16): 1653-1662

Baker, Laurence C. M. Kate Bundorf, Daniel P. Kessler, "Vertical Integration: Hospital Ownership of Physician Practices is Associated with Higher Prices and Spending," *Health Affairs*, May 2014; 33(5): 756-63

Banco, Erin. "Biden Admin remakes Vaccination Strategies after Mass Vaccination Sites Fizzle," *Politico*, March 29, 2021

Barken, Frederick M. *Out of Practice: Fighting for Primary Care Medicine in America*, ILR Press/Cornell University Press, Ithaca, 2011,

Barnett, Michael L. Asaf Bitton, Jeff Souza and Bruce. E. Landon, "Trends in outpatient care for Medicare Beneficiaries and Implications for Primary Care, 2000-2019, *Annals of Internal Medicine*, December 2021; 174(12): 1658-1665

Basu, Sanjay. Russell S. Phillips, Seth A. Berkowitz, Bruce E. Landon, Asaf Bilton, Robert L. Phillips, "Estimated Effect on Life Expectancy of Alleviating Primary Care Shortages in the United States," *Ann Int Med*,174(7), July 2021, 1-8

Basu, Sanjay. Seth A. Berkowitz, Robert L. Phillips, Asaf Bitton, Bruce E. Landon, Russell S. Phillips, "Association of Primary Care Supply with Population Mortality in the United States, 2005-2015," *JAMA Internal Med*, 2019; 179(4), 506-514

Beasley, John W. and others, "Information Chaos in Primary Care: Implications for Physician Performance and Patient Safety," *J Am Board Fam Med*, November 2011; 24(6): 745-751

Beaulieu, Nancy D. Leemore S. Dafny, Bruce E. Langdon, Jesse B. Dalton, Ifedayo Kuye, J. Michael McWilliams, "Changes in the Quality of Care After Hospital Mergers and Acquisitions," *NEJM*, January 2, 2020; 382(1): 51-9

Becker, Marshall H. Robert H. Drachman, John P. Kirscht, "A Field Experiment to Evaluate Various Outcomes of Continuity of Physician Care," *AJPH*, November 1974; 64(11): 1062-70

Becker, Marshall H. Robert H. Drachman, John P. Kirscht, "Continuity of Pediatricians: New Support for an Old Shibboleth," *Journal of Pediatrics* April 1974; 84(4): 599-605

Beckman, Howard. "Three Degrees of Separation," *Ann Int Med*, December 15, 2009; 151: 890-891

Bell, Howard. "The Prior Authorization Burden, *Minnesota Medicine*, November-December 2014, 18-25

Bendix, Jeffrey. "The Prior Authorization Predicament," *Medical Economics*, July 10, 2014, 29-34

Bentz, Charles. Personal Communication to Gregg Coodley, March 31, 2021

Berdahl, Carl T. Molly C. Easterlin, Gery Rayn, Jack Needleman and Teryl K. Nuckols, "Primary Care Physicians in the Merit-based Incentive Payment System (MIPS): a Qualitative Investigation of Participants' Experiences, Self-Re-ported Practice Changes and Suggestions for Program Administrators," *JGIM* 2019; 34(10): 2275-81

Bergeson, Joette Gdovin. Karen Worley, Anthony Louder, Melea Ward, John Graham, "Retrospective Database Analysis of the Impact of Prior Authorization for type 2 diabetes Medications on Health Care Costs in a Medicare advantage prescription Drug Plan Population," J Manag Care Pharm, June 2013; 19(5): 374-84

Berman, Stephen. "Continuity, the Medical Home and Retail-Based Clinics," *Pediatrics*, November 2007; 120(5): 1123-1125

Berwick, Donald M. Andrew D. Hackbarth, "Eliminating Waste in US Health Care," *JAMA*, April 11, 2012; 307(14): 1513-16

Berwick, Donald M. "Era 3 for Medicine and Health Care," *JAMA*, 315(13), April 5, 2016

Bindman, Andrew B. Kevin Grumbach, Dennis Osmond, Karen Vranizan, Anita L. Stewart, "Primary Care and Receipt of Preventive Services." *J Gen int Med*, 1996: 11: 269-276

Block, Susan D. Nancy Clark-Chiarelli, Antoinette S. Peters, Judith D. Singer, "Academia's Chilly Climate for Primary Care," *JAMA*, September 4, 1996; 276(9): 677-682

Bloom, BS. J. Jacobs, "Cost Effects of Restricting Cost Effective Therapy" Medical Care 1985; 23(7): 872-880

Bodenheimer, Thomas. Bernard Lo, Lawrence Casalino, "Primary Care Physicians Should Be Coordinators, Not Gatekeepers," *JAMA*, June 2, 1999; 281(21): 2045-2049

Bodenheimer, Thomas. Robert A. Berenson, Paul Rudolf, "The Primary Care-Specialty Income Gap: Why it Matters," *Ann Int Med*, 2007; 146: 301-306

Bodenheimer, Thomas., "Coordinating Care – A Perilous Journey Through the Health Care System," *NEJM*, March 6, 2008; 358(10): 1064-1071

Bodenheimer, Thomas. "Primary Care – Will It Survive?" *NEJM*, August 31, 2006; 355(9): 861-4

Boyd, Cynthia M. Jonathan Darer, Chad Boult, Linda P. Fried, Lisa Bout, Albert W. Wu, "Clinical Practice Guidelines and Quality of Care for Older Patients with Multiple Comorbid Diseases.

Implications for Pay for Performance," *JAMA* 2005: 294: 716-724

Breslau, Naomi. "Continuity Reexamined: Differential Impact on Satisfaction with Medical Care for Disabled and Normal Children," *Medical Care*, April 1982; 20(4): 347-60

Bronstein, Janet M. and others, "Primary care visits and ambulatory care sensitive diabetes hospitalizations among adult Alabama Medicaid beneficiaries," *Primary Care Diabetes,* 2022; https://doi.org/10.1016/jpcd.2021.10.005

Bryant, Sharon E. "Filling the gaps: Preparing nurse practitioners for hospitalist practice," *Journal of the American Association of Nurse Practitioners*, January 2018; 30(1): 4-9

Buchbinder, Sharon Bell. Modena Wilson, Clifford G. Mellick, Neil R. Powe, "Primary Care Physician Job Satisfaction and Turnover," *AM Journal Managed Care* 2001; 7: 701-713

Burger, Janice. Communication to Gregg Coodley, January 26, 2011

Burstein, David S. David T. Liss, Jeffrey A. Linder. "Association of Primary Care Physician Compensation Incentives and Quality of Care in the United States, 2012-2016," *JGIM*, 2021; 37(2): 359-366

Cabana, Michael D. Sandra H. Jee. "Does continuity of care improve patient outcomes," *Journal Of Family Practice,* December 2004; 53:12, 974-980

Capps, Cory. Daniel Dranove, Christopher Ody. "The Effect of hospital acquisitions of physician practices on prices and spending." *Journal of Health Economics*, 2018: 59: 139-152

Casalino, Lawrence P. and others, "US Physician Practices Spend More than $15.4 Billion Annually to Report Quality Measures," *Health Affairs*, March 2016; 35:3: 401-404

Casalino, Lawrence P. "The Unintended Consequences of Measuring Quality on the Quality of Health Care," *NEJM*, October 7, 1999; 341(15): 1147-1150

Casalino, Lawrence P. Dhruv Khullar, "Value-Based Purchasing and Physician Professionalism," *JAMA*, November 2, 2019; 322(17): 1647-48

Casalino, Lawrence P. and others, "What Does It Cost Physician Practices to Interact With Health Insurance Plans," *Health Affairs*; 28(4), w533-543 (published online 14 May 2009; 10.1377/hlthaff.28.4.w533)

Casalino, Lawrence P. and others, "Small Primary Care Physician Practices Have Low Rates of Preventable Hospital Admissions," *Health Affairs*, September 2014, 33(9): 1680-88

Cassell, Eric J. *Doctoring: The Nature of Primary Care Medicine*, Oxford University Press, 1997,

Catlin, Mary K. John A. Poisal, Cathy A. Cowan, "Out of Pocket Health Care Expenditures, By Insurance Status, 2007-10, *Health Affairs*, January 2015; 34(1): 111-116

Centers for Medicare and Medicaid Services, "Comprehensive Primary Care Initiative," https://innovation.cms.gov/innovation-models/comprehensive-primary-care-initiative

Chang, Chiang-Hua. Theres A. Stukel, Ann Barry Flood, David C. Goodman, "Primary Care Physician Workforce and Medicare Beneficiaries' Health Outcomes," *JAMA*, May 25, 2011; 305(20): 2096-2105

Chen, Candice. Imam Xierali, Katie Piwnica-Worms, Robert Phillips, "The redistribution of graduate medical education positions in 2005 failed to boost primary care or rural training," *Health Affairs (Millwood)* January 2013, 32(1): 102-110

370

Christakis, Dimitri A. Jeffrey A. Wright, Thomas D. Koepsell, Scott Emerson, Frederick A. Connell, "Is Greater Continuity of Care Associated With Less Emergency Department Utilization?" *Pediatrics*, April 1999; 103(4): 738-742

Colla, Carrie H. Toyin Ajayi, Asaf Bitton, "Potential Adverse Financial Implications of the Merit-based Incentive Payment System for Independent and Safety Net Practices," *JAMA*, September 8, 2020; 324(10): 948-950

Colwill, Jack M. James M. Cultice, Robin L. Kruse, "Will generalist physician supply meet demands of an increasing and aging population," *Health Affairs (Millwood)* 2008; 27(3): w232-w241

Colwill, Jack M. "Where Have all the Primary Care Applicants Gone?" *NEJM*, 326(6): 387-393

Coodley, Gregg. Communication to Fanno Creek Clinic, February 9, 2018

Coodley, Gregg. Conversation with patient BH, June 8, 2021

Coodley, Gregg. Communication to Bill Sherer, January 25, 2011

Coodley, Gregg. Communication to Fanno Providers, February 11, 2011

Coodley, Gregg. Communication to Fanno Providers, October 6, 2011

Coodley, Gregg. Communication to Kristen Dillon and others, March 15, 2021

Coodley, Gregg. Communication to Kristen Dillon, March 1, 2020

Coodley, Gregg, Personal Communication, February 7, 2022

Coodley, Karen. Communication to Gregg Coodley, March 31, 2021

Cooper, Zack. Stuart Craig, Martin Gaynor, Nir J. Harish, Harlan M. Krumholz, John Van Reenen, "Hospital Prices Grew Substantially Faster than Physician Prices for Hospital-Based Care in 2007-14," *Health Affairs*, February 2019; 38(2): 184-89

Corder, J. Collins. "Streamlining the Insurance Prior Authorization Debacle," *Missouri Medicine*, July/August 2018; 115(4): 312-314

Cowan, Marie J. and others, "The Effect of a Multidisciplinary Hospitalist/Physician and Advance Practice Nurse Collaboration on Hospital Costs," *Journal of Nursing Administration*, 36:2, 79-85, February 2006

Cristiano Lima, Aaron Schaffer. "Amazon Foes Fear Company's Health Care Acquisition will Cement its Power." *Washington Post*, July 22, 2022

Crosson, Francis J. Kate Bloniarz, David Glass, James Matthews, "MedPACs Urgent Recommendation: Eliminate MIPS, Take a Different Direction," *Health Affairs Blog*, March 16, 2018, 10.1377/HBOG20180309.302220

Cryts, Aine. "Nearly 70% of Physicians Working for Hospitals or Corporate Entities New Survey Reveals," *Medscape Medical News*, July 1, 2021

Cryts, Aine, "3 in 4 Doctors Are Employed by Hospitals, Corporate Entities: Report," *Medscape*; https://www.medscape.com/viewarticle/972604_print

Cunningham, Paige Winfield. Alexandra Ellerbeck, "The Health 202: One hundred million eligible Americans still haven't gotten vaccinated," *Washington Post*, July 1, 2021

CVS Caremark Clinical Services, Communication to Gregg Coodley, April 18, 2021

372

Davis, Karen. Kristof Stremikis, Michelle M. Doty, Mark A. Zezza, "Medicare Beneficiaries Less Likely to Experience Cost And Access-Related Problems Than Adults with Private Coverage," *Health Affairs*, August 2012; 31(8): 1866-1875

DeCamp, Matthew. Lisa Soleymani Lehmann, "Guiding Choice – Ethically Influencing Referrals in ACOs," *NEJM*, January 15, 2015; 372(3): 205-7

DeCamp, Matthew. Lois Synder Sulmasy for the American College of Physicians Ethics, Professionalism and Human Rights Committee, "Ethical and Professionalism Implications of Physician Employment and Health Care Business Practices: A Policy Paper From the American College of Physicians," *Ann Int Med*, 2021; 174: 844-51

Deshpande, Satish P. Jim DeMello, "A Comparative Analysis of Factors that Hinder Primary Care Physicians' and Specialist Physicians' Ability to Provide High-Quality Care," *Health Care Manager*, 2011; 30(2): 172-178

DesRoches, Catherine M. Peter Buerhaus, Robert S. Dittus, Karen Donelan, "Primary Care Workforce Shortages and Career Recommendations from Practicing Clinicians," *Academic Medicine*, May 2015; 90(5): 671-677

DeVoe, Jennifer. George E. Fryer, J. Lee Hargraves, Robert L. Phillips, Larry A. Green, "Does Career Dissatisfaction affect the Ability of Family Physicians to Deliver High-Quality Patient Care," *Journal of Family Practice*, March 2002; 51(3): 223-228

DeVoe, Jennifer. George E. Fryer, Robert Phillips, Larry Green, "Receipt of Preventive Care Among Adults: Insurance Status and Usual Source of Care," *Am J Public Health* 2003; 93: 786-791

Dewan, Mantosh J. John J. Norcini, "We Must Graduate Physicians,

Not Doctors," *Academic Medicine*, March 2020; 95(3): 336-339

Dilger, Benjamin T. Margaret C. Gill, Jill G. Lenhart, Gregory M. Garrison, "Visit Entropy Associated with Diabetic Control Outcomes," *J Am Board Fam Med* 2019: 32: 739-745

Dill, Michael J. Edward S. Salsberg, "The Complexities of Physician Supply and Demand: Projections Through 2025," Association of American Medical Colleges, November 2008, http://www.aamc.org/workforceposition.pdf

Donaldson, Molla S., Karl D. Yordy, Kathleen N. Lohr KN, Neal A. Vanselow, Editors. *Primary Care: America's Health in a New Era*, Committee on the Future of Primary Care, Division of Health Care Services. Institute of Medicine, National Academy Press, Washington, DC, 1996, 31

Dorsey, E. Ray. David Jarjoura, Gregory W. Rutecki, "Influence of Controllable Lifestyle on Recent Trends in Specialty Choice by US Medical Students," *JAMA*, September 3, 2003; 290(9): 1173-78

Dorsey, Joseph L. "The Health Maintenance Organization Act of 1973 (P.L.93-222) and Prepaid Group Practice Plans," *Medical Care*, 13:1(Jan. 1975), p1-9

Drugs.Com., March 26, 2021

Dyrbye, Liselotte N. "Burnout Among U.S. Medical Students, Residents and Early Career Physicians Relative to the General U.S. Population," *Academic Medicine*, March 2014; 89(3): 443-451

Edwards, Samuel T. John N. Mafi, Bruce E. Landon, "Trends and Quality of Care in Outpatient Visits to Generalist and Specialist Physicians Delivering Primary Care in the United States, 1997-2010," *JGIM*, February 25, 2014; 29(6): 947-55

Eisenberg, John M. "Physician Utilization: The State of Research about Physicians' Practice Patterns," *Medical Care* 2002; 40(11): 1016-1035

Emanuel, Ezekiel J. Farzad Mostashari, Amol S. Navathe, "Designing a Successful Primary Care Capitation Model," *JAMA*, May 21, 2021:E1-E2

Epstein, Arnold M. "Pay for Performance at the Tipping Point," *NEJM*, 356(5): 515-517

Epstein, David. "The Role of 'Hospitalists' in the Health Care System," *NEJM*, 336:6, February 6, 1997, 444

Ettner, Susan Louise. "The Timing of Preventive Services For Women and Children: The Effect of having a Usual Source of Care," *Am Journal Public Health* 1996; 86: 1748-56

Express Scripts Clinical Team, Communication to Gregg Coodley, April 19, 2021

Feinwachs, David. "It's time to bring competition back to health care," *Medical Economics*, February 2022; 7-8

Fincher, Ruth-Marie E. "The Road Less Traveled – Attracting Students to Primary Care," *NEJM*, August 12, 2004, 351(7): 630-632

Fletcher, Robert H. and others, "Patients' Priorities for Medical Care," *Medical Care,* February 1983; volume XXI(2): 234-242

Fogelman, Alan M. "Strategies for Training Generalists and Subspecialists," *Ann Int Med* 1994: 120: 589-583

Forrest, Christopher B. "Strengthening Primary Care to Bolster the Health Care Safety Net," *JAMA*, March 1, 2006; 295(9): 1062-4

Frakt, Austin B. Ashish K. Jha, "Face the Facts: We Need to Change the Way We Do Pay for Performance," *Ann Int Med*, 168(4), February 20, 2018

375

Franklin, Janet. "The ABCS of HHS-HCCs: Taking a Closer Look at the Commercial Risk Adjustment," *Journal of the AHIMA*, October 2014; 86(10): 76-9

Franks, Peter. Carolyn M. Clancy, Paul A. Nutting, "Gatekeeping Revisited – Protecting Patients from Overtreatment," *NEJM*, August 6, 1992; 327(6): 424-429

Franks, Peter. Kevin Fiscella, "Primary care physicians and specialists as personal physicians: health care expenditures and mortality experience," *Journal of Family Practice*, August 1998; 47(2): 105-115

Freeborn, Donald K. "Satisfaction, commitment and psycho-logical well-being among HMO physicians," *Western Journal of Medicine*, January 2001; 174: 13-18

Frey, Bruno S. "Does Monitoring Increase Work Effort? The Rivalry with Trust and Loyalty," *Economic Inquiry*, Volume XXX1, October 1993: 663-670

Gaffney, Adam. and others, "Medical Documentation Among US Office-Based Physicians in 2019: A National Study," *JAMA Internal Medicine*, May 2022; 182(5): 564-566

Garbutt, Jane M. and others, "Pediatric Providers' Attitudes Toward Retail Clinics." *J Pediatr,* 2013; 163: 1384-8

Garibaldi, Robert A. Carol Popkave, Wayne Bylsma, "Career Plans for Trainees in Internal Medicine Residency Programs," *Academic* Medicine, May 2005; 80(5): 507-512

Gemelas, Jordan C. "Post ACA Trends in the US Primary Care Physician Shortage with Index of Relative Rurality," *Journal of Rural Health*, 2021: 37: 700-704

Geyman, John P., "Beyond the Covid-19 Pandemic: The Urgent Need to Expand Primary Care and Family Medicine," *Fam Med*, January 2021; 53(1): 48-53, p50

Gill, James M. Arch G. Mainous, Musa Nsereko, "The Effect of Continuity of Care on Emergency Department Use," *Arch Fam Med*, April 2000; 9: 333-338

Gill, James M. Arch G. Mainous, "The Role of Provider Continuity in Preventing Hospitalizations," *Arch Fam Med*, July/ Aug 1998, 7: 352-7

Go, JT. and others, "Do hospitalists affect clinical outcomes and efficiency for patients with acute upper gastrointestinal hemorrhage," *J Hosp Med*, 2010; 5: 133-139

Goldsmith, Jeff Charles. *Can Hospitals Survive? The New Competitive Health Care Market,* Dow Jones-Irwin, Homewood, IL, 1981

Gondi, Suhas. Karen Joynt Maddox, Rishi K. Wadhera. " Reaching for Equity-Moving from Regressive to Progressive Value-Based Payment," *NEJM*. July 14, 2022; 387(2):97-99

Gondi, Suhas. Zirui Song, "Potential Implications of Private Equity Investments in Health Care Delivery," *JAMA*, March 19, 2019; 321(11): 1047-8

Goodrx.com

Goodson, John D. "Unintended Consequences of Resource-Based Relative Value scale Reimbursement," *JAMA*, November 21, 2007, 298(19): 2308-2310

Goodwin, James S. Yu-Li Lin, Siddhartha Singh, Yong-Fang Kuo, "Variation in Length of Stay and Outcomes among Hospitalized Patients attributable to Hospitals and Hospitalists." *JGIM*, 2012, 28(3): 370-6

Gottlieb, Sidney. HouseCalls Plan of Care Report to Gregg Coodley. March 29, 2021

Gottschalk, Andrew. Susan A. Flocke, "Time spent in Face-to-Face Patient Care and Work Outside the Examination Room," *Ann Family Medicine*, November/December 2005; 3(6): 488-493

Gray, Bradley M., Jonathan L. Vandergrift, Jennifer P. Stevens, Bruce Landon. "Evolving Practice Choices by Newly Certified and More Senior General Internists." *Ann Int Med*, July, 2022. 175(7): 1022-1027.

Greenfield, Sheldon. and others, "Variations in Resource Utilization Among Medical Specialties and Systems of Care: Results from the Medical Outcomes Study," *JAMA*, March 25, 1992; 267(12): 164-1630

Gregory, Douglas. Walter Baigelman, Ira B. Wilson, "Hospital Economics of the Hospitalist," *Health Services Research*, June 2003; 38:3: 905-918

Grembowski, David. and others, "Managed Care and Primary Physician Satisfaction" *J Am Board Fam Pract* 2003: 16: 383-93

Gross, David A. Stephen J. Zyzanski, Elaine A. Borawski, Randall D. Cebul, Kurt C. Stange, "Patient Satisfaction with Time spent with their physician," *Journal of Family Practice*, August 1998; 47(2)

Grumbach, Kevin. and others, "Resolving the Gatekeeper Conundrum: What Patients Value in Primary Care and Referrals to Specialists," *JAMA*, July 21, 1999; 281(3): 261-266

Grumbach, Kevin. Dennis Osmond, Karen Vranizan, Deborah Jaffe, Andrew B. Bindman, "Primary Care Physicians' Experience of financial Incentives in Managed Care Systems," *NEJM*, November 19, 1998; 339: 1516-21

Grumbach, Kevin. Thomas Bodenheimer, Deborah Cohen, Robert L. Phillips, Jr, Kurt C. Strange, John M. Westfall. "Revitalizing the U.S. Primary Care Infrastructure," *NEJM*, September 23, 2021; 385(13): 1156-8

Gugielmo, Wayne J. "A Mixed Job Report for Primary Care," *Medical Economics*, May 16, 2008, p8

Gunderson, Richard. "Hospitalists and the Decline of Comprehensive Care," *NEJM*, 375; 11: 1011-1013

Gunta, Satya Preetham and Others. "Association of number of primary care physicians with preventable hospitalizations and premature deaths," *Postgraduate Medicine*, 2021, https://doi.org/10.1080/00325481.2021.2021038

Gusmano, Michael K., Miriam Laugesen, Victor G. Rodwin, Lawrence D. Brown, "Getting the Price Right: How Some Countries Control Spending in A Fee-For-Service System," *Health Affairs*, November 2020; 39(11): 18671874

Guttler, Sanford. "The Role of 'Hospitalists' in the Health Care System," *NEJM*, 336:6, February 6, 1997, 445

Haas, Jennifer S. E. Francis Cook, Ann Louise Puopolo, Helen R. Burstin, Paul D. Cleary, Troyen A. Brennan, "Is the professional Satisfaction of General Internists Associated with Patient Satisfaction," *JGIM* 2000; 15:122-128

Hall, Oswald. "The Stages of a Medical Career," *American Journal of Sociology* 53 (March 1948), 327

Hare, Allison J. Srinath Adusumali, Saehwan Park, Mitesh S. Patel, "Assessment of Primary Care Appointment Times and Appropriate Prescribing of Statins for At-Risk Patients," *JAMA Network Open* 2021:4(5) e219050.doi10.1001/jamanetworkopen.2021.9050

Hauer, Karen E. and others, "Factors Associated with Medical

Students' Career Choices Regarding Internal Medicine," *JAMA*, September 10, 2008; 300(10): 1154-64

Haymond, JaNae. Communication to Lane Hickey, November 30, 2018

Healthnet Medicare Programs, Patient Transition Fill, to Gregg Coodley, March 22, 2021

Heatherington, Jeff. Press Release, December 18, 2017

Heckler, Tom. Communication to Gregg Coodley, 1997

Himmelstein, David U. Adam Wright, Steffie Woolhandler, "Hospital Computing and the Costs and Quality of Care," *American Journal of Medicine*, 2010; 123: 40-46

Hockenberry, Jason. "Cost of Compliance with CMS Physician Quality Monitoring-Too High," *JAMA Health Forum* 2021; 2(5)>e210684.doi:10.1001/jamahealthforum.2021.0684

Hoff, Timothy. *Practices under Pressure: Primary Care Physicians and Their Medicine in the Twenty-First Century*, Rutgers University Press, New Brunswick, 2010

HouseCalls, Communication to Gregg Coodley, June 16, 2021

HouseCalls, Communication to Gregg Coodley, June 17, 2021

Howard, Jenna. and others, "Electronic Health Record Impact on Work Burden in Small, Unaffiliated Community-Based Primary Care," *JGIM* 2012: 28(1): 107-13

Howell, Scott, Peery T. Yin, James C. Robinson, "Quantifying the Economic Burden of Drug Utilization Management on Payers, Manufacturers, Physicians and Patients," *Health Affairs*, 40(8): 1206-14

Howrey, Bret T. Yong-Fang Kuo, James S. Goodwin, "Association of care by hospitalists on discharge destination and 30-day outcomes following acute ischemic stroke," *Medical Care* 49:8, August 2011, 701-707

Hussey, Peter S. Eric C. Schneider, Robert S. Rudin, D. Steven Fox, Julie Lai, Craig Evan Pollack, "Continuity and the Costs of Care for Chronic Disease," *JAMA Internal Medicine*, May 2014; 174(5): 742-8

Iannuzzi, Michael C., James C. Iannuzzi, Andrew Holtsbery, Stuart M. Wright, Stephen J. Knohl, "Comparing Hospitalist-Midlevel Practitioner Team Performance on Length of Stay and Direct Patient Care Cost," *J Grad Med Educ*, 2015 March; 7(1)65-9

Ibrahim, Tod. "The Case for Invigorating Internal Medicine," *American Journal of Medicine*, September 1, 2004; 117: 365-369

Iglehart, John K. "The Expansion of Retail Clinics-Corporate Titans vs. Organized Medicine," *NEJM*, July 23, 2015; 373(4): 301-3

Iliffe, Steven. *"From General Practice to Primary Care: The industrialization of Family Medicine*, Oxford University Press, 2008,

Incze, Michal A. Rita F. Redberg, Mitchell H. Katz, "Over prescription in Urgent Care Clinics – The Fast and the Spurious," *JAMA Internal Medicine*, September 2018; 178(9): 1269-1270

Institute of Medicine, *Primary Care: America's Health in a New Era*, National Academy Press, Washington, D.C., 1996

Johnston, Kenton J. Timothy L. Wiemken, Jason M. Hockenberry, Jose F. Figueroa, Karen E. Joynt Maddox, "Association of Clinician Health System Affiliation With Outpatient Performance Ratings in the Medicare Merit-Based Incentive

Payment System," *JAMA*, 2020; 324(10): 984-992

Johnston, Kenton J. Jason M. Hockenberry, Karen E. Joynt Maddox, "Building a Better Clinician Value-Based Payment Program," *JAMA*, January 12, 2021; 325(2): 129-130

Jones, Laney K. Irene G. Ladd, Christina Gregor, Michael A. Evans, Jove Graham, Michael R. Gionfriddo, "Understanding the medication prior-authorization process: A case study of patients and clinical staff from a large rural integrated health delivery system." *Am J Health-Syst Pharm*, April 1, 2019, 76(7): 453-459

Jones, Laney K. Ilene G. Ladd, Michael R. Gionfriddo, Christina Gregor, Michael A. Evans, Jove Graham, "Medications requiring prior authorization across health insurance plans," *Am J Health-Syst Pharm*, 2020; 77: 644-648

Journal of the American Medical Association "Reorganizing an academic medical service: Impact on cost, quality, patient satisfaction and education," *JAMA* 1998, 279, 1560-1565

Kaissi, Amer. Tom Charland, "The Evolution of Retail Clinics in the United States, 2006-2012; *Health Care Manager*, 2013; 32(4): 336-42

Kalan, Louise. Tracy A. Klein, "Characteristics and perceptions of the US nurse practitioner hospitalist workforce," *J Am Assoc Nurse Pract*, 2020 Nov 16

Kane, Leslie. "Medscape National Physician Burnout, Depression and Suicide Report 2019," *Medscape*, January 16, 2019; https://www.medscape.com/sildeshow/2019-lifestyle-burnout-depression-6011056

Kane, Leslie," Physician Burnout and Depression Report 2022: Stress, Anxiety and Anger," *Medscape Internal Medicine*,

382

January 21, 2022

Kasper, Judith D. "The Importance of Usual Source of Care for Children's Physician Access and Expenditures," *Medical Care*, May 1987; 25(5): 386-398

Kassirer, Jerome P. "Doctor Discontent," *NEJM*NEJM; 339(21): 1543-44

Kassirer, Jerome P. "Primary Care and the Affliction of Internal Medicine," *NEJM*, March 4, 1993; 328: 9: 648-650, p648

Kassler, William J. Steven A. Wartman, Rebecca A. Silliman, "Why Medical Students Choose Primary Care Careers," *Acad Med*, January 1991; 66(1): 41-43

Kendall, Patricia L. Hanan C. Selvin, "Tendencies Towards Specialization in Medical Training," quoted in *The Student Physician*, ed. Robert K. Merton, George G. Reader, Patricia L. Kendall, Harvard University Press, 1957, 153-174

Khullar, Dhruv. Amelia M. Bond, Eloise May O'Donnell, Yuting Qian, David N. Gans, Lawrence P. Casalino, "Time and Financial Costs for Physicians to Participate in the Medicare Merit-based Incentive Payment System: A Qualitative Study," *JAMA Health Forum* 2021;2(5):e210527.doi:10.1001/jamahealthforum.2021.0527

Khullar, Dhruv. Gregory C. Burke, Lawrence P. Casalino, "Can Small Physician Practices Survive? Sharing Services as a Path to Viability," *JAMA*, April 3, 2018, 319(13):1321-22

Kilgore, C. "Some Internists Bid Farewell to Rounds," *Internal Medicine News*, March 1, 1995,1, 33

Koch, TG. BW Wendling, NE Wilson. "How Vertical integration affects the quantity and cost of care for Medicare beneficiaries." *Journal of Health Economics*, 2016; 52: 19-32

Kocher, Robert. Nikhil R. Sahni, "Hospitals' Race to Employ Physicians – The Logic behind a Money-Losing Proposition," *NEJM*, May 12, 2011; 364(19): 1790-3

Kralewski, John E. Bryan E. Dowd, YI Xu, "Medical Groups Can Reduce Costs By Investing in Improved Quality of Care for Patients with Diabetes," *Health Affairs*, August 2012; 31(8): 1830-35

Kralewski, John E. Terence D. Wingert, David J. Knutson, Christopher E. Johnson, "The Effects of Medical Group Practice Organizational Factors on Physicians Use of Resources," *Journal of Healthcare Management*, May/June 1999; 44(3): 167-183

Kripalani, Sunil. Frank LeFevre, Christopher O. Phillips, Mark V. Williams, Preetha Basaviah, David W. Baker, "Deficits in Communications and Information Transfer Between Hospital-Based and Primary Care Physicians: Implications for Patient Safety and Continuity of Care," *JAMA*, February 28, 2007, 297:8, 831-841

Ku, Benson S. Benjamin G. Druss, "Associations Between Primary Care Provider Shortage Areas and County-Level COVID-19 Infection and Mortality Rates in the USA," *J Gen Int Med*, 2020; 35(11): 3404-5

Kuo, Yong-Fang, James S. Goodwin, "Association of Hospitalist Care with Medical Utilization After Discharge: Evidence of Cost Shift from a Cohort Study," *Ann Int Med*, August 2, 2011, 152-159

Lafferty, Fred W. *The Major Cause of Rising Health Care Cost with Decreasing Quality: A Scarcity of Primary Care Physicians*, Page Publishing, New York, 2015

Lambrew, Jeanne M. Goron H. DeFriese, Timothy S. Carey, Thomas C. Rickets, Andrea K. Biddle, "The Effects of Having a Regular Doctor on Access to Primary Care," *Medical Care* 1996; 34(2): 138-151

Larson, Eric B. and others, "The Future of General Internal Medicine: Report and Recommendations from the society of General Internal Medicine (SGIM) Task Force on the Domain of General Internal Medicine," *JGIM*, 2004; 19:69-77

Leigh, J. Paul. Richard L. Kravitz, Mike Schembri, Steven J. Samuels, Shanaz Mobley, "Physician Career Satisfaction Across Specialties," *Arch Int Med*, July 22, 2002; 162: 1577-1584

Levinsky, Norman. "Recruiting for Primary Care," *NEJM*, March 4, 1993; 328;9: 656-660; p658

Liao, Joshua M. Risa J. Lavizzo-Mourey, Amol S. Navathe, "A National Goal to Advance Health Equity Through Value-Based Payment," *JAMA*, June 22/29. 2021; 325(24): 2439-2440

Liao, Joshua M. Amol S. Navathe, "Does the Merit-Based Incentive Payment System Disproportionately Affect Safety-Net Practices," *JAMA Health Forum* 2020: 1(5)e200452. Doi:10.1001/jamahealthforum.2020.0452

Lima, Cristiano. Aaron Schaffer. "Amazon Foes fear Company's Health Care Acquisition will cement its Power." *Washington Post*, July 22, 2022

Lin, Chen-Tan. and others, "Is Patients' Perception of time Spent With the Physician a Determinant of Ambulatory Patient Satisfaction," *Arch Int Med*, June 11, 2001; 161: 1437-1442

Lin, Susan X. Kathleen Klink, Peter Wingrove, Stephen Petterson and Andrew Bazemore, "Shifting Sources of US Primary Care Physicians, *American Family Physician*, 2015, www.aafp.org/afp

Lindenauer, Peter K. Michael B. Rothberg, Penelope S. Pekow, Christopher Kenwood, Evan M. Benjamin and Andrew D. Auerbach, "Outcomes of Care by Hospitalists, General Internists and Family Physicians, *NEJM*, 357:25, December 20, 2007, 2589-2600, p2589

Linder, Jeffrey A., Jun Ma, David W. Bates, Blackford Middleton, Randall S. Stafford, "Electronic Health Record Use and Quality of Ambulatory Care in the United States,"

Liss, David T. Toshiko Uchida, Cheryl L. Wilkes, Ankitha Radakrishnan, Jeffrey A. Linder, "General Health Checks in Adult Primary Care: A Review," *JAMA*, June 8, 2021, 325(22): 2294-2306

Lo, Chun-Han and others, "Association of Primary Care Physicians Per Capita with Covid-19 Vaccination Rates Among US Counties," *JAMA Network Open*, February 10, 2022:5(2):e2147920.doi.10.1001/jamanetworkopen.2021.47920

Luft, Harold S. Su-Ying Liang, Laura J. Eaton, Sukyung Chung, "Primary Care Physician Practice Styles and Quality, Cost and Productivity," *American Journal of Managed Care*, April 2020; 26(4): e127-e134

Macinko, James. Barbara Starfield, Leiyu Shi, "Quantifying the Health Benefits of Primary Care Physician Supply in the United States," *International Journal of Health Services*, 2007;37(1), 111-126

MacLean, Catherine H. Eve A. Kerr, Amir Qaseem, "Time Out – Charting a Path for Improving Performance Measurement," *NEJM*, May 10, 2018; 378(19):1757-1761

Mainous, Arch G. Richard Baker, Margaret M. Love, Denis Pereira Gray, James M. Gill, "Continuity of Care and trust in One's Physician: evidence from Primary Care in the United States and the United Kingdom," *Fam Med*, January 2001; 33(1): 22-27

Margolis, Jay M. and others, "Effect of a Medicaid Prior Authorization Policy for Pregabalin," Am Journal of Managed Care 2009; 15(10): e95-102

Marshall-Olson, Angela. Communication to Gina Johnson, May 3, 2018

Martin, Sara. Robert L. Phillips Jr., Stephen Petterson. Zachary Levin, Andrew W. Bazemore. "Primary Care Spending in the United States, 2002-2016," *JAMA Internal Medicine*, July 2020; 180(7): 1019-1020

Maslach, Christina. Wilmar B. Schaudel, Michael P. Leiter, "Job Burnout," *Annu Rev Psychol* 2001; 52:397-422

McDonald, Clement J. Michael H. McDonald, "Electronic Medical Records and Preserving Primary Care Physicians' Time," *Arch int Med*, February 13, 2012; 172(3): 285-287

McHarris, Louise. Interview with Gregg Coodley, July 22, 2021

McWilliams, J. Michael. ME Chernew, AM Zaslavsky, P Hamed, BE Landon, "Delivery system integration and health care spending and quality for Medicare beneficiaries," *JAMA Internal Medicine*, 2013; 173(15): 1447-56

Medical Economics, "AAFP Fires Back at the 'Convenience Care Revolution' Begun by Retailers," *Medical Economics*, July 25, 2013; 14

Medical Economics, "EHRs Continue to Hinder Physician Job Satisfaction," Medical Economics, July 25, 2014; 7

Medical Group Management Association, "Annual Regulatory Burden Report," October 2019; https://www.mgma.com/Resources/Government-

Programs/mgma-Annual-Regulatory-Burden-Report

Medical Group Management Association. Annual regulatory
burden report. Accessed April 13, 2021.
https://www.Mgma.com/Resources/Government-
Programs/MGMA-Annual-Regulatory-Burden-Report

Meier, Diane. "Private Equity and Healthcare Delivery," *JAMA*,
December 28, 2021; 326(24): 2533-34

Melnick, Edward R. Christine A. Sinsky and Harlan M. Krumholz,
"Implementing Measurement Science for Electronic Health
Record Use," *JAMA*, June 1, 2021; 325(21): 2149-2150

Meltzer, David O. "Hospitalists and Primary Care," *J Gen Int Med*
30(5): 541-2, 2015

Meltzer, David O. Jeanette W. Chung, "The Population Value of
Quality Indicator Reporting: A Framework for Prioritizing
Health Care Performance Measures," *Health Affairs*, January
2014; 33:1: 132-139

Meltzer, David. "Hospitalists and the Doctor-Patient Relationship,"
Journal Of Legal Studies, June 2011, volume 30, S2, 589-606

Menac, Verena H. Monica Sirski, Dhiwya Attawar, "Does
Continuity of Care Matter in a Universally Insured
Population," *Health Services Research*, April 2005, 40;2: 389-
400

Merritt, Karissa. Yalda Jabbarpour, Stephen Peterson, John. M.
Westfall, "State Level Variation on Primary Care Physician
Density," *American Family Physician*, August 2021; 104(2):
133-134

Meyers, David S. Carolyn M. Clancy, "Primary Care: too important
to Fail," *AIM* 2009:150(4), 272-3

Miller, Robert H. Christopher West, Tiffany Martin Brown, Ida Sim, Chris Ganchoff, "The Value of Electronic Health Records in Solo or Small Group Practices," *Health Affairs*, September/October 2005;24(5):1127-1137

Millis JS. Citizens Commission on Graduate Medical Education, American Medical Association, Chicago, 1966

Moda Health, Provider Communication: Request for Prescription Change or Information, to Gregg Coodley, April 2, 2021

Monroe, Julie. "Nurse Practitioner versus Doctor: In-Depth Career Comparison," *Nursing Process.org*, 2021

Moore, Carlton. Juan Wisnivesky, Stephen Williams, Thomas McGinn, "Medical Errors Related to Discontinuity of Care from an Inpatient to an Outpatient Setting," *JGIM*, August 2003; 18: 646-651

Moore, Gordon. Jonathan Showstack, "Primary Care Medicine in Crisis: Toward Reconstruction and Renewal," *Ann Int Med* 2003: 138: 244-247

Morra, Dante. Sean Nicholson, Wendy Levinson, David N. Gans, Terry Hammons, Lawrence P. Casalino, "US Physician Practices versus Canadians: Spending Nearly Four Times as Much Money Interacting with Payers," *Health Affairs*, August 2011; 30(8): 1443-1450

Muhlestein, David B. Nathan J. Smith, "Physician Consolidation: Rapid Movement from Small to Large Group Practices, 2013-15," *Health Affairs*, September 2016; 35(9): 1638-42

Mullan, Fitzhugh. "The 'Mona Lisa' of Health Policy: Primary Care at Home and Abroad," *Health Affairs*, 17(2): 118-126

Murphy, Daniel R. and others, "Electronic Health Record-based Messages to Primary Care Providers: Valuable Information or

Just Noise," *Arch Int Med*, February 13, 3012; 172(3): 283-5

Murray, Alison. Jana E. Montgomery, Hong Chang, William H. Rogers, Thomas Inui, Dana Gelb Safran, "Doctor Discontent: A Comparison of Physician Satisfaction in Different Delivery System Setting, 1986 and 1997," *J Gen Int Med* 2001; 16: 451-459

Nakasahima, William F. "The Role of 'Hospitalists' in the Health Care System," *NEJM*, 336:6, February 6, 1997, 445

National Center for Health Statistics, Health, United States, 2010 with special feature on Death and Dying, Hyattsville, Md, 2010

Navathe, Amol S., Claire T. Dinh, Anders Chen, Joshua M. Liao, "Findings and Implications from MIPS Year 1 Performance Data," *Health Affairs Blog*, January 18, 2019, 10.1377/HBLOG20190117.305369

Nixon, Richard. Transcript of Tape Conversation between President Richard Nixon and John D. Ehrlichman(1971) that led to the HMO Act of 1973 (https://en.wikisource.org/wiki)

Nyweide, David J. William B. Weeks, Daniel J. Gottlieb, Lawrence P. Casalino, Eliot S. Fisher, "Relationship of Primary Care Physicians' Patient Caseload with Measurement of Quality and Cost Performance," *JAMA*, December 9, 2009; 302(22):2444-2450

O'Malley, Ann S. Jeanne Mandelblatt, Karen Gold, Kathleen A. Cagney, Jon Kerner, "Continuity of Care and the Use of Breast and Cervical Cancer Screening Services in a Multiethnic Community," *Arch Internal Medicine*, July 14, 1997; 157:1462-70

O'Malley, Ann S. and others. "Practice-site-level measures of primary care comprehensiveness and their associations with patient outcomes," *Health Services Research*, 2021; 56: 371-377

Oliver, Christine. Communication to Gregg Coodley, May 5, 2021

OptumRx, to Gregg Coodley, July 3, 2021

Palms, Danielle L. and others, "Comparison of Antibiotic
Prescribing in Retail Clinics, Urgent Care Centers, Emergency
Departments and Traditional Ambulatory Care Settings in the
United States," *JAMA Internal Medicine*, September 2018;
178(9): 1267-69

Pamela Hartzband, Jerome Groopman, "Physician Burnout,
Interrupted," *NEJM*, June 25, 2020; 382(26): 2485-7

Panagioti, Maria. and others, "Controlled Interventions to Reduce
Burnout in Physicians: A Systemic Review and Meta-analysis,"
JAMA Internal Medicine 2017; 177(2): 195-205

Papanicolas, Irene. Liana R. Woskie, Ashish K. Jha, "Health Care
Spending in the United States and Other High-In-come
Countries," *JAMA*, March 13, 2018; 319(10): 1024-1039

Park, Jeongyoung. Karen Jones, "Use of Hospitalists and Office-
Based Primary Care Physicians Productivity," *JGIM*, August
2014; 30(5): 572-81

Patel, Vaishal. Eric Jamoom, Chun-Ju Hsiao, Michael F. Furukawa,
Melinda Buntin, "Variation in Electronic Health Record
Adoption and Readiness for Meaningful Use," *J Gen Intern
Med*, 2013; 28(7): 957-64

Pegus, Cheryl. Communication to Gregg Coodley, January 27, 2021

Perrin, James M. and others, "Primary Care Involvement Among
Hospitalized Children," *Arch Pediatr Adolesc Med* 1996; 150:
479-486

Petersdorf, Robert G. "Primary Care Applicants – They Get No
Respect," *NEJM*, February 6, 1992; 326(6): 408-9

Petersen, Laura A. LeChauncy D. Woodard, Tracy Urech, Christina Daw, Supicha Sookanan. "Does Pay-for-Performance Improve the Quality of Health Care?" *Ann Int Med*, August 15, 2006; 145(4): 265-272

Petterson, Stephen M. Winston R. Liaw, Robert L. Phillips, David L. Rabin, David S. Meyers, Andrew W. Bazemore, "Projecting US Primary Care Physician Workforce Needs: 2010-2025." *Ann Fam Med*, 2012: 1): 503-509

Petterson, Stephen M. Winston R. Liaw, Carol Tran, Andrew W. Bazemore, "Estimating the Residency Expansion Required to Avoid Projected Primary Care Physicians Shortages by 2035," *Ann Family Medicine*, 13(2), March/April 2015, 107-114

Pfizer, Communication to Gregg Coodley, April 5, 2021

Pham, Hoangmai H. Deborah Schrag, Ann S. O'Malley, Benny Wu, Peter B. Bach, "Care Patterns in Medicare and Their Implications for Pay for Performance," *NEJM*, March 15, 2007; 356(11): 1130-1139

Pham, Hoangmai H. Joy M. Grossman, Genna Cohen, Thomas Bodenheimer, "Hospitalists and Care Transitions: The Divorce of Inpatient and Outpatient Care," *Health Affairs*, 2008; 27:5: 1315-1327

Phillips, Robert L. Jr. Andrew W. Bazemore, "Primary care and why it matters for the US health system reform," *Health Affairs (Millwood)* 2010 May: 29(5): 806-810

Phillips, Robert L. Jr. Linda A. MacCauley, Christopher F. Koller, "Implementing High-Quality Primary Care: A Report from the National Academies of Sciences, Engineering and Medicine," *JAMA*, June 22/29, 2021, 325(24): 2437-8

Phillips. Julie. "The Impact of Debt on Young Family Physicians:

Unanswered Questions with Critical Implications," *J Am Board Fam Med*, March 8, 2016; 177-179

Physicians Advocacy Institute. "Updated physician practice acquisition study: national and regional changes in physician employment, 2012-2018."*Physicians Advocacy Institute*, February 2019 (http://www.physicians advocacyinstitute.org/Portals/0/assets/docs/011919-Avalere-PAI-Physcian-Employment-Trends-Study-2018-Update.pdf?ver=2019-02-19-162735-117).

Piero, Mathilde H. and others, "Outcomes-based trial of an inpatient nurse practitioner service for general medical patients," *Journal of Evaluation in Clinical Practice*, 2001, 7(1), 21-33

Poses, Roy M. Wally R. Smith, "How Employed Physicians' Contracts may Threaten Their Patients and Professionalism," *Ann Int Med*, July 5, 2016; 165(1): 55-57

Post, Brady. Tom Buchmueller, Andrew M Ryan, "Vertical integration of hospitals and physicians," *Med Care Res Rev*, 2018; 75(4): 399-433

Prime Therapeutics, Communication to Gregg Coodley, March 22, 2021

Privett, Natalie. Shanice Guerrier, "Estimation of the Time Needed to Deliver the 2020 USPSTF Preventive Care Recommendation in Primary Care," *Am Journal of Public Health*, January 2021; 111(1): 145-9

Providence Medicare Advantage Plans, Communication to Gregg Coodley, April 8, 2021

Pussey, William Allen. "The Disappearance of Doctors from Small Towns," *JAMA* 88, February 12, 1927, p505

Ratanawongsa, Neda. "Association between Clinician Computer Use and Communication with Physicians in Safety-Net Clinics," *JAMA Internal Medicine*, 176(1): 125-127

Ratwani, Raj M. Michael Hodgkins, David W. Bates, "Improving Electronic Health Record Usability and Safety Requires Transparency," *JAMA*, December 25, 2018; 320(24): 2533-34

Ravindranath, Mohana. and Susannah Luthi, "Pharmacies Score Customer Data in Vaccine effort. Some are crying foul," *Politico*, April 3, 2021

Raymond, John R., Joseph E. Kerschner, William J. Hueston, Cheryl A. Maurana, "The Merits and Challenges of Three Year Medical School Curricula: Time for an Evidence-Based Discussion," *Acad Medicine,* October 2015; 90: 1318-23

Reid, Rachel O. J. Scott Ashwood, Mark W. Friedberg, Ellerie S. Weber, Claude M. Setodji, Ateev Mehrotra, "Retail Clinic Visits and Receipt of Primary Care," *JGIM*, 2012; 28(4): 504-12

Reinhardt, Uwe E. "The Rise and Fall of the Physician Practice Management Industry," *Health Affairs*, January/February 2000; 19(1): 42-55

Relman, Arnold. "Medical Professionalism in a Commercialized Health Care Market," *JAMA*, December 12, 2007; 298(22): 2668-2670

Resneck, Jack S. "Refocusing Medication Prior Authorization on Its Intended Purpose," *JAMA*, February 25, 2020, 323(8): 703-704

Rezler, Agnes G. Summers G. Kalishman, "Who goes into Family Medicine," *Journal Of Family Practice*, December 1989, 29;6: 652-6

Rich, Eugene C. Ann S. O'Malley, Claire Burkhart, Lisa Shang,

Arkadipta Ghosh, Matthew J. Niedzwiecki, "Primary Care Practices Providing a Broader Range of Services Have Lower Medicare Expenditures and Emergency Department Utilization," *JGIM*, 2021; 36(9): 2796-2802

Rieger, Erin Yildirim. and others. "Primary care physician involvement during hospitalization: a qualitative analysis of perspectives from frequently hospitalized patients." *BMJ Open* 2021; 11:e053784.doi:10: 1136/bmjopen-2021-053784

Rittenhouse, Diane R. Andrew W. Bazemore, Zachary J. Morgan, Lars E. Peterson, "One-Third of Family Physicians Remain in Independently Owned Practice, 2017-19," *J Am Board Fam Med*, 2021; 34: 1033-34

Rivo, Marc L. "Internal Medicine and the Journey to Medical Generalism," *Ann Int Med* 1993; 119: 146-152

Roberts, Eric T. Alan M. Zaslavsky and J. Michael McWilliams, "The Value-based Payment Modifier: Program Outcomes and Implications for Disparities," *Ann Int Med* 2018; 168: 255-265

Robinson, James C. Kelly Miller. "Total Expenditures per Patient in Hospital-Owned and Physician-Owned Physician Organizations in California," *JAMA*, 2014.312(16): 1663-69

Robertson, Sandy L. Mark D. Robinson, Alfred Reid, "Electronic Health Record Effects on Work-Life Balance and Burnout Within the I3 Population Collaborative," *Journal Of Graduate Medical Education*, August 2017:479-484

Rodriguez, Hector P. Sean P. McClellan, Salma Bibi, Lawrence P. Casalino, Patricia P. Ramsy, Stephen M. Shortell, "Increased Use of Care Management Processes and Expanded Health Information Technology Functions by Practice Ownership and Medicaid Revenue," *Medical Care Research and Review* 2016; 73(3): 308-328

Rohrer, James E. Kurt B. Angstman, Gregory M. Garrison, Julie A. Maxson, Joseph W. Furst, "Family Medicine Patients Who Use Retail Clinics Have Lower Continuity of Care," *Journal of Primary Care and Community Health*, 2013; 4(2):150-3

Rosenbaum, Sara. Daniel R. Hawkins, "The Good Doctor – Jack Geiger, Social Justice and U.S. Health Policy," *NEJM* 384:11,March 18, 2021, 983

Rosenblatt, Roger A. and Others, "The Effect of the Doctor-Patient Relationship on Emergency Room Use Among the Elderly," Am J Public Health, January 2000; 90(1): 97-102

Rosenblatt, Roger. L. Gary Har, Laura-Mae Balwin, Leighton Chan, Ronald Schneeweiss, "The Generalist Role of Specialty Physicians: Is there a Hidden system of Primary Care?," *JAMA*, May 6, 1998, 279(17): 1364-1370

Rosenthal, Elizabeth. "Apprehensive, Many Doctors Shift to Jobs with Salaries," *New York Times*, February 13, 2014

Rosenthal, Meredith B. Richard G. Frank, "What is the Empirical Basis for Paying for Quality in Health Care," *Medical Care Research and Review*, April 2006; 63(2): 135-157

Rosenthal, Michael P. and others, "Influence of Income, Hours Worked, and Loan Repayment of Medical students' Decision to Pursue a Primary Care Career," *JAMA*, March 23/30, 1994; 271(12): 914-917

Rotenstein, Lisa S. Nate Apathy, Bruce Landon, David W. Bates, "Assessment of Satisfaction with the Electronic Health Record Among Physicians in Physician-Owned vs. Non-Physician-Owned Practices," *JAMA Network Open*, 2022: 5(4):e228301.doi.10.1001/jamanetworkopen.2022.8301

Rotenstein, Lisa S. A. Jay Holgren, N. Lance Downing, Christopher A. Longhurst, David W. Bates, "Differences in Clinician

Electronic Health Record Use Across Adult and Pediatric Primary Car Specialties," *JAMA Network Open*, 2021; 4(7): e2116375.doi:10.1001/jamanetowrkopen.2021.16375

Rourke, Elizabeth, "In Clinical Care, What Will Amazon Deliver?" *NEJM*, December 23, 2021; 385(26)2401-3

Rosenbaum, Lisa. "Reassessing Quality Assessment – The Flawed System for Fixing a Flawed System," *NEJM*, April 28, 2022; 386(17): 1663-1667

Rowland, Christopher. "Diagnosis for Small Family Doctors: Less Money, Greater Hardship and Patients on Video," *Washington Post*, September 2, 2020

Roy, Christopher L. and others. "Patient Safety Concerns Arising from Test Results that Return after Hospital Discharge," *Ann Int Med*, July 19, 2005;143:121-128

Rundall, Thomas G. John R.C. Wheeler, "The Effects of Income on Use of Preventive Care: An Evaluation of Alternative Explanations," *Journal of Health and Social Behavior*, December 1979; 20(4): 397-406

Ryan, Sheryl. Anne Riley, Myungsa Kang, Barbara Starfield, "The Effects of Regular Source of care and Health Need of Medical Care use Among Rural Adolescents, Arch Pediatr Adolesc Med, 2001: 155: 184-190

Saddawi-Konefka, Daniel. Ariel Brown, Isabella Eisenhart, Katherine Hicks, Eileen Barrett, Jessica A. Gold, "Consistency Between State Medical License Application and Recommendations Regarding Physician Mental Health," *JAMA* 325(19), May 18, 2021, 2017

Safran, Dana Gelb. and others, "Organizational and Financial Characteristics of Health Plans: Are They related to Primary Care Performance," *Arch Int Med*, January 10, 2000; 160: 69-76

Salsberg, Edward. Paul H. Rockey, Kerri L. Rivers, Sarah E. Brotherton, Gregory R. Jackson, "US Residency Training before and after the 1997 Balanced Budget Act," *JAMA* 2008: 300(10) 174-180

Sandy, Lewis G. Steven A. Schroeder, "Primary Care in a New Era: Disillusion and Dissolution," *Ann Int Med* 2003; 138: 262-267

Saran, Dana Gelb. "Defining the Future of Primary Care: What Can We Learn from Patients," *Ann Int Med* 2003; 138: 248-255

Saultz, John W. Jennifer Lochner, "Interpersonal Continuity of Care and Care Outcomes: A Critical Review," *Annals of Family Medicine*, March/April 2005; 3(2): 159-166

Sax, Harold. "Leaving (Internal) Medicine," *Ann Int Med*, January 3, 2006: 144(1): 57-58

Schellbase, Kenneth. Thomas D. Koepsell, Thomas E. Norris, "Providers' Reactions to an Automated Health Maintenance Reminder System incorporated into the Patient's Electronic Medical Record," *J Am Board Fam Pract* 2003; 16:312-7

Schoen, Cathy. Robin Osborn, Michelle M. Doty, Meghan Bishop, Jordon Peugh, Nandita Murukutla, "Towards Higher-Performance Health Systems: Adults Health Care Experience in Seven Countries, 2007," *Health Affairs*, 26(6) 2007: w717-734

Schroeder, Steven A. William Frist for the National Commission on Physician Payment Reform, "Phasing out Fee-for-Service Payment," *NEJM*, May 23, 2013; 368(21):2029-2032

Scott, Kirstin W. E. John Orav, David M. Cutler, Anish K. Jha. "Changes in Hospital-Physician Affiliations in US Hospitals and their Effects on Quality of Care," *Ann Int Med*, January 3, 2017; 166(1): 1-8

Schwartz, Aaron L. Rachel M. Werner, "The Imperfect Science of

Evaluating Performance: How Bad and Who Cares," *Ann Int Med*, January 4, 2022: doi:10.7326/M21-4665, 1

Seabury, Seth A. Dana P. Goldman, Iftekhar Kalsekar, John J. Sheehan, Kimberly Laubmeier, Darius N. Ladawalla, "Formulary restrictions on atypical Psychotics: impact on costs for patients with schizophrenia and bipolar disorder in Medicaid," *Am J Managed Care*, 2014, 20(2):e52-e60

Segal, Jodi B. Aditi P. Sen, Eliana Glanzberg-Krainin, "Factors associated with Overuse of Health Care Within US Health Systems: A Cross-Sectional Analysis of Medicare Beneficiaries from 1016 to 2018," *JAMA Health Forum,* 2022; 3(1): e214543.doi.10.1001/jamahealthforum.2021.4543

Shah, Sachin D. Adam S. Cifu, "From Guideline to Order Set to Patient Harm," *JAMA* March 27, 2018; 319(12): 1207-8

Shanafelt, Tait D. and others, "Relationship between Clerical Burden and Characteristics of the Electronic Environment with Physician Burnout and Professional Satisfaction," *Mayo Clin Proc* 2016; 91(7):836-848

Shanafelt, Tait D. Lotte N. Dyrbye, Colin P. West, "Addressing Physician Burnout: The Way Forward," *JAMA*, March 7, 2017; 317(9): 901-2

Shanafelt, Tait. and others, "Longitudinal Study Evaluating the Association Between Physician Burnout and Changes in Professional work Effort," *Mayo Clinic Proc*, April 2016;91(4): 422-431

Sharma, Gulshan. Kathlyn E. Fletcher, Doug Zhang, Yong-Fang Kuo, Jean L. Freeman, James S. Goodwin, "Continuity of Outpatient and Inpatient Care by Primary Care Physicians for Hospitalized Older Adults," *JAMA*, April 22/29, 2009:301(16) 1671-1689

Shea, Steven. Dawn Misra, Martin H. Ehrlich, Leslie Field and Charles K. Francis, "Predisposing Factors for severe, uncontrolled Hypertension in an Inner-City Minority Population, *NEJM*, 1992, 327, 776-81

Shi, Hanyuan. Kevin C, Lee, "Bolstering the pipeline for primary care: a proposal from stakeholders in medical education," *Medical Education Online*, July 5, 2016, 21:32146, http://dx.dai.org/10.3402/meo.v21.32146

Shin, Jaeun. Sangho Moon. "Do HMO Plans Reduce Expenditure in the Private Sector," *Economic Inquiry*, Jan. 2007; 45(1): 82-99

Shipman, Scott A. Christine A. Sinsky, "Expanding Primary Care Capacity by Reducing Waste and Improving The Efficiency of Care," *Health Affairs*, November 2013; 32(11): 1990-97

Shrank, William H. Teresa L. Rogstad, Natasha Parekh, "Waste in the US Health Care System: Estimated Costs and Potential for Savings," *JAMA*, October 15, 2019; 322(15): 1501-9

Shryock, Todd. "Permission Denied: Why Prior Authorizations aren't going away," *Medical Economics*, May 2021; 16-20

Sidorov, Jaan. "It Ain't Necessarily So: The Electronic Health Record and The Unlikely Prospect of Reducing Health Care Costs," *Health Affairs*, July/August 2006; 25(4): 1079-1085

Siegel, Eleanor. "Emergence of Emergicenters," *Boston Globe*, June 8, 1981

Sinsky, Christine A. Lotte N. Dyrbye, Colin P. West, Daniel Satele, Michel Tutty and Tait D. Shanafelt, "Professional Satisfaction and the Career Plans of US Physicians," *Mayo Clinic Proc*, November 2017; 92(11): 1625-1635

Sinsky, Christine. and others, "Allocation of Physician Time in Ambulatory Practice: A Time and Motion Study in Four Specialties," *Ann Int Med*, 2016; 165: 753-760

Sinsky, Christine. Michael Tutty, Lacey Colligan, "Allocation of Physician Time in Ambulatory Practice," *Ann Int Med*, May 2, 2017; 166(9); 683-4

Sinsky, Christine A., Tait D. Shanafelt, Liselotte N. Dyrbye, Adrienne H. Sabety, Lindsey E. Carlasare, Colin P. West, "Health Care Expenditures Attributable to Primary Care Physician Overall and Burnout Related Turnover: A cross-sectional analysis," *Mayo Clin Proc*, February 25, 2022; https://doi.org/10.1016/jmayocp.2021.09.013

Snyder, Dane A. Jonathan Schuller, Zeenath Ameen, Christina Toth, Alex R. Kemper. "Improving Patient-Provider Continuity in a Large Urban Academic Primary Care Network," *Academic Pediatrics*, March 2022; 22(2): 305-312

Soumerai, Stephen B. "Benefits and Risks of Increasing Restrictions on Access to Costly Drugs in Medicaid," Health Affairs, January/February 2004; 23(1): 135-146

Soumerai, Stephen B. Jerry Avorn, Dennis Ross-Degnan, Steven Gortmaker, "Payment Restrictions for Prescription Drugs Under Medicaid: Effects on Therapy, Cost and Equity," *NEJM*, August 27, 1987; 317(9): 550-556

Soumerai, Stephen B., Thomas J. McLaughlin, Dennis Ross-Degnan, Christina S. Casteris, Paola Bollini, "Effects of Limiting Medicaid Drug-Reimbursement Benefits on the Use of Psychotropic Agents and Acute Mental Health Services by Patients with Schizophrenia," *NEJM* September 8, 1994: 331(10): 650-655

Starfield, Barbara. Leiyu Shi, James Macinko, "Contribution of Primary Care to Health Systems and Health," *The Milbank Quarterly*, 2005, 83(3), 457-502

Starfield, Barbara. "Is Primary Care Essential?" *Lancet*, 1994: 344: 1129-1133

Starr, Paul. *The Social Transformation of American* Medicine, Basic Books, New York, 1982

Stefani, KM. JR Richards, J Newman, KG Poole, SC Scott, Scheckel CJ, "Choosing Primary Care: Factors Influencing Graduating Osteopathic Medical Students," *Am Osteopath*, June 1, 20220; 120(6): 380-387

Stevens, Jennifer P., David J. Nyweide, Sha Maresh, Laura A. Hatfield, Michael D. Howell, Bruce E. Landon. "Comparison of Hospital Resource Use and Outcomes Among Hospitalists, PCPs and other Generalists," *JAMA Internal Medicine*, 2017; 177:12, 1781-1787

Stewart, Ada D. "Prioritizing Primary Care Can Save the U.S. Health Care System," *American Family Physician*, July 2021; 104(1): 14-15

Stone, Valerie E. George R. Seage, Thomas Hertz, Arnold M. Epstein, "The Relation Between Hospital experience and Mortality for Patients with AIDS," *JAMA*, 268: 19, 2655-2661

Strange, KC. SJ Zyzanski, CR Jaen, "Illuminating the 'black box': A description of 4454 patient visits to 138 family physicians," *J Fam Pract* 1998; 46: 377-389

Tahir, Darius. "Medical Boards get pushback as they try to punish doctors for Covid misinformation," *Politico*, February 1, 2022

Todd, F. H. "Organization," *JAMA* 39 (October 25, 1902), 1061

Toevs, Kim. Communication to Gregg Coodley, March 18, 2021

Tolkien, J.R.R. *The Two Towers,* Ballantine Books, New York, 1965

Tolkien, J.R.R. *The Fellowship of the Ring,* Ballantine Books, New York, 1965

402

Tollen, Laura. Elizabeth Keating, "Covid-19, Market Consolidation and Price Growth," *Health Affairs,* August 3, 2020.doi:10.1377/forefront.20200728.592180

Truls Ostbye, Kimberly S. H. Yarnall, Katrina M. Krause, Kathryn I. Pollak, Margaret Gradison, J. Lloyd Michener, "Is There Time for Management of Patients with Chronic Diseases in Primary Care," *Ann Fam Med*, May/June 2005; 3(3): 209-214

United Healthcare, Retrospective Drug Utilization Review, to Gregg Coodley, March 30, 2021

United Healthcare, Retrospective Drug Utilization Review, to Gregg Coodley, March 22, 2021

United Healthcare Clinical Engagement Services Team, Communication to Gregg Coodley, April 26, 2021

United Healthcare, Communication to Gregg Coodley, March 31, 2021

United States Department of Health and Human Services, Characteristics of Office-Based Physicians and their Practices, United States 2005-2006, Vital and Health Statistics 13(166), April 2008

van Walraven, Carl. Ratika Seth, Peter C. Austin, Andreas Laupacis. "Effect of Discharge Summary Availability During Post Discharge Visits on Hospital Readmission," *JGIM*, March 2002; 17: 186-192

Vinh, Khanhuyen P. Stephen L. Walston, Jeff Szychowski, S. Robert Hernandez, "The Effect of Hospitalists on Average Length of Stay," *Journal of Healthcare Management*, 2019 May-Jun; 64(3), 169-184

Wachter, Robert M. "Reflections: The Hospitalist Movement a Decade Later," *Journal of Hospital Medicine*, 1:4, July/August

2006, p248-252, p.251

Wachter, Robert M. "The State of Hospital Medicine in 2008," *Med Clin N Am*, 2008; 92: 265-273

Wachter, Robert M. Lee Goldman. "The Emerging Role of 'Hospitalists' in the American Health Care System," *NEJM*, August 15, 1996; 335:7, 514-517, p514

Wachter, Robert M. Lee Goldman. "The Role of 'Hospitalists' in the Health Care System," *NEJM*, 336:6, February 6, 1997, 445-6

Wachter, Robert M. Patricia Katz, Jonathan Showstack, Andrew B. Bindman, Lee Goldman. "Reorganizing an Academic Medical Service: Impact on Cost, Quality, Patient Satisfaction and Education." *JAMA*, May 20, 1998; 279(19): 1560-65

Wadhera, Rishi K. Jose P. Figueroa, Karen E. Joynt Maddox, Lisa S. Rosenbaum, Dhruv S. Kazi, Robert W. Yeh, "Quality Measure Development and Associated spending by the Centers for Medicare and Medicaid Services," *JAMA*, April 28, 2020; 323(16): 1614-1616

Walgreens, Communication to Fanno Creek Clinic, April 9, 2021

Wall Street Journal, May 2003, http://online.wsj.com/article/SB10539733189909600.html)

Wallace, Jacob, J. Michael McWilliams, Anthony Loll, Janet Eaton, Chima D. Ndumele. "Residual Confounding in health Plan Performance Assessments: Evidence from Randomization in Medicaid," *Ann Int Med*, January 4, 2022: 175: 314-324

Walter, Louise C. Paul Heineken, "Pitfalls of Converting Practice Guidelines into Quality Measures," *JAMA* September 15, 2004; 292(11): 1301-1302

Wang, Bill. Ateev Mehrotra, Ari B. Friedman, "Urgent Care Centers

Deter Some Emergency Department Visits But, on Net, Increase Spending," *Health Affairs*, April 2021; 40(4): 587-595

Wasson, John H. and Others, "Continuity of Outpatient Medical Care in Elderly Men: A Randomized Trial," *JAMA*, November 2, 1984; 252(17): 2413-2417

Weeks, William B. Amy E. Wallace, Myron M. Wallace and H. Gilbert Welch, "A Comparison of the Educational Costs and Incomes of Physicians and Other Professionals," *NEJM*, May 5, 1994; 330, 18: 1280-6

Weiss, Linda J. Jan Blustein, "Faithful patients: The Effect of Long Term Physician-Patient Relationships on the costs and Use of Health Care by Older Americans," *American Journal of Public Health*, December 1996; 86:2, 1742-48

West, Colin P. Carol Popkave, Henry J. Schultz, Steven E. Weinberger, Joseph C. Kolars. "Changes in Career Decisions of Internal Medicine Residents During Training," *Ann Int Med* 2006; 145: 774-779

Wetterneck, Tosha B. and others, "Worklife and Satisfaction of General Internists," *Archive Internal Medicine*, March 25, 2002, 162:649-656

Wharam, J. Frank Dennis Ross-Degnan, Meredith B. Rosenthal, "The ACA and High Deductible Insurance-Strategies for Sharpening a Blunt instrument," *NEJM*, October 17, 2013; 386(16): 1481-1484

Whitcomb, Michael E. Joshua J. Cohen, "The Future of Primary Care Medicine," *NEJM*, August 12. 2004; 351(7): 710-712

Whitehead, David C. Ateev Mehrotra, "The Growing Phenomenon of 'Virtual-First' Primary Care," *JAMA, December 21, 2021; 326(23): 2365-66*

Wilensky, Gail R. "Reforming Medicare's physician payment system," *NEJM* 2009; 360: 653-55

Wilensky, Gail R. "The Future of Medicare Advantage," *JAMA Health Forum*, May 5, 2022; 3(5):e221684.doi.10.1001/jamahealthforum.2022.1684

Wilkinson, Elizabeth. Anuradha Jetty, Stephen Peterson, Yalda Jabbarpour, John M. Westfall. "Primary Care's Historic Role in Vaccination and Potential Role in COVID-19 Immunization Programs," *Ann Fam Med*, 2021; 19: Online. https//doi.org/10.1370/afm.2679

Wolfson, Bernard J. "Can a Subscription Model Fix Primary Care in the United States *Washington Post*, June 3, 2021

Wray, Charles M. Meena Khare, Saloment Keyhani, "Access to Care, Cost of Care, and Satisfaction With Care among Adults with Private and Public Health Insurance in the US," *JAMA Network Open*, 2021; 4(6) e2110275.doi:10.1001/jamanetworkopen.2021.10275

Yarnall, Kimberly S. H. Kathryn I. Pollak, Truls Ostbye, Katrina M. Krause, J. Lloyd Michener, "Primary Care: Is There Enough Time for Prevention?" *Am Journal of Public Health*, April 2003; 93(4):635-641

Young, Gary P. Michele B. Wagner, Arthur L. Kellerman, Jack Ellis, Doug Bouley; for the 24 hours in the ED Study Group, "Ambulatory Visits to Hospital Emergency Departments: Patterns and Reasons for Use," *JAMA*, August 14, 1996; 276(6): 460-465

Young, Gary J. E. David Zepeda, Stephen Flaherty, Ngoc Thai. "Hospital Employment of Physicians in Massachusetts is Associated with Inappropriate Diagnostic Imaging," *Health Affairs*, May 2021; 40(5): 710-718

Yu, Wendy Y. Sheldon M. Retchin, Peter Buerhaus, "Dual Eligible Beneficiaries and Inadequate Access to Primary Care Providers," *Am J Manag Care*, 2021; 27(5): 212-216

Zhou, Mo. Allison H. Oakes, John FP Bridges, William V. Padula, Jodi B. Segal, "Regional Supply of Medical Resources and Systemic Use of Health Care Among Medicare Beneficiaries," *JGIM*, 2018: 33(12): 2127-2131

Zhu, Jane M. Daniel Polsky, "Private Equity and Physician Medical Practices – Navigating a Changing Ecosystem," *NEJM*,384:11, March 18, 2021, 981

Zitek, Tony. Ignasia Tanone, Alexzza Ramos, Karina Frama, Ahmed S. Ali, "Most Transfers from Urgent Care Centers to Emergency Departments are Discharged and Many are Unnecessary," *Journal of Emergency Medicine*, 54(6): 882-888

Zuger, Abigail. "Dissatisfaction with Medical Practice," *NEJM*, January 1, 2004; 350(1): 69-75

ABOUT ATMOSPHERE PRESS

Atmosphere Press is an independent, full-service publisher for excellent books in all genres and for all audiences. Learn more about what we do at atmospherepress.com.

We encourage you to check out some of Atmosphere's latest releases, which are available at Amazon.com and via order from your local bookstore:

The Great Unfixables, by Neil Taylor

Soused at the Manor House, by Brian Crawford

Portal or Hole: Meditations on Art, Religion, Race And The Pandemic, by Pamela M. Connell

A Walk Through the Wilderness, by Dan Conger

The House at 104: Memoir of a Childhood, by Anne Hegnauer

A Short History of Newton Hall, Chester, by Chris Fozzard

Serial Love: When Happily Ever After... Isn't, by Kathy Kay

Sit-Ins, Drive-Ins and Uncle Sam, by Bill Slawter

Black Water and Tulips, by Sara Mansfield Taber

Ghosted: Dating & Other Paramoural Experiences, by Jana Eisenstein

Walking with Fay: My Mother's Uncharted Path into Dementia, by Carolyn Testa

FLAWED HOUSES of FOUR SEASONS, by James Morris

Word for New Weddings, by David Glusker and Thom Blackstone

It's Really All about Collaboration and Creativity! A Textbook and Self-Study Guide for the Instrumental Music Ensemble Conductor, by John F. Colson